GW00858054

IF LOVING YOU

WAS EASY

Written by Cassandra M Porter

This book is dedicated to all those who have left footprints on my heart, those that have encouraged me to chase my dreams and God my creator who has blessed me with the ability to share this talent.

Special thank you to my long time friend who encouraged me, believed in me and invested in me to help me make this a reality. Also sending out a big thank you to my best friend who is like a sister to me. Love you always.

Remember that love is out there, somewhere for each and every one of us.

One day we will all find our perfect fit.

Love is patient, love is kind. It does not envy, it does not boast, it is not proud. It is not rude, it is not self-seeking, and it is not easily angered, it keeps no record of wrongs. Love does not delight in evil but rejoices with truth. It always protects, always trusts, always hopes, always perseveres.

(1 Corinthians 13:4-7)

Chapter 1.

Janet

It happened again! Oh my gosh what was wrong with me? How does someone have that power over you, without even being close to you! Especially when you haven't seen them in the past three years! I took a deep breath, he looked so delicious walking towards the entrance of Selfridges department store, dressed in a black pinstriped suit with a pink shirt, complimented with a black tie, and black Paul Smith loafers. His leather man bag by his side. Strutting his sexy body delicately to the rhythm of the summer wind. My heart pounded in my chest at the sight of him and the brief moment we had shared five years ago came flooding back to me....

We had known each other for two years whilst at college and had formed a close friendship from the start, which made us the best of friends. Every moment after lectures we were together; in the social room watching the college team play basketball or just chilling in the greasy cafeteria. Our daily routine always started with each other, waiting for the same train and consistently being at each others houses. His house practically became my second home, his mother, my mother! Then suddenly it all came to a halt after our stretch at college ended. Marcus made the decision to attend Brunel University, to study Law and I had gone to Coventry. It was devastating at first because he was like my right arm, we would talk on the phone every night, talking about every and anything. But being at university, we had to get used to the distance and the substitution of talking on the phone, instead of the freedom of popping round one another's house when needed. Uni life changed us and eventually the calls withered away. It soon became a bonus to speak to him once every few months. I didn't hold it against him because I knew the pressures we were both under and the expectations we had to meet. But then that night finally came when we could not contain our feelings anymore. The passion took over and our lust got the better of us!

We had met up at a charity dinner for the Black and Aware foundation, which was a huge business event for Ethnic minority business owners and inspiring entrepreneurs. The annual event was held in the Britannia Hotel, near Manchester City Centre. It was a beautiful hotel, definitely fit for purpose. I was sitting with some friends which I had known from work and previous networking events, discussing recent political events, drinking champagne and adoring the music which the DJ was playing. We sat and watched the couples and groups of people in the middle of the dance floor, admiring them move their bodies in time with the music. There was this one couple who must have been in their late fifties, really having a go on the floor, showing the younger couples how to move to the jazz music precisely. The atmosphere was so calming; it was nice to see so many successful and inspiring black people and happy couples of all ages, socialising together, enjoying the music and splendour of the venue.

My eyes were lit with delight as I looked across the room, eagerly scanning the rest of the guests, admiring the women all dressed up in ballroom gowns and the men looking all refined in their tuxedos exploiting different colours and varieties of accessories. My heart sank as a realised I was subconsciously looking for one body in particular. No longer being discrete I turned my body to the left, trying to look in-between the mass of silhouettes dancing on the dance floor. Then suddenly through the array of colours from the gowns in the large banqueting hall I felt a pair of eyes looking in my direction. He had noticed me first and was watching me attentively. As our eyes locked he smiled and proceeded to rise up from the table he was sitting at with four other people. He walked across the hall cruising over towards me slowly, trying not to look eager but his expression told me otherwise. I knew he was happy to see me. I could tell by the way his mouth was formed, desperately trying to contain his excitement. We had not seen each other for ages. I admired him walking towards me wearing a perfectly fitted black tuxedo with a silk gold cummerbund and bow tie, as his round cufflinks reflected at me with every stride he took. I took a deep breath as he finally reached my table. Frantically rubbing my sweaty palms on the tablecloth, I rose to meet him as he leaned forward

2

and gave me a big tight embrace, the kind of hug where your body melts and you don't want to let go, you lose all perception of your surroundings and fall into a fairytale! At that moment I realised that I missed him so much. Slowly he released me from his incredibly tight grip, smiling we sat down and caught up on the latest developments in each others lives, taking it in turns to lead the conversation, disclosing enough information about our recent experiences for us to enquire more at a later stage. After talking for about an hour with numerous interruptions Marcus suggested that it was time we got up and enjoyed the music instead of warming the seats. It was certainly true; I had not paid an arm and a leg for my immaculate hair and two hundred and fifty pounds to sit down in my silver low-cut ball gown. Standing up, pleased at his suggestion I took Marcus up on his offer and I am glad that I did. We danced so close that we merged like two butterflies dancing in the summer breeze; our bodies pulsating with sweat. No matter what song played, we danced. We danced until our feet hurt, it was like we were afraid to let each other out of our grip, as though we would fall into an abyss and never feel each other again. The best thing about the night was that we both had reservations at the hotel, meaning that we could dance until the end. The older crowd had begun to disperse, some resigning to their seats and a few had retired to their rooms. It was mainly the young couples remaining on the dance floor, enjoying the moments surrounded by the warm glow of the dimmed lights and astounding white décor which made you feel like a princess. It was perfect.

I closed my eyes and fully inhaled the way in which Marcus body moved. It was so sensual. I could feel his every muscle against the most sensitive parts of my slim structure. He was so seductive without even knowing it. Damn, we were two young professionals here for a business event and here I was feeling like we were the only two people in the room. I pondered on the thought of him feeling the same way I felt. But why would he? We had been best friends back in college and we hadn't seen each other in three years, why would he feel the way my body was reacting to him now? Maybe it's the several glasses of champagne talking or maybe it was my inner-self coming out! Whatever it was, it was driving me crazy!

"You feel so soft" Marcus whispered into my ear while he ran his soft hands against my back.

"I can't believe the turn out, it is nice to be here" What was I mumbling! I wanted to tell him that he was making my body hot all over and was causing fluctuations between my legs.

"Yeah. It is a nice venue and they actually hired a decent DJ. Janet are you okay because you seem a bit distracted?"

"I'm fine Marcus, honestly. I just haven't drank like this for ages or even danced like this for a long, long time"

"Yeah, not since that time you had a date with that producer guy!" He slyly laughed.

Yeah he knew everything about my past relationships or brief encounters, he was practically my diary throughout college. In a way it was a good thing. There was nothing to hide; we already knew everything we had both done. We knew each other inside out. I pushed him playfully away.

"Trust you to remember that Marcus!"

"Oh I don't forget anything babe... You know, you look really beautiful tonight"

"Thanks, so do you. I must admit you scrubbed up well!" I joked. Finally he had noticed. I had especially searched for this gown for weeks, making sure that it hugged in all the right places, strictly because I knew Marcus would be here alone. We had spoke about coming here last month during one of our irregular brief conversations and he had informed me that he normally would bring one of his 'admirers' but he wanted to catch up and spend time with me, rather than accommodate some woman tonight who was probably trying to win over his affection with the hope of securing the key to exclusivity. After the song 'At your Best' by Aaliyah had stopped playing, the DJ changed the genre and put on some revival.

"Hey, you ready to leave? You look like you are going to fall over"

"Yeah, I take it your tired as well! It's almost three o'clock and my feet are starting to burn me"

"Exactly, let's just slip away" He whispered, holding me by the waist like a delicate flower. That was fine with me.

We slipped out the banquet hall and past a young dark skinned man in a grey tuxedo, talking to one of the daughters of the organisers. Holding on to the intention of trying to get a telephone number or the number of her hotel room she was staying in. Marcus and I laughed as we walked up the stairwell towards the elevator, remembering the days when that would have been him. The doors to the lift opened and we staggered inside, pressing the button for the third floor. Wall to floor mirrors surrounded the inside of the elevator and I caught the gaze of my reflection. Damn, my eyes looked tired but more importantly I never noticed how perfect Marcus was even from behind. The length of his back was astonishing; it complemented his long neck and wide manly shoulders. The tux was definitely a good look on him! Exhale.

As we reached the third floor the elevator doors opened. Stepping out I lead the way walking through the long corridor, passing numerous pieces of antique oak furniture and various original art pictures by artists which I had never heard of. I stopped at my door, room 345. Oh my gosh I really needed to take off these heels. I could hardly stand up.

"Jay, where's your key?"

I reached into my purse and took out the key card. Fumbling with the security door for the green light to come on, I was becoming impatient. Eventually, after three attempts it finally opened. A relieved Marcus held it open while I entered. My hotel room was small but had a warm, cosy atmosphere. There was a double bed in the middle of the room, the side table with the TV above and all the commodities surrounding. The en-suite bathroom was to the front of the room near the door. Luckily I had left some scented candles burning in the room as it helps me to relax and I must admit it also helped to set the mood…

"Right, let me make you some coffee, you don't want to have a pulsating headache in the morning and you know what you're like" Marcus said as he slid out of his suit jacket.

Oh, I loved the way he took charge. My mind suddenly pondered on what he was like in-between the sheets. I could just imagine, by the way he moved his mocha chocolate extra toned body I would expect him to have mad skills, especially as all the women he had been with did not want to let him go so easily. Marcus stood across the bed beside the dresser where the small kettle and complimentary refreshments were situated, waiting for the water to boil. As soon as it did he poured it into the two mugs and turned to sit down beside me. He grinned as he handed me my coffee and sat at the edge of the bed sipping his drink. I was feeling so horny right now, Marcus body had done things to me during that dance that I haven't felt for over a year. The way he had held me told me that I was having the same effect on him. But hey, we're friends and that's how it would remain.

"Jay, you know something?" He looked delicious as he sat and turned towards me to talk. Focus!

"What's up?"

"I'm glad that… you had a nice time tonight. I haven't seen you for so long and you still look the same. You know, all that work you been doing lately. You haven't had time to relax and enjoy yourself"

"I know, it's been hectic recently..." Before I could finish my sentence he cut in.

"You look really beautiful tonight. I enjoyed dancing with you. We haven't really danced together like 'that' before. I mean it was nice"

"Marcus, you dance like that 'all' the time with your girlfriends"

"Hey, don't hate! But nah, it was never like 'that'…your body…"

He took his cue and lent closer, touching my chin, then he slowly pressed his smooth lips against mine. Ohhh, he felt so good. I had to

6

respond the only way I knew how to, the way my body wanted me to, I was melting with pure desire. I grabbed him closer as our tongues danced together. I could feel his warm soft hands gliding up my back. The sensation made me grip the back of his neck forcing him even closer. He guided me gently down onto my back as I gazed into his soul, watching the passion racing in his dreamy light brown eyes. Right then I knew he wanted me as much as I wanted him! He took his hands and slowly slid my dress up, kissing and stroking my thighs until he reached the middle. He entered so carefully with his tongue, exploring places which I had forgot existed. My body tingled as he caressed my erogenous zones, my body responding like it had never been touched before! I was wet all over. I could not fight the feeling any longer and my body gave in. After my body exploded, he continued to kiss his way further up and he then completely removed my dress. I wanted him now; I wanted to feel him inside of me, deep inside of me. Marcus continued with what he had started tasting and kissing me all over my body, slowly but passionately. I held his back so tight I could feel his blood racing.

"Take me" I whispered into his ear.

Marcus reached inside his trouser pocket and took out a condom from his wallet and slowly took off the rest of his clothes, seducing me with his every movement. My breath sped up anticipating his silhouette, waiting for him to be ready for me. Once he had it on I could see the full size of his manhood! Wow, what an impressive package it was. He climbed on top of me slowly, damn I was going to explode again and he hasn't even put it inside of me yet. I can't believe I am feeling like this. Finally he entered deep inside my love nest, our bodies intertwined like two locks of hair. Damn he felt so good. "ooooohh", he slid deeper and deeper. Sweat was dripping down our bodies but neither one of us was ready to climax. We were both trying to hold back the intense feeling of releasing the passion which we had been holding inside for a lifetime. It feels too good to stop. I moved in and kissed his small but erected nipples as he moaned out with pleasure. His hands caressed my body as if I was a smooth lace of the finest silk. We continued to make love between the sheets, it was so perfect. It felt so right and in the heat of the moment we sweated and changed positions, holding each other firmly. "Oohh Marcus" I whispered.

"Ahhhhh Janet, you feel so right"

We exchanged kisses on each others necks whilst he held my firm breast and I got lost in ecstasy. I grabbed his defined buttocks and commanded him to thrust deeper, "right there marrrrc" I couldn't get the rest of the word out. It was a feeling I had yearned and craved for what seemed an eternity. The passion continued until I was no longer in control of my sexual emotions. I began to tremble, I moaned out loudly and held him tighter, sinking my nails into his back. I knew he could feel my emotions releasing. The feeling of complete and total euphoria was overpowering. I don't know how but Marcus sensed what my body was going through. At the same time I felt him shudder, "oooohhh" he growled, grasping my hands and squeezing tightly, allowing us to climax together. We laid on the ruffled bedding in silence for the next twenty minutes waiting to catch our breath and come back to our senses. He continued to be affectionate by softly playing with my hair and stroking my arms until reality struck me...I suddenly rose up untangling our locked bodies.

"Don't say a word!"

"But Jay..."

"Look, I'm sorry the drink got the better of me. I didn't mean to..."

"Jay, I enjoyed every moment of it. Don't apologise"

"But Marcus, we shouldn't of."

"But we did! You wanted it and I know I sure wanted it... what are you saying?"

"I'm saying... we shouldn't have done this" He looked on at me, confused.

"Do you want me to go?"

I sighed "Yeah... I think, I think it's best"

What was wrong with me! Marcus eased his body out of the bed and searched for his clothes which were lying all over the room. Once he found them he quickly put them on, composed himself and walked towards the door. He paused for a brief moment, like he was trying to find something appropriate to say but he decided against it and continued to open the door before walking out closing it behind him. Without looking back, he was gone.

Why did I let him walk out of the door? Truth was I enjoyed it all too. I longed to hold him that close and feel him inside of me like that for years and now the moment had finally arrived and I practically kicked him out. Why did I do that? I was scared. I didn't want to spoil the friendship we had recently rekindled and I could not handle the aftermath or the possibility that we will never be the same again.

Now here he was walking across Oxford Street. We hadn't spoken a word of the night afterwards and our friendship grew further and further apart. Marcus got a promotion and moved to Luton to work at another branch with his law firm *Braxton and Co*, after that we never had enough time to call due to our busy schedules. I was confused, I had no idea that he was back in London. The sight of him made my heart flutter like a schoolgirl. I wanted to go over to him and say hello. The last time he phoned it was a quick hello to make sure I was okay and that was it. Now there he was in the flesh and looking as good as I could remember, maybe even better. He had a fresh haircut with his goatee beard and moustache perfectly joined together. His Mocha chocolate skin shining like the glow of a radiant fire. My gosh! What am I doing looking at his every perfection! If only I could pluck up the courage to go over and say 'Hi', I'm sure he wouldn't ignore me. But my feet would not move. I had frozen at the sight of him. He had that power over me, he was my kryptonite and he had made me as weak as I could ever be. No one else has ever had that effect on me to this day.

He was now out of vision as he entered the huge doors to Selfridges and became lost within the crowd. I can now breathe again. I dived into my purse frantically looking for my phone, dismissing the fact that I was blocking other peoples walk way as they angrily brushed past me. I just have to phone Leyah and tell her that Marcus was back in London.

Chapter 2.

Keshia

How do I get myself into these situations? Is it my fault or is it Bobby's? Nah, it's defiantly not mine. If he would only pay attention to what he is supposed to then we wouldn't be in this situation now.

"So Keshia, when are you going to give me the pleasure of your company again so I can take you out for dinner?"

"Look Clayton, I'm really busy this week, but I can try come over quickly tomorrow evening" I replied, staring at my ceiling, casually holding the phone to my ear whilst watching my pre-recorded dose of America's Next Top Model.

"You're always passing through! You never actually spend 'TIME' with me. I want to hold you, I want to feel your warm lips against mine again. I can't remember what you feel like and it's been so long baby!"

"Babes, I'm trying but I've just been too busy, it's not easy being me! Look, I have to prioritise my time and besides it wasn't that long ago! I'm sure you can remember."

"That's what you think! I need to sample the goods again" He blurted out sounding frustrated.

"Clayton, just wait a little longer!" I rolled my eyes. Truth was I didn't really want to give him anymore! Yeah we had two passionate nights together, but that was all it was. I was in need for some attention and special feelings on those nights and yes, Clayton was at the right place at the right time. It was nice, but not worth doing it again. I mean I had to juggle him around with Bobby, who was trying extra hard lately to make things right again. Especially after that bitch Naomi had tried to seduce him into her bed. I never really knew what actually did happen but it made me seek elsewhere for what I was missing and Clayton was only happy to oblige. But now I didn't know how to let him go… it would break his heart. It's my own fault, I was too affectionate with him, I couldn't help it, it was nothing personal, just how I do things. Now he wanted to take me out more and I always had to find a new excuse. I mean he never knew about Bobby because he never asked and then we never spoke about forming a relationship either. So it's his fault that he let his feelings get caught up in our fling.

"I will speak to you soon Clayton. Bye" Leaving him with that false promise I hung up the phone.

Now Bobby was sweet, sexy and a charmer. We had been dating for two years on and off and we had been through our fair share of madness with girls trying to split us up, the malicious rumours and the family members who wanted to keep us apart. But we got through it, sort of! Now here we were trying to make things work again! He was moving back into my flat this week and we promised to try and make things work this time. He promised to be more dedicated to the relationship and commit everything he had to make it work. Yes I believed him, why not. I loved him and he loved me and love conquers all doesn't it?

"Hey baby, I'm going to bring the rest of my stuff on Thursday, so we can go out Friday night. I won't be down until late tonight though because I'm going out with the boys. Before you start, it's Miles' birthday so were just going out for a drink"

"But babes, we haven't spent any time together at all this week and you promised you would" I declared as I responded to his rushed phone call.

"Yeah, I will be down later tonight" Bobby stated, trying to convince me.

I took a deep breath. "When I'm sleeping!" I moaned pulling the blanket over my bare legs after feeling the slight draft which christened my room.

11

"Baby, don't be like that! I won't go if you don't want me to"

"Nah, you go babes, I don't want them to think I'm not letting you out like last time! You know how they talk rubbish. Go and enjoy yourself "

Now I knew that his *'boys'* encouraged him to chat up other women, especially his best mate Danny, because he could definitely not attract them on his own! Now Danny, he was such an arse. He hated on my relationship with Bobby from day one and that was only because he could not get me himself.

When I met Bobby, at a garden party in Hammersmith five years ago, he was with that fool Danny. He had tried to proposition me with his best useless lyrics, but I politely turned him down, much to his disapproval. As soon as I was able to slip away from him my eye caught a hold of this sexy 5'9, brown skin, firm bodied honey across the smoke filled room. He had the body of a model, actually no a chocolate Adonis. I will never forget that moment... He was wearing dark blue denim jeans and a white shirt with his crucifix chain hanging down his muscular chest. I'm telling you I was on him like a bee to honey. That night I was looking sexy dressed in my black ¾ length skirt which hugged my wide but sexy hips, a black and red corset top which flattered my small breasts and made them look a size bigger. I wore my hair flowing straight above my shoulders with copper highlights perfectly complementing my complexion. Amazingly I was the one who went over to him and introduced myself. I just needed to say something and somehow the courage leapt out of me like a trapped tiger, as my feet carried me over to him with uncertainty. I was thankful that he didn't reject me. He whispered in my ear through the loud music that he had been watching me all night and was actually happy that I had come over. I was flattered. After breaking the ice we conversed outside in the early hours of the humid morning for about an hour while everyone else was dancing away to the classic sounds. I found him so mentally stimulating. It turned out that he was an actor and had been in many huge plays across England. In turn I informed him of my recent funding events for underprivileged youths. A few minutes into the conversation and I had realised that we had so many things in common. From that day on we developed a relationship which was plagued with hurt and insecurities from past relationships. Being together was a challenge for both of us, one which we were willing to face but knew would be hard.

Bobby was a good man deep down, but he was overpowered by the pain Hazel had caused him earlier. Now she was a right bitch, she had tried to trap him with a pregnancy but then later confessed that she had slept with one of his friends. That news had broken him down, however it didn't stop her. She had tried to convince him that it was his but he didn't believe her. He knew that she wasn't sure who the father was, but wanted it to be his because the other guy wasn't interested in being a father. Her pleas were worthless and she ended up having a termination. After that experience he couldn't find it within himself to trust a woman again. He always claimed that it burned so much because he never cheated on her and it made it worse that she had been with someone he knew. So honestly I didn't really blame him for his feelings and reluctance to commit to our relationship. Janet said that I was mad to put up with some of the things he did, but I just understood his situation and knew that he needed support and assurance to trust me and then we could move our relationship to the next level. My past was also haunting me but hey you have to try and move on and get over it.

Moving in together was a big step, although he had practically lived with me when we were together eight months ago it was not official and it caused more problems than good. But that was only because Bobby was not ready to fully commit at the time, still wanting to walk the streets like he was a bachelor. He couldn't cope with me asking him, what time he would be home, what he wanted for dinner, telling him that it was his turn to wash up, reminding him to tidy up after himself and constantly telling him to put the toilet seat down. Looking back at it now, what was actually going to be different this time? He would still have his bad habits! Only I would have to put up with it, welcome it, get used to the fact that this was how it was going to be! Before he decided to move in with me, Bobby was flat sharing in Walthamstow with two other guys in a dingy small detached house. He was not used to his own space, but was accustomed to an environment full of testosterone, blossoming in the unwelcoming smell of dirty dishes in the sink and months of neglected cleaning. I tell you something for sure, I am not going to miss that two hour drive down there. No more suffering nights in the presence of a male occupancy.

13

I looked around my surroundings, examining my comfortable space. My flat was only a one bedroom, but it was big enough for the both of us. I'd been living here for three years now and I had made it into my own. Having to share it was a bit daunting for me. I was organised and Bobby had a lot of stuff, despite him basically living in one room at his place he had accumulated enough stuff as someone who had a three bedroom house! He had already moved in half of his belongings during the past week, of which I had been weaving through in order not to break my neck. There were musty smelling books stacked in boxes in the corridor, his keyboard and other musical instruments lying all around the flat and even pictures of him and famous actors, which he was adamant he was going to hang up on my flawless walls. Somehow I did not think so! I walked around in my pink slippers laughing, remembering that it had led to numerous discussions about where he was going to put a lot of his 'junk'! Frustrated with seeing the scattered cardboard boxes around the flat, I decided to hang up his clothes and neatly stack his shoes and trainers which were all still in their boxes, nicely in the built-in wardrobe, where tons of my own shoes were stacked. I was all hot and sticky when I had finished. Living with Bobby was going to be a big step, but it would be nice to come home knowing that my boyfriend would be there or would be coming home soon. I welcomed having to cook everyday instead of rushing for a quick bite to eat before sitting bored in front of the television, constantly flicking channels trying to find something interesting to watch. Only problem was, now I would have to ensure that I constantly looked presentable. I had to lose the frumpy unkept look which I normally transformed into come evening. It meant that I wouldn't be able to come home, take out my contact lenses and resort to wearing my half crooked pair of D&G glasses and relax in my over-worn house t-shirt and tracksuit bottoms. No, no, I can't do any of that just yet, how he met me is how I've got to stay! Me letting myself go now that we have moved in together, is a recipe for disaster. It could easily turn him off and send him into the arms of another woman and I know there would always be a dozen who are willing to take him up. Its not that he hasn't ever seen me first thing in the morning with my headscarf around my head and no make-up on or anything like that. But I just didn't want anything to go wrong again. I wanted everything to be perfect. I wanted him to remain attracted to me, keep the relationship alive. Not that we had a boring sex life, our sex life was very exciting when he was actually here! But I didn't want the flame to burn out!

In a way it felt like an invasion of my space but on the other hand it was like I embraced the warm feeling it gave me. I was sharing my world with someone I loved. I was replacing my lonely days with joy and excitement. I was building my life with another, changing for the better. Making my home 'our' home.

Chapter 3.

Leyah

'Knock, knock, knock... baby...' The sounds of Joe blasted from my stereo as my cousin Rachel relaxed in the living room, listening to some old CD's, whilst I got Asia ready for her father to come and collect her. The weekend was my time for freedom, not that I did anything in particular with it, but I was a time for me to chill.

"You got some good tunes here Leyah!"

"I know, I love my music, it gets me through. It makes me think back to when we were younger and all the house parties we used to attend. Now those were the good old days, when you could just go out and have fun!" I smiled, reminiscing as Rachel went through my album collection on my computer. "Asia! Come here and finish your dinner, you father is coming for you shortly"

Asia is my baby girl, I love her to bits. Her father on the other hand was a waste of space! We had Asia during a relationship we had four years ago. He charmed me, whined and dined me and then got me pregnant. That's when I found out that he had a woman or to be precise a fiancée. I was hurt and also four months pregnant when I eventually figured it out. Some people ask me, how did I not work that one out, but it was not simple. He had hidden it well. I mean we were together mainly everyday, if I did not see him I could guarantee that I spoke to him. He knew exactly how to play the game and have me eating out of his hands. He told me all the right things and took me to all the beautiful places. We even went to Barbados together, which I later found out he had lied to his woman and told her some story about going to research the property market over there as a surprise for his mother. Man I must have really been a fool for true! The only good thing about him is that he takes responsibility for his daughter. His relationship with his fiancée is still prevailing though. She is actually a bigger fool than me! But I suppose whatever makes you happy and he *MUST* be making her happy or giving it to her damn good for her to stay through his lies and scandals. Come on, Asia is almost three and Reese is a charmer, he has sex appeal oozing out of his body. I'm so over him now but I do understand what that stupid Shantel is going through. It's because I know what it is like. I know exactly what he has to offer and YES it is all that and then some! I mean this man knows how to work every part of his body and then make every part of your body scream with desire, while making it look effortless.

He doesn't really love Shantel, he couldn't. He loves himself more. For him to treat her the way he has and still continue the same behaviour, he surely has no form of respect or remorse. The only reason he is still with her is because I kicked his arse to the kerb after I found out that he was engaged and had been the whole time throughout our one-year relationship, plus her parents own a number of estate agents and he needs the enhanced recognition. Would I have stayed with him if he weren't engaged? I'm not really sure how to answer that....maybe, or on the other hand maybe not. I had always said from young that I wanted to have kids with one man and that would be the person who I would spend my whole life with. I grew up without my father in my life and I did not want that for my children. But life then dishes you out its own hand and your fate is at the mercy of silly mistakes and chances. Not to say that my Asia was a mistake, but it could have been planned a lot better, first being that Reese wasn't the father and we had never met. Just then my doorbell rang. I looked at the clock on the kitchen wall sceptically.

"Damnit, he's here early" I announced as I rushed out of the kitchen to open the door.

"Look I will be back about eight. Let me go and buy some blank disks and come back" Rachel announced as I made my way past the front room to open the door. I knew Rachel was just trying to avoid Reese, she could not stand him. None of my family or friends could, but Rachel could not hide her repugnance towards him so she avoided him like the plague because she was known to be very opinionated. She could not hold her tongue!

"Alright then Rache" I opened the door and greeted Reese while Rachel kissed Asia goodbye and then forced a 'hi' and 'bye' to Reese as she brushed past him at the door and into the sunset street.

He stood at my door, with the automatic safety light exposing his presence for all to see as he leaned causally on the wall.

"Hi, sorry I'm a bit early, it's just that I left work at six and decided to come straight down"

I rolled my eyes. "Look it's fine, your only half an hour early. She's not quite ready yet. Just finishing off her dinner"

"Daddy" Asia bellowed from the kitchen having heard her dad's voice.

"Where's daddy's little princess?" He smiled as he passed through the front door and towards the kitchen which was opposite and in clear view of Asia sitting at the table on her pink princess booster seat.

Now I didn't really let Reese into my house, because there was no need for him to come inside, but he took it upon himself to enter. Maybe this was the real reason why he had come early. To come and snoop to check that no man was living here. I know his tricks and I know the way he thinks, he had expressed many a time that he did not want any man around his baby. Like I am supposed to remain a nun for the rest of my life. He must be mad!

Reese finished placing a tender kiss on her forehead before giving her instructions. "Princess, finish your dinner. Then you can come and have some fun at daddy's and I've got a little surprise for you if you eat all your food"

Asia rushed to eat her food, taking big gulps with her plastic children's cutlery, anticipating her surprise. Reese turned and looked at me suspiciously, causing the temperature to dramatically drop.

"What's wrong with you now? I like how you just invited yourself into my house and don't start your foolishness" I said to him sternly, turning my back to walk into the living room.

"What are you on about now woman? I am just looking at you, you look different. You look like your blossoming... there seems to be a radiance about you today"

I sucked my teeth. "Please Reese! What do you want? Those tricks certainly do not work with me anymore"

He smiled, following close behind me, loving the fact that he had been sussed. "I came early because I just wanted to have a word with you"

"About what?

"Well, we have to try and be civilised for Asia's sake and...it's not good for her not to see us interacting together positively" Reese said in his authoritarian tone.

"What is your point? I am always civilised towards you despite the way which you treated me by lying and deceiving me, forgetting to mention that you had a FIANCEE!" I bickered at him.

"Leah, Leah, I know I hurt you and I am truly sorry for what I did, it's just that I grew to love you so much that I couldn't bare to lose you. You became a huge part of my life and you were like...."

"Stop bullshitting me Reese, it doesn't make one bit of difference now. All that matters is that we are both happy and Asia is not neglected because of your stupidity!"

"Leah Leah I know but..."

He always used to call me Leah Leah when we were together. The way he said it used to make me feel all warm inside and he knew it, that's why he was calling me it now. He was definitely scheming and trying to make me succumb to whatever point he was trying to put across.

"Look I don't know what it is that you are hoping to achieve here…" I tried to finish my words but he cut in before I could.

"Leyah, listen. I just want to say that I think we should act more like a family for Asia's sake! I mean try and give her some memories of the three of us together. Just in case something happens in the future, at least she will have pictures and memories of us all together." He blurted out as he invited himself to take a seat on my leather sofas.

"Well I am sure you have ruined any chances of us being a *FAMILY* and it will all just be lies because you have made it this way" I scorned at him, the heat beginning to rise within me as the anger took hold of me once again.

"Come on Leah Leah, we have to try for our daughter's sake, I mean lets just try and do things together for her."

I could not believe what this fool was coming out with, how dare he try and act like the mature parent here. He was the reason why our daughter had to live in a single parent home and spend weekends at her fathers. Why should I be made to look like I was the one that was stopping things from progressing and stopping her from being happy! Damn he irritates me!

"Look, I hear what you are saying and I agree that we need to do something together for Asia, but I am not going to lie to *YOUR WOMAN* sorry *FIANCEE* about anything" I shouted. He ignored my anger and continued with his point.

"I'm not asking you to. Asia is my daughter and you are her mother she understands that. S he also understands that I would do anything for my baby girl. So that is not a problem. Look I have tickets to go to the aquarium on Sunday. It would be nice if you could come"

Reese put me on the spot and I could see the persistence in his eyes. I lowered my head confused. He knew he had backed me into a corner and I could not retreat without saying yes.

I brushed off my dress. "Wow, you had it all planned out then, didn't you?"

"Not exactly, I was going to take her with Mum, but her arthritis is playing up again. So I thought it would be a good opportunity for us to make a go… you know… and do something together"

As I was about to give him another piece of my mind, with my arms folded and ready for the attack, Asia came running into the front room right into her father's loving arms.

"Princess Mummy is coming with us to the aquarium" Reese slyly said, avoiding any eye contact with me fully knowing that Asia would be excited at the prospect of me coming with them.

"Yeah, mummy, mummy, see the fishies?" She said jumping up and down on her dad's lap excited.

"Yes darling, mummy is going to come and see the fishies with you" I said sarcastically "Now go and get your shoes and coat on"

"Okay" She said as she jumped off her dads lap and ran upstairs to get her coat.

I applauded him sarcastically, Clap! Clap! "You are so conniving, you really haven't changed! You knew that I couldn't say no in front of my baby" I snapped at him.

"I know! Well I didn't plan to tell her like that, she just came in at the right moment. Don't worry about it, it will be fun. I won't try and feed you to the sharks if that's what you're worried about" He humoured. "I just want Asia to have fun memories with us"

Somehow what he said seemed genuine, although I knew he must have an ultimate plan under that scheming head of his. I will just go along for Asia's sake and as he said it might even be fun.

"Look, I'm coming but don't be sneaking around, tell Shantel exactly who you are going with!"

"Listen I will! I am done with all the lying and hiding. She will know and I will be the one to tell her. Okay?"

I nodded my head in agreement.

"Well-then I will come and pick you up on Sunday for eleven o'clock. Is that okay?"

"Yeah, I will make sure I am ready. And don't think that this is for your benefit, I still dislike you and you are still the number one bastard in my life, this is not about us!"

I had to ensure that Reese full and well knew that I was only doing it for Asia and not holding on to the small hope that it would bring us back together. I knew that he always had it in the back of his mind that one day I would beg him back. But I had gained some inner strength over the past couple years, especially seeing him and Shantel still together after everything he'd done. It has also made me a lot stronger and icier towards men. I am no longer a doormat for them, which is a huge change.

Asia came running down the stairs with her favourite coat that her dad bought her and her pink kickers, ready to leave. Reese didn't need to take any clothes for Asia because she had her own room at his house with everything she needed, it was like her second home. He had managed to buy a huge four-bedroom house in Shirley, courtesy of his success in property development. He had purchased the type of house he had always wanted and had impressively made numerous investments to maintain his empire.

"Well Leyah I will see you on Sunday. Asia give your mummy a big hug and kiss from the both of us" He said while he let out a cheeky devious smile. I sucked my teeth at him, showing my disapproval.

I waved them good-bye as he drove off in his brand new black Range Rover Sports Jeep, the engine roaring down my quiet street. As soon as I closed the door, I went straight into the living room and sat down for a while. I needed to fully digest the arrangements that I had just made with

Reese. I mean this man had caused so many problems within my life and now I have to try and play happy families with him and it was not even my idea! Wait until I tell the girls about this. I'm not even sure if I should go. What if he fails to tell Shantel and I go through another experience like the last time when he came to the parents evening without letting her know. Now that was drama. She phoned me up cussing and swearing down the phone, accusing me of using Asia as a way to get back with him and at one point she even accused me of having an affair with him. As if I would do that again!

Chapter 4.

Marcus

I stretched out my arms, frustrated at the outcome of today's trials. My mind was not focused at all. There was only one thing that was directly occupying my thoughts. I needed to phone Janet. I can't let someone else tell her that I am back! Damn, I haven't seen her since she kicked me out of her hotel room five years ago. I closed my eyes and reminisced on the tender moment we shared... I miss her and we have talked since then but it hasn't been the same. The friendship changed, we haven't even spoken a word of that night and it was amazing, I mean it was better than I imagined it to be. She felt so smooth and tasted so good. I just don't know what I did wrong, I mean it was not like I was the only one who wanted it to go further that night. Maybe she feels like she made a huge mistake! Every time I try to mention it she just cuts me off! Damn that woman sure knows how to run cold on a brother! How do I tell her? I don't even know how she will feel. I don't even know where to start! The last time we spoke I know I should have told her, but I just couldn't get the words out. It's not like we have anything romantic or had anything romantic going on. It was just that one night and I haven't forgotten it ever since. Yeah it was special but she has made it clear that she does not want to discuss what happened, and so I can only oblige her request.

How do I even tell her? What if she reacts irrational? I do not want to keep this from her any longer. I know she is going to be angry at me for it already! I'm going to call her tonight, maybe I'll go round and visit her, take her out for a drink...

Chapter 5.

Janet

I sat at my desk looking out at the riverfront watching the yuppie couples dining, drinking their lattés and cappuccinos. My work was so demanding these days, I hardly had time to sit and think at my desk without receiving a thousand and one calls. I was a Human Resources Manager for a large Media company and the office was always vibrant and busy. My desk was swamped with paperwork. I could just about locate my phone. I looked up at the picture that was sitting on my desk of Me, Leyah, Yasmin, Gregory and Marcus at our college prom. This picture always put a smile on my face and would warm up my coldest of days. The clothes we were all wearing were so embarrassing! Marcus had this slanted high top which was dyed blonde at the top. I remember he used to have all the latest haircuts before any of the other guys in college. Greg was funny, the joker of the group always making people laugh. He was wearing this awful cream pinstriped suit with a yellow satin shirt and his dark sunglasses! I remembered seeing him a few months ago, working as an engineer for B.T. I was shocked when he told me he has four kids with three different women! I shook my head recalling his behaviour at college; I always knew he would be one of those men! Diverting my attention back to the photo, the girls and I all looked hot as usual. Sporting hairstyles which we would never resort to now, but it was the lick back in those days. Yasmin was wearing this skin tight little black dress, don't ask me where she was going in that. I remember the whole night she kept on pulling it down, all it did was ride up and entice the horny college boys. Wow, those were the days, how I miss those moments. Looking at the picture made me remember seeing Marcus earlier, so I decided that I had got over the initial shock of seeing him and I was ready to spread the news that he was back in London. I located my office phone under all the paperwork and dialled the familiar number.

"Hey Keshia, you never guess who I saw today?"

"Who? No don't tell me... Winston?' She laughed.

"Oh hell nah! Not that dry head thieving bastard! I wish I did see him!... Nah I saw Marcus..."

"Ohhh girl. Where? Did he look good? Was he with a woman?" Keshia said eagerly.

"Oh my gosh, did he look good! That is an understatement! You know he always looks sexy. But I couldn't find it in myself to speak to him. I mean I was so shocked that I saw him, I thought he was still out of London. We talked a few months back and he didn't mention that he would be coming back anytime soon. Well I haven't spoken to him in ages but that's not the point."

"Look Jay, why didn't you go and say hi, I don't understand! Don't tell me that the man still makes you weak, he must have been with a woman for you not to say anything to him"

"You don't understand. I mean I froze I had an exhale moment, my breath stopped and I had to exhale from the bottom of my lungs. The man had me hypnotised just with his distant presence"

"Now look, if a man can do that to you, why in the hell did you two not get it together after that night?" She said in a puzzled voice.

"It wasn't that simple...come on now he was my best friend, he knew everything about me and..."

"And nothing! He wanted you and you definitely wanted him and you just let him go. You let him slip from beneath your hands, damn I would have taken care of him for you" Keshia laughed.

"I'm sure you would've! Listen, I don't know what to do. Should I call him or wait for him to call me? I mean I would like to catch up with him. Sit and talk about what he's been up to"

"Yeah I'm sure you would, look what happened the last time you did that!"

"Nah, I'm not out for getting into his pants, I just want to see him and be able to have a friendship like how we used to. I'm over that night. I mean it was me who didn't want to discuss it further afterwards. I just wanted it to disappear, to be a pleasurable memory that we both held. Imagine if we got together and it didn't work out, then all our history together would have been ruined. It was for the best. I did what was right. Now we are still are friends and I love him dearly" I said trying to convince myself.

"Look Jay, I'm gonna be straight with you. You lost a damn good man. Well you let a damn good man go. He was perfect and he is one of the very few good men out there. I always knew that you two would have that one passionate night but I thought it would bring you together. You can't let your past bad relationships haunt you forever. Get over them and take a chance for once in your life. Call him and ask him round for a drink… make sure that you are looking as fine as ever and just seduce him!"

"*KESHIA* !"

"No seduce him with your words! Damn I know he must still be feeling the effects of that night and you did basically kick him out afterwards! Shit the man must feel that he can't even approach you face to face anymore!"

"Keshia, what are you saying? You think I should call him?"

"Hell yeah! You better call him and apologise for your behaviour that night! Okay I'm chatting rubbish now. But call him and tell him that you were thinking about him and wanted to see how he was doing. Don't tell him that you saw him. Let him tell you that he is back in London."

"Yeah, you're right. I'm not going to say I saw his fine, sexy ass. I'm just going to call him like I was thinking bout him. I miss him, we were so close back in the day"

27

"I know, that's why you have to do this. Come on, you know him almost better than he knows himself"

"Yeah your right. Okay got to go. I'm going to call him now before I explode!"

"Good. Tell him I said hi."

I put down the phone and thought about how I was going to approach it, as I recited it in my mind the phone began to ring…

"Keshia I'm going to do it now…"

"Hey" Said a deep sexy voice down the line.

"Hello? Keshia?" I said puzzled.

"Nah babes this isn't Keshia. It's me…. Marcus"

Oh my gosh, my heart skipped a beat and I froze for a quick minute. "Marcus, oh my gosh babes, long time no hear. I thought you forgot about me!" I stuttered.

"Hell nah. I could never forget about you Jay. You're my girl for life!"

I laughed, he was still the same. He still presented with the same humour, like we had never been separated for so long. The way which he said I was his girl made me lose focus for a while.

"How have you been? I missed you girl!" He confessed sounding all sexy.

"I've been okay. Just working and getting on with things, you know how it is. Bought a new house..."

"Yeah I heard, good on you girl. You know I'm back in London now…"

"Really! How comes? You back for good or passing through?"

"Well...I'm back here for good, you know. Luton is dead! I love London and I missed my girl Janet" Marcus said cheekily. "Jay, look here. I haven't seen you in over three years. Damn what you look like now girl? You still as fine as I remember?... I'm just playing with you!"

"I know Marcus, you always make me smile and I miss that about you. I miss the way we used to talk back in the day"

"I know Jay, so do I" I could hear the sincerity in his tone. "You know you are so special to me and you will always be. Look we need to meet up, let's go out for a drink. What you doing tonight?"

"Tonight? Errm... well…"

"That's good nothing. Lets meet up at Embargos at nine and I will not take no for an answer" Marcus demanded.

"Marcus, you can't just demand that I meet you tonight, with no warning! I might have plans!"

"Jay please! Come on just meet me, we haven't seen each other for years, now you're going to try sit there and make up an excuse for not meeting me, when you well and truly know you have nothing else to do tonight, so stop pussyfooting and meet me at nine!"

Damn, I loved it when he was so firm and authoritive. I could feel my insides warming up just picturing his expressions on his face as he spoke.

"Okay, Okay. I will meet you. But I'm only having one drink, I have work in the morning"

"Babes, one drink is not enough but I respect that you have to work in the morning, while I will be resting in my bed, nursing my hangover" He sniggered. "But what if I promise that you will have two drinks and I will ensure that you make it to work on time and sober tomorrow. Nine o'clock sharp!"

Marcus had a way with his words and I loved the way he spoke to me, I just had to oblige his offer.

"You are trouble. I haven't seen you in years and you haven't changed one bit Mr Walters!" I smiled. "I will be there"

"Right then, word is bond. I will see you there Ms Lloyd… and hey don't keep me waiting"

That was it. Oh my gosh, I had a date with Marcus later that same evening. What was I going to do? How would I handle seeing him again after so long? Damn I need to leave work early and sort myself out. Wait why should I? He knows what I look like first thing in the morning, we have spent many nights sleeping in the same bed after a long night of raving. But I can't let him see me looking a wreck, not that I look one at the moment but I need to look presentable. Right, that's decided I need to hit Oxford Street and pick up something new for tonight. Damn, what do I even want to come of tonight?

Chapter 6.

Keshia

The moon was glistening through the blinds in the living room, as Bobby and I sat down in the comfort of each others presence, reflecting on the moment; happy to be with each other, happy to be holding our bodies close. We huddled together relaxed on the sofa watching CSI. It felt nice to have him back. At times everything was just so peaceful, no noise and no phones ringing. I hated when his phone always rung, interrupting every moment it could. Its like the caller just wanted to irritate me at every chance and Bobby knew I hated the fact that his phone was so hot. As soon as he put it down it down, it would ring again! Now all I do is just shoot a look in his direction and he knew to cut the conversation short. Tonight there would be no interruptions, just me and him, our night.

"Baby lets go to the Indian restaurant in Camden and then come home. Then I will run you a nice hot bubble bath and wear something special for you" I whispered seductively.

"Yeah, that sounds good beau. Let's do that, then come back and enjoy the rest of the night. I'm just not sure that I will be much company. I've had such a strenuous day. I had to work out for that role all day today" He said while he was rubbing the back of my hand.

"I know baby, that's why I'm gonna come home and help you relax, give you a nice massage..." I said running my hands seductively over his strong defined back.

"You, your so much trouble. B e careful before you start something up in here, and you end up starving for the rest of the night!" He laughed, stroking my soft thigh as he teased my lips with his inviting breath.

"Mmmm, how you know that's not what I want"

He looked deep into my eyes. "Beau, you know I love you so much and I love being with you, I'm just glad that we are back together and I promise I will be everything you expect me to be"

"Baby I know. I feel the same. You know how much I love you too. I just want everything to be perfect, and we know what we want now" I said trying to reassure him and myself.

I glimpsed the Sky display on the 42inch plasma, it was now eight thirty. CSI had finished, so I decided to get up and start getting ready, leaving Bobby on the comfortable sofa in his Arsenal shorts with his leg raised up flicking through the channels. It didn't take him long to get dressed, he wasn't a finicky man, but he always dressed good. Always went out to impress just in case he bumped into a film director or a talent scout. Not that it ever happened! As it was a pleasant mild evening, I decided to put on my black low neck dress with my thick brown buckled belt and my tanned brown Miss Sixty boots. I admired my reflection in the full length mirror, damn Bobby had one fine ass woman. I must admit I looked good tonight and I wanted to. I wanted to make an extra effort because I wanted this night to be perfect. I didn't want anything to go wrong tonight, I just wanted to be alone with my baby beau.

We gave our order to the well mannered greasy haired waiter, whilst we sat at the simple dressed table with one red rose and ate the complimentary popadoms with mango chutney. As I temporarily cured my hunger we discussed the plans for booking our holiday and the ideas we had for redecorating the flat. Although all the decorating ideas were his I just sat there agreeing, rubbing his soft palm enjoying the fact that I was making decisions with someone else other than myself. When our piping hot meal came we sat there feeding each other and staring into one another's eyes, silently declaring our love. He could be so romantic at times and I loved that so much about him, he would be the perfect husband one day, with a lot of training! We both sat in the busy restaurant flirting like it were our first date, everything was just perfect and after we would go home and continue this lovely romantic evening just the two of us. As I finished drinking my white wine to wash away the taste of the naan bread, interrupting my plans right on schedule just as if the bad omen was listening, waiting to spoil the moment Bobby's phone began to ring...

"Hey what's going on?" His face changed. "What? Don't lie, didn't I tell her about moving with that fool...I told you it would bring nothing but trouble, she don't know who she is fucking with and now I have to sort this all out because that man don't play, he will shoot her for that shit!"

His voice had changed and at that point I knew the night was not going to end how I expected it to, as per usual. I let out a huge sigh and shook my head in disapproval as the candle on the table felt my pain and the flame flickered out. Although Bobby had his head focused and was doing good for himself now, considering the things he used to get up to back in the day, he was still that bad boy underneath. He still knew how to hold his own. I must admit this turned me on about him, the fact that he was not a man who pretended he was something he was not. He was a little thuggish and sometimes he still had to resort back to that mentality in order to let people know he hasn't gone soft in his old age.

"Look, shush man. I'll sort it out. I'll phone you back". He shut his phone off, licking his lips to get ready for the next instalment.

"Don't even say what I think you're going to say" I said as I pushed up my face, furiously crossing my arms and rolling my eyes like they were looking for the back of the sockets.

"Baby look, I know your gonna cuss but I have to sort this out before it gets out of hand. Shanny is going to get her head buss, she's gone and mess with Riddlers money and he don't play! I have to go down there and chat to him" He said with conviction, his arms describing his irritation.

"That's not your business Bobby, why do you always get involved in her mix up. I don't know why you run around with that girl. She's just involved in so much shit, look at her with her criminal lifestyle and shit, thinking she's better than others and you sit and collude with all that rubbish" I started to raise my voice and Bobby could see that I was becoming aggravated. He reached into his back pocket and took out his LV wallet, raising his hand for the bill.

"Beau calm down. Let's pay for this and get out of here"

"Yeah let's get out of here! Why? So that you can run to her defence like a good little puppy. What about us, what about our plans? Now your just gonna leave me!"

By this time the nearby Asian couples started to look in our direction as our voices began to rise over the Bollywood music playing in the background.

"Beau it's not like that, I can't just stand back and let her get fucked up, you don't understand he will kill her!"

"That's not *YOUR* problem, *I AM YOUR* problem. I am *YOUR* woman, not her!" I was fuming, forgetting about the other people in the restaurant as I slammed my stained napkin on the table.

"Don't start saying your shit now please. I am not in the mood"

"Yeah, you're never in the mood when it comes to supporting me and being there for me. Thanks, thanks a lot" I stressed, anger clearly visible in my tone. Just then the waiter reluctantly handed us our bill with two small breath mints on the tray.

Now Shanny was some girl who he claimed he knew from five years ago. Truth was that he went to a weekender with his best mate and met her there. Danny was on her case first and she obviously didn't like him but that's how she got close to Bobby. By speaking to him on a regular basis about the situation and how Danny was phoning her line everyday begging to take her out and buy her things. Bobby couldn't see it but I warned him that it was just a way for her to try and get close to him. Then they found out that they knew some of the same people and that's where it all started. I know her type. I knew from the first day that I saw her. She was a '*hyped girl*' and was always around loads of drama. Bobby secretly loved this, he liked being around all the hype at times. I was too serene for him. I wasn't someone who was always around drama. I was just peaceful, looking for someone to build a life with minus the female headache.

Bobby put enough money on the table to pay for the bill and leave a generous tip. He placed his hand on his head before taking a deep breath and leading the way out the restaurant door, thanking the weary staff on the way out. As we walked down the cobbled streets I angrily strutted my heels making as much noise as I could to emphasise my frustration. He didn't even try to defuse the situation until we got to his car five minutes later. He closed his door, which was shortly followed by my hard slam of the passenger door, sending an echo throughout the rest of the vehicle.

"Kesh, I'm not going to be long, imma go sort this out and come straight back. You're carrying on like I don't come home to you every night"

I turned to face him. "That's not the point Bobby. This always happens and that bitch knows what she is doing. Oh actually let me retract that because she doesn't even know that we are together again does she?" I questioned.

"Ohhh, Kesh, stop chatting shit. How could she not know we are living together for Gods sake!"

"Yeah but its not like you told her, just like that other bitch. Why don't you tell your so called friends that you have a woman and that you live with her? Huh Bobby! Why is it that you have to lie all the time? Why can't you tell them?"

"Ohhh your just chatting shit now, listen to yourself. All I'm going to do is sort this mess out and come straight home to you!"

By this point it was evident that Bobby was going to do what he wanted to do regardless of how I was feeling or how much it would ruin our night. Truth was he loved females needing him, he loved the fact that the women loved him and tonight was going to be another night where I was going to be home alone, sitting in my lonely bed until about three or four o'clock in the morning when he would eventually come strolling in with some cocked up story. I knew this scenario all to well and until he

35

locked off all those women who he knows are trying to get him our relationship would remain at this stagnant point!

After he dropped me back home I decided that I was not going to let this get me down. I pulled out a bottle of Pinot Grigio from the wine rack and played one of my old school slow jam CD's before throwing myself down on the lonely sofa. I was fed up with this shit already. Nothing ever changes! Here I am on a lively Friday night sitting on my own like a lonely miserable woman but the difference is I have a man! But where is he? With another woman! Yeah he says that he is sorting out her so called beef, which I must add she managed to get herself into, therefore she should get herself out of it or suffer the consequences. Then I thought about it for a while... why should I sit here horny thinking about my man gallivanting? I know exactly what to do to occupy my time....

The sound of a tired voice spoke down the phone. "Hey, what you doing calling me so late?"

"Sorry, were you sleeping?" I whispered with sex on my mind.

"Oh hell nah, not really nah! Why what's up?" I could hear him clearing the sleep from his voice.

"I just needed someone to talk to. How you been?"

"I've been okay, just missing you really. What you got on?"

Yes this is what I'm talking about. I didn't even need to initiate anything, Clayton could read my mind and he knew exactly what this call was about! "Nothing much, just some little black French knickers and a tight little vest. Why what you got on?"

"Damn I can just picture you now, with your long sexy legs with that firm arse of yours and those big juicy nipples"

I could hear the desperation in his voice, he wanted me and he wanted me bad. I knew I shouldn't be doing this, especially with Clayton but I needed to feel special tonight. I needed to feel like I was the only one that mattered and Clayton knew how to execute this with precision, even over the phone. Come on I'm not doing anything wrong and in theory I'm not doing anything that Bobby hasn't already done or hasn't done of a similar nature. I needed to get mine and mine was on the other end of this telephone tonight and if phone sex was the only way which I could achieve this, then phone sex it would have to be…

Chapter 7.

Leyah

It was almost eleven o'clock and I was ready and waiting, pacing up and down my living room peering through my wooden blinds out into the dull street with over grown hedges. I looked on watching my neighbour Paul effortlessly wash his Ford Escort with his tanned tattooed hands, taking so much pride in his modified car as he rubbed off the daily dirt. I looked up into the sky feeling a little guilty that I couldn't even tell mum that I was going out with that bastard Reese today. Damn, she would come straight down here and give him a peace of her mind, like she did every occasion she could. The man repulsed her and I can't blame her. He hurt her daughter and my poor mother had to help me to get over him. For weeks I would not eat, all I would do is lay in my bed crying, pregnant with his child, asking God why me! Reality struck me as I watched Mrs Henry's fifteen year old granddaughter strutting down the road with her luminous skirt, matching leg warmers and white vest. What was I actually thinking! How could I even think about going out in public on a family outing with this fool? He better not get used to this because this is the first and the last time. I walked back over to the bookshelf, I can't let this man take control over my life again! I stopped and looked out the window again, noticing Reese's sparkling Black Jeep pull up outside. The rays of the sun reflecting off his flawless bodywork. I grabbed my short denim jacket off the banister as I rushed out into the hall checking myself in the handcrafted mirror and re-spraying my Marc Jacobs perfume before taking my time to stroll out the door, acting like I was not sitting by the window waiting. As the light breeze touched my skin like a piece of soft wool my anger faded away and I was introduced to an optimistic mood. The weather had actually kept to its promise and remained sweltering. The sun appearing through the perfect white clouds in the clear blue sky. Asia was sitting in her safety seat in the back wearing a Baby Phat dress in her favourite colour pink. She waved her little palm frantically through the window, surprised that her mother was actually coming out with the two of them. I opened the heavy passenger door and entered, sitting on the cream leather seat.

"Hey, you're on time" I said stunned, then I turned and directed the rest of the conversation at my beautiful princess, sitting with hair in two white bobbles which was one of the only styles Reese could perfect. "Baby girl, did you miss mummy?' She responded giving me a shy smile and exposing her pearly whites.

"Leah, I'm always on time babes, you know me!" He said offended as he eased the gear into drive.

"Humm don't I just! So what did you tell her and what did she say?" Reese coughed nervously which meant that he was about to make up a story. "And don't lie to me. You didn't tell her did you?"

"Well, I told her and she was like… she doesn't know why you should come. So I explained to her why I wanted you to come for Asia's sake and then we had a big disagreement… and then she told me not to come home if I go today!"

"Look I don't want to be causing any problems between you and her, you're the one who has to go home to that afterwards and you are not sleeping on my sofa tonight" I said firmly, watching him grip the steering wheel tighter.

"Did I ask if I could? Please, she can't keep me out of my own house even if she wanted to! It's sorted anyways. Like I tell her all the time, my baby girl comes first!"

"Hmmm, so when a r e you two having kids so that she can say the same crap to you? Then what would you do then? Forget about your baby girl?"

"Don't be silly. Look can we just forget it and concentrate on our day" He stressed, looking into his side mirrors before turning onto the open dual carriageway.

"Well like I said to you before, I don't want any more drama on my door!"

"Don't worry bout it Leyah. Forget all that. We are going to have fun today, aren't we Princess?"

"Yeah daddy"

The roads were only plagued with a few cars on this wonderful day which was a surprise. Maybe everyone had set off earlier to head to the popular destination of Brighton. Luckily the journey was not too far from my house, meaning that I did not have to tolerate sharing a confined space with this bastard for too long. We sat in silence most of the way listening to some old school R&B as I looked out the window watching the cars fall behind us on the motorway while Reese clocked 120 miles per hour in the fast lane. The drive was awkward, but we occasionally engaged in some small talk to make the journey seem quicker. I watched the horizon as the sea got closer and the smell of fresh salt water and seaweed hit my senses. We had finally reached Brighton and it was only twelve o'clock. The streets were packed with people trying to enjoy the sporadic weather. Amazingly Asia was actually awake, taking in her surroundings excitedly. We neared the sea front and Reese drove around looking for a parking space amongst the packed streets. Eventually he spotted a green people carrier exit a spot, leaving it open for him to steal before anyone else spotted it. I climbed out and stretched my limbs while Reese went and assisted Asia. Thankfully we were parked a short distance away. Mentally remembering where we had parked Reese led the way towards the Aquarium. Asia was skipping along quickly trying to keep her fathers pace. As we walked past the happy people skating along the pavement and the children eating their ice-creams, Reese could not let the silence be blissful.

"Look Leyah thanks for coming with us, it means a lot"

"Like I said before, I'm not doing it for you I'm doing it for our daughter. Did you even bring a camera?" I said in a sarcastic manor, shaking my head.

"What do I look like? Look I know your only doing what's best, that's what I love about you. You just…"

I stopped in my tracks. "Okay, stop right there! Don't be reminiscing about things, lets just do this get it over and done with. So we can both go back to our normal lives, okay?"

"Okay. Sometimes I just would like to talk to you about how things are going, you know. We can at least maintain a friendship so to speak"

"Reese, why are you chatting BS? What is it that you want to find out? Just be open. We don't need a friendship, we have a daughter together and we only interact because of her or else I would not be talking to your lying, cheating, scandalous arse no way!"

"Leyah, I'm sorry yeah. I'm sorry for what I did to you in the past. I'm sorry for being a bastard to you. I admit I got caught up and did not realise the implications of my actions. I regret it like I have told you over and over again. I just want us to move on from that!"

"What do you mean move on? Move on and do what? I'm here with you now, this is moving on! We have to do what we have to do. You say sorry like it's your middle name. I just can't believe you at times!"

"Leah Leah, I'm sorry" Reese said sympathetically as we regained our pace to Asia who had run ahead.

I ignored him, rolling my eyes as we finally reached the entrance of the aquarium. Reese handed the young brunette cashier the tickets with Asia holding onto his hands jumping up and down excitedly. I must admit, Reese seemed more genuine today than he has in a long time. I wonder if everything is okay between him and his fiancée. I wonder what he is up to. Look how he has got me, always thinking like a paranoid fool!

We walked around the aquarium looking at the beautiful sea life. Asia was so excited and was enjoying every moment of it. Reese was taking loads of pictures and got a few passers-by to take some of all three of us like he intended. As we reached to the gift shop we purchased a few souvenirs and Asia sat and got her face painted like her favourite Disney character Nemo. I must admit it was fun. I watched Asia's little face light up when she saw her reflection in the mirror and the smile on Reese's face. After we exited our tour of the aquarium we decided to walk along the busy pier to get something to eat. Passing one of the amusement stands Reese could not resist trying to win a teddy bear.

"Look I bet I can win my princess one of those teddy's. Which one do you want baby?"

"Errm, the pink one daddy" She pointed, excited at the thought of another new teddy.

"Reese you can't win one of them, come on lets go in case you make a fool of yourself " I laughed, trying to pull him away as he shrugged me off.

"Please! Don't insult me. Watch and learn darling!"

Reese began to frantically try throwing the plastic rings on the bottles for twenty minutes and must have spent about fifty pounds doing so until he finally managed to get three rings on the bottles. Well the man let him off on one of the rings for trying so hard and gave him a prize for the sheer determination. People looked on bemused at my hysterics.

"Well! Well done. You actually won a prize"

"Shush you. I told you I would do it and I wasn't leaving until I fulfilled my promise"

"Please, it wouldn't have been the first time you didn't fulfil your promises" I always had to get a dig at him anyway I could. He just looked at me and didn't even bother to retaliate to that one.

We continued to walk, stopping to buy some ice lollies before arriving at the rides. I stood enjoying my cherry brandy lolly while Reese took Asia on a few of the children's rides. Her little face looked like she was bursting with so much fun. I looked on admiring her happiness and innocence. Deciding to be a part of it we all went on the teacup and saucers and the merry-go-round. We were laughing and joking together like there was no tension between us, like we were the perfect family. Damn let me come back to reality!

This is what that bastard wanted! For me to think about the good times we could have so that he could sneak back into my heart like a serpent in the grass and sting me full on! I am not going to let him do that to me again!

The sun was beginning to descend and it was getting late so we decided to start walking back to the car. Asia was tired and I was happy that she had such fun. I could tell that she was pleased having both her parents together, enjoying themselves. She had this constant grin on her face, her little dimples prominent on her small cheeks that favoured her fathers too much. During the drive home Reese started talking about the old days and the fun which we used to have. I had to remind him that he was doing the same things with his *woman* and that what we did actually meant nothing! But I have to admit we did have some fun. I actually never experienced so much fun in all the past relationships I had been in. Even though our time was all a huge lie I was happy until the day I found out about him and Shantel!

"Leyah, you look distracted"

"Nah I'm fine" I muttered turning from the window to answer him. I didn't want him to have the pleasure of knowing that I was reminiscing on the good times we used to have.

"Well, thanks for coming today. You know it meant a lot to Asia and me"

"I didn't do it for you Reese. I did it for my little girl, she is all that matters in this relationship"

"Oh… so we have a relationship now then!" Reese said trying to wind me up.

"Shut up Reese, you wish" I sort of sniggered.

"Indeed I do" He laughed. "I know that it was hard for you to come out today, but we have had mad fun babes. I hope that we can do this again… I mean Asia would like it."

"Reese, stop! You know this was a one off and I don't think your fiancée would like to know that you are associating with me, not that I would anyway!"

Reese let out a sly laugh "That's what I love about you, you're so head strong and feisty at times!"

"Humm, and your woman doesn't know how to stick up for herself, because if I was the one in her shoes I would've of buss your head a long time ago and you would've felt my wrath big time!"

"Damn, I'm glad you're not then" He laughed again. "Leyah, you look very nice today if you don't mind me saying so"

I turned my face and blushed. Fact was I knew I did and yes I spent a lot of time thinking about what I was going to put on today. Shit I had to look good because I knew he would be watching me and Reese is the type of man who cannot let a good compliment miss his lips. My tight light denim jeans which made my backside look so round and peachy did me justice today. I liked the fact that Reese noticed me and was still sexually attracted to me. He made it so obvious at times being unable to control his stares. It made me feel good and to be honest I also enjoyed flirting with him because I know he regrets the fact that I didn't stay after finding out about Shantel but hey, he has to live with the fact that he missed out on a good thang!

Reese turned the powerful jeep into my road, pulling up outside my door and parking up. He put his gear in park, pulled up the handbrake and turned off the engine as the stars glistened outside in the night sky.

"Leyah, I'm going to carry Asia in the house. She's sleeping and I don't want you to struggle with her"

"Reese shut up" I laughed. "Look, your delaying going home so don't play dumb. I know your tricks now! You were driving at thirty miles per hour all the way back."

"Okay, so I am. Can you at least let a man keep his pride! Is it okay if I come in for a bit?"

"I suppose that's the least I can do, even though I don't need to feel obliged to do *anything*, but come on then" I unlocked the passenger door and climbed out into the night.

Reese carried Asia upstairs and put her in her bed, it was 8.45pm. We had been out all day. I didn't intend to stay out so long. I hung up my jacket exposing my goose pimpled arms as Reese came bouncing down the stairs like he lived here.

"Can I get a cup of coffee please? All that driving has made me tired" He stated as we both entered into the tidy kitchen.

He sat himself down on the small dining table, playing with the place mat.

"Hummm, you better not fall asleep because you know that woman will be at my doorstep" I spun around suspiciously. "Wait a minute how comes I haven't heard your phone ring once? She normally blows off your phone!"

"I turned off my phone because today was our day" He said trying to convince me that it was okay, avoiding any eye contact.

"Are you mad! I'm surprised she isn't waiting outside the door. Look have this coffee and then go straight home, it's late, she must be having kittens. You must have about thirty messages on your phone. Why would you do that?"

"Look Leyah, I just wanted some time to myself just put her behind me for a while you know. Clear my head..." He confessed, looking tense before I cut him off.

45

"Clear your head for what? You don't need to clear your head. You know EXACTLY what you are doing. Next time you want to clear your head, please do not involve me!" I demanded.

"Don't worry bout it, its nothing. She knows the score and it's not like we are going to end up sleeping together anyway" He said with slight suggestion. Watching me intensively, hoping that I would take the bait.

"That's not the point, from when she gets that in her head its just headache. Look call her and tell her you're elsewhere"

"Leyah, are you asking me to lie?" He said comically.

I had to slightly snigger at the fact that I was actually asking him to. I was colluding with the gutter rat. "NO, I'm not! I'm just saying tell her that you're somewhere and go THERE!"

"Don't worry I'm off in a bit. I won't get you involved in my dramas anymore. I know that you have put up with a lot from me and I do not want to get you involved for nothing. You're a good woman and I don't want to hurt you anymore"

Now I knew this emotional blackmail of his all too well. I would feel sorry for him and let him get his way. But not this time, he had to go! He sipped on his coffee as I looked on in anticipation hoping that he would just hurry up and get out.

"Reese just go now and save the argument"

"Okay Leyah. I respect your wishes, thanks for the nice day" Putting his mug down on the counter he retreated and walked towards the front door with his head down, like a sick pup. "I'll call you...bye"

He shut the door behind him without a fuss or dispute, which surprised me. Normally he would protest against my wishes. I wonder what the deal really is with him and Shantel at the moment. Why does he not want to go home just yet? I mean he has work in the morning and given the circumstances he should be running home. Oh well that's not my problem, he made his bed, now he has to lie in it.

Chapter 8.

Janet

I looked at the watch on my wrist anxious about being on time. It was nine fifteen and I had just pulled up outside Embargos in a taxi driven by the most daring cab driver I have ever witnessed. I swear there is no way he had a driving licence the way which he was driving. I hurriedly stepped out the red Mazda and into the after work party district. I dusted off my blue off the shoulder top which I had grabbed up Westend after work and straightened my black high waisted skirt which complimented my black and blue stilettos. I don't know why I was making such an effort, it was only a drink. I strutted carefully past these two white men who gave me a wolf whistle as I wined passed. I hadn't seen Marcus 'officially' for near enough a year and I know he will be looking fine as usual.

The door was opened for me by the middle aged Columbian door man and I walked through the heavy glass doors into the dimly lit bar. I scanned the room to look for Marcus, as I turned to my left I noticed him waving towards me from a secluded corner of the bar. I strutted towards him with a huge smile on my face as he mirrored my action with his arms open.

"Hey beautiful. Damn you look good" He said as he twirled me around.

"Same to you babes" I expressed as I we held each other in a tight embrace for about twenty seconds. Anyone who saw us could tell that we had missed each other immensely.

I subconsciously licked my slightly glossed lips. I looked on and admired Marcus, still as suave as ever. He was wearing a chocolate brown suit, with a pink shirt with the top two buttons undone displaying his sexy chocolate skin. Damn, he knew how to pull off a good suit. My eyes drifted as I sat there thinking ' how did I ever let him slip away after that night?' What really was going through my mind! This was something worth risking. We had never fully regained the friendship we had after that night. Everything changed. Now, here we were meeting together after all this time. What really was on his mind? Did he just want to catch up or does he have something he needed to tell me to my face? My suspicion grew stronger as I smiled happy to see him. Well it can't be anything worst than how I treated him, I thought. He's back in town and I'm sure I could make reparations. Did I even want to? Fear was over shadowing my senses. Please God let me get through this evening.

I loved quiet spots like this, although it was in the heart of the wine bar district, Embargos was for the grown and sophisticated, the working folk who wanted to be secluded from all that 'young hype'. Everyone in here looked like they had just come from work or had enough money not to work, yet the environment was not pretentious.

"Here babes. I ordered you a brandy cocktail. You still like them don't you?" He murmured so close up to my ear that it sent a slight shiver down my spine as I accepted the drink.

"Yes I do. I don't like how you know me so well" I said cheekily, with a flirtatious smile on my lips whilst flicking my fringe from my face.

"Come on, give me some ratings. We spent so much time together in college of course I know you like the back of my hand. Actually I think I know you better than I know myself babe"

We both laughed, walking over to the huge vacant comfortable white leather sofa, surrounded by dimmed honey lighting and a few people in deep conversation. We sat down adoring the sounds of the live band playing on the back stage. We sat for an hour engrossed in conversation, discussing the latest progressions in my life and his new promotion. Marcus shared his troubles moving back to London and his newly purchased three bedroom house in Streatham. I was so proud of him, who would think that the little street boy Marcus would be so successful! I mean he was always running after women like they were going out of fashion, actually let me correct that, they were running him down. I suppose they could see the potential in him because he was always hard working. He did actually put his head down despite his reputation and he always had high ambitions. I'm so glad that he has succeeded. The conversation became light, discussing the bands collaboration of music. As I peered over my tall glass I could see that Marcus was itching to say something; he looked as though he couldn't contain his self any longer. I was right! Just like he could read my thoughts he opened his mouth and mentioned that night…

"What happened in Manchester Jay?"

"Marcus, look I'm sorry about what happened that night. I just…."

"Jay, actually don't worry bout it. I haven't held it against you. I understood where you were coming from, you had to protect your own interest"

"Hey! Don't put it like that! I did not act selfishly, I mean… I was just scared"

"Scared of what Jay? I would never hurt you" He said with a sincere look on his sweet face, his brows sighing in disbelief.

"I know, but I was scared to lose you as a friend. You meant the world to me and I didn't want to risk that changing"

Where was I going with all this honesty! I've only had a few drinks now I was here pouring out my feelings which I had suppressed for so long. What am I doing? I sound pitiful.

He leaned his chair closer, drowning out the sounds of the background distractions. "Jay, I felt the same way. That night felt so right. I mean I felt at one with you. I thought the feelings were mutual…"

"They were… I… look it was a long time ago. Now you've moved on, I've moved on. Let's just leave it!"

"This is what you do every time, brush it under the carpet. Jay we need to talk about it. I need to know how you feel about me"

"Why? Look I told you. I didn't want to ruin our friendship, you have always been special to me, we have been there for each other since college and I didn't want that to change"

"Okay. So that's how it is yeah? You care for me like a best friend?" He said frustrated.

"Yes!" I lied.

"And nothing more?"

"Why are you interrogating me? I have told you already!"

"Okay, okay... I'm just asking. Let me get you another drink"

He rose up and went over to the well stocked bar to get me another cocktail. Watching him I sat thinking. Why don't I just tell him the truth? The truth that I am in love him and always have been and that night just made my feelings stronger. I just can't seem to get the words out. He doesn't really need to know how deep it actually is does he? What if he feels the same? He hasn't really spoken about his true feelings. Well I haven't actually given him the opportunity to do so. Maybe I should just tell him... Nah! As he stood at the bar with his body leaning partially over the counter, I sat there admiring his physique letting my thoughts run away, picturing us together happily married and visualising what our children would look like. Would they inherit his strong sexy features with his gorgeous brown eyes that shone like the sun through a glassed stained window. Would our daughter be as pretty as him? Would our son be athletic and charming like him! I shook the thoughts out of my head. Argh, I'm driving myself mad! I forced the vision back into my 'what if' memory bank as Marcus came walking back over, reclaiming his seat.

"Here Jay. Look I'm sorry for pestering you about it. Your right we should just move on, I won't mention it again. But I just needed to know. From the first time I met you I knew we had something special and I am glad that we are still friends to this day babe. I'm just sorry that we haven't been as close the past few years…"

"That's fine, it's my fault as much as yours, but mainly yours! Most important thing is that we are here now"

"I know, thanks for coming. I mean I didn't actually give you a choice did I?"

I had to laugh at that because he actually didn't, although I wanted to meet up with him anyway. I'm glad he actually made the first move.

"Jay, look I have something I need to say to you. It's been on my mind for ages and I feel bad that it has taken me so long to pluck up the courage to say something"

Wow, he rushed his words out so fast and his face looked serious. He leaned closer, looking around uncomfortably. What was he possibly going to say? A thousand things ran through my head but I could read Marcus like a book. His left eyebrow was raised and he was biting his bottom lip nervously which indicated that it was something which I would not be too happy to hear.

He took a deep breath and began talking… "Jay… remember I told you about the girl that I'm seeing at the moment?"

"Oh yeah, the *'personal assistant!'* I said sarcastically, rolling my eyes.

"Yeah, well its going okay, and err… we have been together for almost six months now but err…urmm… we getting married next spring"

OH MY GOSH! My heart stopped beating. What was this that he was telling me! Please say that this is all a bad dream. I cannot believe what he just said, what happened to not wanting to hurt me! My lips won't move… good evening heartache! Why, why, why?

"Jay, I'm sorry...thing is, I haven't known her for that long and I'm not sure about the relationship, but Jay" He took a deep breath. "She's pregnant…"

51

I couldn't utter a single word. I just sat there with a blank expression on my face, frozen on the spot. I can't believe it got worst!

"I'm only doing what's right for the child, what choice do I have?"

My world had just crumbled before my eyes. How could he, how could he get that woman pregnant! He has only known her for a minute, how could he be getting married! She is a professional bitch! She has never liked me. Ever since she's been around she has been trying to throw a deeper wedge between Marcus and me. Now look! I can't breath... but I need to say something. I can't let him know how much this is hurting me! Compose yourself, I must get it together! I shifted in my seat increasing the space between us.

"Wow...that's a surprise. Marcus the sweet boy, getting married and having a child, damn! You're going to have to throw away your players card now!"

"I know. It's not something which I planned, I mean I can't believe it myself, Jasmine told me and I just couldn't believe it. Me, going to be a father. I had to propose to her, my mother just wouldn't let it go. I mean she tried to make me tie the knot before the baby is born, but I don't think I can handle that"

"What do you mean? Come on now, your going to do it next year, you must love her" My gosh those words were so hard for me to get out, I don't think I even want to hear the answer. I retreated back into the sofa, scared of the oncoming verbal slaughter.

"To be honest with you... I'm not actually sure. It's all happened so fast, I haven't had time to evaluate my feelings. All I know is that I'm going to be a father in six months for sure. Jay...I'm doing the right thing aren't I?"

"How can you ask me! You must know what you're doing, you obviously knew what you were doing when you slept with her unprotected" I snapped not realising that my feelings were being exposed right now.

"I know. You know what Jay, your right. I'm not going to make no excuses but she was supposed to be on the pill, but I should have known better and now I'm just taking responsibility for my actions"

"What you saying she trapped you?"

"I'm not saying that, but she did tell me she was on the pill. You remember that one girl in college that time that lied to me and told me she was pregnant"

"Oh my gosh, yeah now that was funny, she was the girlfriend from hell. She wouldn't stop at anything to get you back! Damn!" At this point I actually cracked a smile and a giggle as I rose back out from the shadows. "I'm happy for you I suppose. I'm just shocked that you're tying the knot before all of us! You're the last person anyone could see getting married!"

"Excuse you, your going on like I am such a hoe" He laughed.

"Oh please, don't play innocent with me. So full time commitment is knocking on your door, smelly nappies, pushing buggies all that heading your way!"

"Don't remind me. I always thought it would be different, you know with someone else…"

His eyes glistened as he looked at me. Was that directed at me? Why would it be? My emotions were getting the better of me so I interrupted the tension and got up rapidly. I can't pretend anymore all this talk was cutting me in two. My voice croaked. "I'm going to the ladies, be back in a minute"

I hurried over Marcus's legs and rushed to the bathroom almost bumping into the foreign waiter holding a tray of drinks. I wiped under my eyes carefully, not wanting the mascara to smudge. Oh my gosh, I just cannot believe what he has just told me. I looked in the mirror. Thank God I didn't tell him how I actually feel about him. I would have looked like a right fool. All this is my own fault, it could have been us together! Why

53

did I kick him out that night, why! Now he is marrying that bitch, I know she planned this. Fuck! How did this happen. I want to cry so bad.

I can't think straight.

Marcus is getting married!

I forced back my tears.

As I walked back to where we were sitting I thought about what he last said, about him wanting it to be with someone else because I wished this was not happening. I wished it were me. He was the perfect man, good job, career minded, he knew how to treat a woman. He was family orientated and God fearing so I understood where he was coming from proposing to her but why now, why her!

"Babes are you okay?" Marcus asked sincerely, the light giving him an angelic appearance as I walked back to the table.

If only he could read how bad I wanted it to be me, how bad I wanted this all to disappear, how much I really loved and cared for him. But of course I couldn't tell him that, so I lied again!

"I'm fine. Look its getting late I need to get to bed, I got a meeting early in the morning"

"Sure. Jay" He reached out and held my hand. "I just want you to know you're very special to me and I'm sorry about leaving it so late to tell you. I didn't want you to hear it from anyone else. I just... didn't know how to tell you... just in case... you know!"

"Marcus, it was a long time ago I'm past that now. I'm happy for you, really I am. It's just a shock because we used to be so close. I just thought you would have spoken to me before making such an important decision. But I know everything is different now"

"No it is not Jay. Not if we don't want it to be"

"Come on lets be real here. Number one your woman, well fiancée does not like me, never has and doubt if she ever will. Our friendship cannot get any better, not if she has anything to do with it. I would love it to be how it was back in college but it never is going to be. I will still love you the same, you will always have a special place in my heart and I hope I will in yours"

He lent forward and held my hand tighter, rubbing it gently with his thumb whilst he searched my eyes for what I was desperately trying to hide.

"Of course you will Jay, I'm telling you. You and Me for life no matter what. You remember what we used to say?"

We both laughed and said it together "We will ride or die together, friends forever, M&J"

After we finished reciting our little pact, I stood up and wrapped my scarf around my shoulders before quickly walking out of the now quiet bar. Marcus was close behind me trying to keep up with my hurried pace. He reached out and held onto my arm, forcing me to slow down before questioning if I had drove. I explained that I had not and he offered me a lift home. My heart was aching me, there was no way I could be around him any longer so I declined. I needed to be alone right now. I believe he understood as he didn't put up a resistance like he would normally do. I needed to digest what I had just heard. Once outside we shared a hug and another goodbye as he gave me a kiss on the cheek before looking into my eyes and rubbing his thumb against the same spot he just sanctified. He was so seductive without even knowing it. The streets were busy and noisy with drunk people falling out the bars in search of food. Marcus ushered me close to protect me from the oncoming barge from an unconcerned young lad. He looked as though he wanted to hold me close and never let me go but reality hit me as I waved goodbye, I flagged down a passing taxi and jumped in, leaving him standing on the cold pavement, alone.

Damn, how did I mess this up! I have lost the best man in my life and I know that no one will ever fill that void of Marcus.

Chapter 9.

Marcus

I sat in my car with my hands clasped on my brow listening to the sounds of the unexpected rain hitting my windscreen. Damn, I know Janet is hurting right now but I had to tell her. I only wish that things were not happening this way. I wish it were Janet I was marrying. But what choice do I have? She has expressed herself clearly that she could never get into anything romantic with me and that night was nothing more than one night. Did she actually mean it or was she shutting me out? Looks like I will never know because here I am engaged to be married to someone who I hardly know. I mean Jasmine is a sexy woman, but I don't love her. I don't. I can't at the moment I love Janet and I think I always have. I can't believe that I have messed up like this, how could I get her pregnant!

I stared through the rain blankly. I had hoped that within time Jay and I would have rekindle what we had that night and it would mould into a full loving beautiful relationship. I always held onto that thought but I had needs and that's how I ended up with Jasmine. She helped take my mind off Jay for a while. Now Jasmine is tall and sexy, she actually looks like a runway model but thing is I don't know if she is for me, she is too materialistic. She is already talking about the designer buggy she wants and a matching Louis Vitton baby bag. Come on now, that's just too much. I don't know how she is going to cope with a baby, she gets her nails done every week, parties like it is the last rave ever and she just knows everybody on the circuit and I mean *everybody*. But it is what it is at the moment, she's moving into my house in the next few weeks once I have sorted out the decorating and it's all final.

I can't believe I am losing my freedom like this. One minute she was coming over for the odd night during the week then the long weekends and now were having a baby, getting married and moving in together permanently. How did I get myself into this! Janet is perfect, she would be the perfect soul mate for me. We know each other so well and she still looks as good as she did in college, well that is a lie, she looks even better! She is doing well for herself. I feel so bad that it took this long for me to tell her. I think that she is hurting more than she is actually telling me. This is the first time she has not let me drop her home ever! I need to call her tomorrow to see if she is okay. I have realised that I need her around me, she is like my daily drug, she always puts a smile on my face no matter what and we have spent too much time apart. If I hadn't moved out of London, things would still be like old times and maybe just maybe I wouldn't be in this predicament I am in now.

Looks like I am going to have to learn to love Jasmine, she is carrying my child after all. I relaxed back into the comfort of my warm nappa leather seat and thought to myself I better just give her a quick call, make sure that she is okay…

Chapter 10.

Keshia

I woke up from my slumber, feeling no guilt at all. Untangling myself from the duvet I turned around and noticed that Bobby was fast asleep as usual after creeping back into the house about five in the morning. Unfortunate for him I was awoken by the sounds of the key unlocking the door. Why do I put up with this shit! It's not like I can't get anyone better! I'm sure I could get a whole lot better than him, but I love him and we should try.

I mean I shouldn't give up too easy.

I should give it a chance.

I've been too hasty in the past, too quick too move on so I'm going to work at this one, but how can I work alone? A relationship takes two and Bobby needs to start playing his part in this.

I slid out of the warm bed and went to the shower across the hall from our room. I stood at the door for a while watching Bobby asleep on the four poster oak bed in the centre of the room, spread with lilac sheets, surrounded by complementary cheap furniture and scented candles. He was definitely a sexy man. He lay there peacefully with not a worry or care on his face. His caramel skin blossomed at me with a radiance that only he could carry off. But that's what the girls loved and he knew this. He did not have to try, he was a charmer without even exploiting anything. I eased myself into the electric shower and adjusted the water to get hot enough to steam the room. I reached over and grabbed my scrunchy, lathering the shower gel into it forming suds which I strategically washed into my skin letting the sweet smell of jasmine and lavender eliminate my stress. The touch of the water on my soft skin made my thoughts get the better of me and I started thinking about the first time Bobby and I made love. A time when there were no other cares in the world, when I was oblivious to all the drama and the girls. I was the only thing which mattered that night and he made me feel so special. I thought I was on cloud nine for weeks. He had me dancing with stars. It was definitely a 'waiting to exhale' moment and damn I had exhaled at least eight times that night! He made my toes curl and my heart flutter. I think that was the moment he got me, the moment which has now led to this. I turned off the shower and stepped out grabbing my lilac towel then drying my skin delicately before creaming myself with rich coco butter lying on the over congested window ledge. I picked up my makeup bag from the cabinet and carefully put on my mascara and blue eye pencil in the partly steamed mirror. Bobby loved this shade on me and I wanted him to see exactly what he stood up last night. Although I was going to work, I wanted to make an effort just to slap it in his face once more. As I exited the bathroom I heard his gruff voice begin to talk...

"Babes, I'm sorry bout last night. I had to go and do something bout the madness. You understand don't you?"

He started talking and I shot him one look before walking over to the wardrobe and selecting the clothes I was going to wear. I answered him angered at his choice of words.

"Bobby, you know what. It doesn't matter what I think anymore. All I can see is you not sticking to your end of the agreement. We have been back together for a few months and you're already letting them bitches interfere with our relationship again. Look if you don't want this to work, then please say because I don't really want to be wasting my time again thinking shit will change!"

He sat up indirectly aggravated at the potential argument. "Kesh, I love you so much and I know you're fed up with me. I promise it won't happen again..."

"Don't promise me anything please, because it doesn't mean a thing! It's just a lie, because you cannot keep to your promises"

"Babes don't be like that I'm trying"

"You're not trying hard enough" I shouted, slamming the wardrobe door. "You left me here all alone again! Last night was supposed to be *OUR* night, no one else but ours and you left me. You left me and ran to the defence of her, putting our relationship in jeopardy for her once again. Do you even care how it makes me feel? No you don't, I'm telling you, you need to do something about it. You need to decide what you want. I am not going to let her be the third wheel in our relationship anymore. So you decide Bobby!"

"What? Woman, what are you going on about, you're carrying on like I'm having an affair with her! I'm not, she is just my friend but if you don't want me to talk to her again, then fine because I love *you* and I will do anything I can to save this relationship"

"Well, let's start with you locking her off. There should be no need for you to contact her anymore should there? She is just going to end up getting you killed!"

"Don't be so dramatic babe. Look I sorted out the madness yesterday, well calmed it down. Riddler said he is going to give her two weeks to repay his money"

"Why? What has she done this time that it will take two weeks for her to make payment and don't even think about giving her any money!" I said with a stern look on my face, because I knew he is a sucker and will do just that. I continued to get dressed angrily.

"Don't be silly babes. Basically she is going to have to sell her car. She sort of run this scam behind his back and it went pear shaped, its all stupid to be honest"

"Yeah, and that's the sort of people you like to hang around with!"

"Look babes, let's just forget it. Let me make up last night to you!"

He had this horny look on his face and I knew just what he was thinking, but hell no! After he left me home alone last night, he is not getting any for a few days!

"Are you serious, because I think you're a comedian right now! You better put on one of your DVDs and exercise your right hand because I'm going to work!"

"Babes, don't mess about! You can't leave me like this!"

He took the covers off his body and exposed his full erection. It was tempting but right now I needed to stick to my words, how dare he choose her over me!

"Babe, lie there and reflect on the sexy black and red lingerie set, with my stockings and black stilettos, which I was going to wear for you *LAST NIGHT* !"

It made me feel good leaving him lying in the bed like a confused child, but I cannot let him get away with this right now, he took the blatant piss. I turned around and walked out of the room without giving into the temptation that was tearing between my legs. I could hear Bobby sighing in the bedroom and pleading with me to come back to bed. I wanted him to suffer so I quickly grabbed an apple and muesli bar from the kitchen and left the house without saying goodbye just to show him how angry I was with him. Normally no matter what, we never left the house without giving each other a kiss, but today was different. He had broken his promise already and for that two faced bitch. Allowing myself to think about Shanny and Bobby together last night made my blood boil so I decided to take a slow walk down to the train station. I needed to calm myself down and ponder on my thoughts for a while. I walked at a brisk pace and reflected on the past ineffectual men that I had been with before Bobby. Now there was Omar, he was so fine, intelligent, ambitious, romantic and had money. Only thing was that he had too many bad relationships which haunted him like a reoccurring dream. I mean he would have been perfect if he was not so conceited. Some men just feel that they have to constantly be the alpha male and remind you at every opportunity. He would continuously go on about how much in bonuses he would be getting at work and how he could buy anything he wanted. The thing which got to me the most was his constant reminders of the things which he bought for his ex's. Now what kind of man actually keeps a full account of everything they have ever bought a girlfriend! Well he bloody did and that used to really annoy me, it's like he was doing it for recognition, not from the kindness of his heart. He bought me a diamond bracelet once and he never let me live that one down. Even when we broke up he tried to ask for it back, now how pathetic was that! Then there was Simon. I should have known he would have been trouble because he had off-key features from the start. This man would phone me up all hours of the night asking me where I was and what I was doing. He would offer to pick me up from work and follow me everywhere I went. I'm sure he was borderline obsessively disturbed because all this happened in the first month of us dating! Now Lionel, he was the bum! The sexy arse no good man that we all come across a t one point in our life. He was so good in bed and adventurous. Hell, we did it almost everywhere, outside in the park, the car, the lift, in the rave, the swimming pool, kitchen table and even on the train. We had some good times, but wherever we went I was footing the bill. He was on job seekers allowance and a part time fraudster, who I must admit was not very good at his criminal trade. He spent most of his day smoking weed and driving about with his brother. Although the sex was great, it became tedious carrying him and I thought about the things he would teach our kids and it was not a good look at all! There was also Teddy, yes the fat lover. He was not that big but squishy like a bear- soft and cuddly. What went wrong with him? He had a good job, good to converse with but he had five children with four different women and he lived at home with his mother! Oh yeah, not to forget Matty, sweet but too soft. Come on everyone needs a man that can defend them and Matty was just too nice for his own good. I could walk all over him without even trying. No one wants a man that they can fully control, one who doesn't put up any resistance. So you know he had to go! I briefly recollected on the many others, but they were not even worth thinking about. I mean you have your first date and you think that they are the best thing ever. They tell you everything you want to hear, like they have a script for men on how to trap women like a spider laying its web. You fall for all the sweet talk and the serenading. Then they go for the kill and then two, three months later you find out that the person you have just given yourself to is a fraud, a fake, you have been bamboozled and by then it is too late. You either bail out and add another failed relationship to your list of annulled encounters or you press on and stick with rubbish which you do not really want, because you are afraid to move onto another relationship due to fear of being labelled as a 'hoe'. Well for me, I don't actually care. If it doesn't work out I move on. I don't waste anytime waiting anymore. Yeah maybe I am a fool for the charmers and I try their goods too quick. But who determines too quick? I mean how long does a woman have to wait to find out that the man is no good and you're totally incompatible in the bedroom! Please, I would rather find out sooner than later!

Things with Bobby have been an entire turn around for me, I mean I have had to do a total 360 on the situation. I went back and I decided to try again! But Bobby is taking too long to adjust, too long to change and I'm searching, I am an impatient person and I want mine now. It is about time for me to be happy. I'm fed up of watching these bitches take all the good men and be happy. I'm a good woman, when is it going to be my turn? Yeah, I am sort of cheating at the moment but it is something which developed when Bobby decided that he wanted to chase those useless girls and be a bachelor like his cousin. That's when I met Clayton. So in theory I'm not actually doing anything wrong. Me and Bobby getting back together just happened so quick, like watching a cheetah in the African Jungle chase its prey. Before I could blink we were talking about moving in together. I just didn't have time or the heart to tell Clayton it was over, I mean he comes in handy sometimes. And it is always good to have a plan B!

Chapter 11.

Leyah

You know there is this period in your life that most women go through, where they meet the most perfect man. He is everything you have ever dreamed, he is handsome, sexy, stylish, sweet, and charming. Your family loves him, he is attentive to your every need, he knows how to maintain a smile on your face and keep you feeling all warm inside. He is the perfect fit to you and you look like a Hollywood couple together, he challenges you physically and mentally. Someone who finishes your sentences for you without being intimidating, that special someone who makes your body tingle without even touching you, strictly on the basis of reminiscence. Every time you think about that person you can't help but to smile, because he will never make you cry. The last person who you think about before you go to bed and the first person who crosses your mind as soon as you wake. That special someone who is real, but sounds like a fairy tale. We all know that someone, we've had one or know someone who has experienced one. Yeah, it's a damn good feeling and you hoped it would last forever, only problem is that he has a woman and he is not yours, but you have developed such a bond that you cant help but think about what life would be like with him for the rest of your life. Come on he ticks all the boxes, it's just that you did not meet him first and it hurts to even think about all the good loving he is giving his girl. Your heart aches at the thought of someone else holding your property, but he is not. He is not 'officially' yours but in your own perfect ideal world he would be.

Life can be strange at times and you will meet someone who appears to be your soul mate only to find that he has eloped with another. That was Reese and me. He was everything I ever desired, everything I had pictured as a teenager, you know at that age when you start planning how you want your life to be and how your husband and family will be.

Only thing was that the penny dropped and hit the floor. Reality struck and although I know he had strong feelings for me, his loyalties were already set. He was with her, she had scooped him up and locked him down. Fortunate for me to some extent the chain was not fully locked and I was able to slip in, unaware of his situation of course. But in a way I don't regret any of the moments we shared, even though it was all mainly based on a lie, a mirage, a piece of science fiction. I loved him, it's just that the bastard got me pregnant before I woke up and opened my eyes to what was beyond my belief.

I remember one particular time, where the moment was too perfect to be true. We were in hot and sunny Barbados enjoying this lovely hotel we stayed at called 'Sand beach Castle'. Everything was like a fantasy, our hotel room was filled with flowers and candles. Reese had really gone all out for this trip. He paid for everything and the surprises kept on coming... It was one of those beautiful cool evenings and I returned from the hotel shopping mall content, having just purchased the sexiest two piece swimsuit ever. It was white with gold diamante trimmings and a gold belt along the top of the bikini knickers. It was so stunning; I just could not leave it on the shelf! When I opened the door to our hotel room all I could hear is the soft sound of R. Kelly's- *Seems like your ready'* playing. Wow! Then I saw his tall, slender shadow in-between the smoke left by the candles walk towards me. He was wearing nothing but a white towel wrapped around his waist, holding a flute of champagne in his left hand. He slowly walked up to me and took the bag out of my hand, handed me the flute then delicately kissed my forehead and without saying a word he ushered me into the bathroom. Once we entered the huge bright room with the most breath taking view of the sea, he looked deep into my eyes and then he bent down slowly, gliding his hands down my legs before slipping off my sandals. He rose up and kissed my lips so seductively that my breath was literally taken out of me. At that point I had to say something or attempt to say something...

"Baby, what's this all about?"

"Shhhh"

He silenced me and run his hands up my thighs to my waist and then up to my warm breasts. He took off my lilac chiffon dress as I stood there marvelling in all the control he was taking. I could view the bubbles rising in the luxurious hot tub at the back of the bathroom, surrounded with white candles and red rose petals floating in the large tub.

I was standing there in just my Victoria Secrets.

He looked me up and down and my body just melted... before I knew it my underwear was off and he walked me towards the bath directing my feet in slowly, before taking off his towel and tossing it to the ground. We were both consumed by the atmosphere, the soft feel of the bubbles and rose petals. It was so romantic. We didn't need to say anything, the music said it all. We just lay there while he stroked my hair and caressed my body for about an hour. My head was totally consumed by him, he was all I could think about and vision, everything at that moment was perfect. There was nothing to worry about, nothing to consider. But that of course did not last for long!

Reese is a good man, just in a situation. I suppose it happens to the best of us, meaning me! It is easy to fall in love with two people I guess. I mean one may have qualities which the other lacks, one may caress you better than the other, they may stimulate every sense in your body, your mind, heart and touch every emotion. So I guess it's not an easy situation to be in and it is not one which is planned. You don't 'really' plan who you fall in love with, it just happens most times. You just lose total control of yourself and become consumed by the loving and tenderness that person gives. It may not be down to looks, desirable features, wealth or even sex. Sometimes the person just steals your heart and that's it! I can say that was it for me. I was blind to everything else, I just wanted him, I wanted everything about him to be with me forever, but there is no such thing as forever is there?

Chapter 12.

Keshia

My eyes were glued in amazement. I slowly licked my glossed lips while taking in everything about him. He was about 6'2, dark toned with small well kept locks. This man had it all. He was dressed in a kaki short sleeved top emphasising his well toned torso with matching combats clinging onto his big manly thighs sitting directly in my visual proximity on the highlighted stage by the staircase, playing his guitar with his sexy manly fingers. The whole audience was captured by his sweet sensual sound. It was like the sound of a sweet humming bird coming from the tropical breeze. It was totally phenomenal. It was sensual, the notes he played rushed through my body like a burning pulse. I looked on mesmerised, stuck in a trance. How did he make it feel so real? He appeared not to be making any effort at all as his lips sang the passionate words of lust. I blinked out of my thoughts. I had made up my mind, as soon as he finishes his performance I'm going to have to say something to him, tell him how his music is making me feel! Janet, Leyah and myself had one of the best tables in the house. We had waited six weeks to reserve a table here at the Velvet Café, this was the place to be at the moment. It was the place for raw, sensational unsigned talent. You would see an array of people performing from poets to comedians in the warm welcoming atmosphere. The venue was decorated with huge dark violet velvet drapes and scarlet candles complementing the large round tables which were plotted carefully on the main floor opening up the small stage at the front. I looked around and admired the huge portraits of various abstracts and city landscapes. The Velvet Café served the most delicious colourful cocktails all presented with perfection and what made it even more unique was the exotic food menu offering a vast selection of meals while you enjoyed the show. We all looked stunning tonight, wearing various simple but snazzy outfits. Making a statement that we were not desperate for a man to come and take care of us, but could handle our own. It was ladies night out for us, a time to catch up on gossip and give out advice that we would not actually follow ourselves, but it was all part of being a good friend. The night also gave rise to scouting the eye candy, seeking the singles which were still out on the shelf. I mean we were all practically single. Well apart from myself, but I still had to hook up a plan B. An alternative. I had to line up a friend in waiting because with Bobby most times nothing he says is long lived.

The dimly lit venue was filled with an enormous encore as the sexy musician finished his set. From the amount of applause he received, you could tell the crowd loved him even the men had to show their appreciation. As he stepped off the stage and into the arms of one of the organisers he was replaced with a less entertaining blonde female hippy looking singer, wearing a pleasantly gorgeous gipsy dress. My eyes desperately tried to follow where the sexy musician was headed as he walked through the tables, but the girls constantly interrupted my quest debating the problems with men and the recent long list of admirers in Leyah's life which she ignored. I gave up and turned my concentration back to the conversation, making a mental note to take a trip to the ladies in ten minutes to find the musician. We sat and enjoyed the sounds of a poet, strongly expressing the lyrics about Love and Pain, feeling every word he spoke intensely as he moved with the words. I looked around the overcrowded room, squinting my eyes through the dark but there was no sign of the sexy musician. Finally our platter of spicy Caribbean chicken dippers and brandy soaked king prawns had arrived, which was delivered by the exhausted glamour puss waitress. As soon as she headed back to the hot kitchen I glimpsed the sexy musician walking through the nearby crowd. My natural instincts jumped out of me as we locked eyes and I signalled him to come over to our table. I quickly reassessed my posture, trying to look casual and not desperate whilst ensuring that my best assets were on full display. He looked over indecisively and then decided against ignoring my rudeness and began walking our way…

"Hi, do I know you?" He said exposing his sexy and powerful voice.

"No. Sorry" I said with a little embarrassment in my tone. "I just wanted to tell you that you were fantastic up there tonight, it was very impressive. My name is Keshia and you are?"

"I'm Kamarni. Nice to meet you Keshia"

He took hold of my sweaty palm and gently gave it a shake whilst I tried to linger onto his touch. Here I am talking with the sexy musician and I'm flirting with him big time, fluttering my heavily mascara eyelashes confidently, picturing that tall torso wrapped around my body. I slowly let go of his hand, fighting back the hot flush that raced though my body remembering that we were not alone.

"Girls meet the star behind the soulful music, which stole my heart" I said with a slight emphasis in my tone, looking dead in his eyes.

"Wow your music is so beautiful"

"Where did you learn to play like that?"

"How long have you been playing?"

"Do you write your own music?"

He laughed. Yes we were all up in his grill. We managed to capture him before all the other hungry women in the club went for the sting. Every single woman in the room was checking out his every asset. Looking for the ring… and *yes* the finger was bare.

Kamarni joined us at our table as I made room for him on the velvet booth, right next to me. His leg accidentally touched mine as he eased his body in. Exhale. We all sat speaking about his music, captured by his every word, listening attentively as he answered our Spanish inquisition. He was so fascinating and not to mention sexy. He spoke so many powerful things in the short time we experienced his presence, showing that he was passionate about his heritage and his love of music. The conversation was inspiring and uplifting for me. He had the ability to recite the appropriate quote to capture the moment and add his own signature to it. His frame alone was enough to make your body shudder

69

like you had just experienced the biggest orgasm ever. I wanted to hear more. I wanted to be consumed in this mans life.

"Well ladies, it was nice speaking to you all but I have to go. You all enjoy the rest of your night and remember to stay blessed…"

That was it, the moment we shared was over and he was rising to get up without even leaving a contact number.

"…See you around, sometime" He said with a sensual tone, looking directly at me as the words floated from his defined smooth lips. I could see the desire in his eyes, through his words. In response I bit my lip seductively and gave him a look, which said 'I sure hope so'. And with that he left, walking through the crowd stopping to talk to the grungy Justin Timberlake lookalike.

"Oh my gosh, snap out of it. You don't have to look so desperate Kesh!" Leyah sniggered snapping her long unpolished fingers at me, waking me out of my mesmerised state.

"Yeah, you are one horny lady and you're the one with the full time, resident man! Look at us two, we haven't got anything and you got everything. We got dicks in jars…"

"Ummm hum and batteries on standby" Leyah added.

"… And there you are being all greedy. Taking all the men, not leaving anything for us. Cor, you undressed him with your eyes a thousand times and exhaled so many times I lost count!"

We all laughed. It was true. I was not satisfied at home or maybe in life. I was always subconsciously searching. Searching for something better, someone with more to offer, more love to give. I wasn't even sure that if I found that man I would be satisfied, but right now all I knew was that I was seeking Kamarni!

"Look Janet, you can talk. Come on, Marcus is back in town and he is the finest brother *EVER* and you just let him slip out your hands again and again!" I preached. "He is one fine chocolate brother and you need

70

to go and grab your man. Heck I'm jealous I didn't meet him first and here you are playing with him!"

"Yep, Kesh has got a point there Jay!" Leyah said nodding in agreement.

Janet immediately rose to her defence. "Look, it just isn't that simple!"

"What! Look if you don't take risks in life, where would we all be?… In this small safety bubble, scared of making a mistake. Well life is about making mistakes, falling over and getting up and trying again. Stop taking the safer option, it is not always the right one. You will regret it when your old and grey, pondering on what if 's!" Listen to me, the big relationship philosopher. I had this habit of dishing out good advice for others but not for myself. But I'm a risk taker, I don't waste time. I react to the moments, not leave them in the air. You haven't lived until you have taken numerous risks.

"Marcus already has a woman! And anyway any possibility of us being an item is out the window because he told me some shocking news the other night when we went out for a drink"

"Oh my gosh! What was it? He's not gay is he?" Leyah joked.

We all laughed, but I could tell that this moment of laughter was overcome by a sense of sadness in Janet's heart. Her eyes always told the truth and the truth was something she did not want it to be.

"Girls" She took a deep sigh. "… Marcus is engaged and to top that he is also expecting a baby!"

We both gasped in disbelief. My mind quickly comprehending what she just disclosed. "What! I can't believe it. Marcus, getting married! How? When? Why? and with who?" The shocked words rolled from my mouth. I knew it was bad news but I would have never guessed it was as devastating as this. And here I was earlier all self consumed with the sexy musician.

"You know that bloody woman I told you about, that he was flexing with!"

71

"Oh, not the personal assistant?" I said scornfully, turning up my nose hoping it was not her.

"Yeah, her! Well she has trapped him, she's pregnant and now he feels obligated to marry her. I just can't believe my Marcus is marrying her. I mean she is such a chicken head. She has nothing but her looks. Marcus has told me things about her from the start. He would have never made her his wife on his own accord. Not to say he isn't a good guy, because he is…. I know she just wanted to trap him… how could he let himself get trapped like this…"

She buried her hands in her head forcing the tears not to ruin her mascara. Janet, was really upset. Despite her breaking down she was talking one hundred miles per hour.

"Look Jay don't worry about it, it won't last. He does not love her. I'm sure even she knows that" Leyah said trying to sound comforting while I pulled out a Kleenex from my bag.

"Babes, that woman is dread! Marcus is your man! It's supposed to be you and him. How did this happen?... Don't worry about it. Let me get another round of drinks, we need it"

We continued to talk for the next two hours while getting through three more cocktail jugs, trying to comfort Janet. This was bad news! Marcus was one of the most eligible bachelors we knew. Him and Janet were perfect for each other. Since we were in College they had this weird relationship, they were always close. I remember they looked so sweet together, they complimented each other fluently. Because of their chemistry all the girls in college used to hate Janet. Marcus was such a handsome, lovable guy. If only Janet didn't take so long to confront her feelings she had towards him, then this would not have happened. He was one of the most perfect men ever. He made me believe that there are actually some good men out in the world.

The bar was still lively when I looked down at my watch noticing the time which had gone so quick. It was now after two o'clock. I enlightened the girls with the time and we got up deciding it was time to make our way home to our separate destinations. I watched the remainder of the crowd sip on their alcoholic beverages and my mind drifted towards all the happy couples that were in the bar, holding hands, whispering sweet words in their woman's ears and touching their partner delicately but enough to declare that they loved them. Love was a beautiful thing but one feeling which did not knock on our doors very often. We just happened to be the three unluckiest beautiful and successful women on this side of town, who I must add seemed to attract the most useless, un-committing men. When was it going to be one of our turns to be happy, to be the ones getting proposed to by a 'decent' man and have that overwhelming feeling that we have met the 'one' and be able to build a life together! The thoughts drifted through my mind until I hastily snapped out of it as I felt Leyah hand me my Red Dior handbag.

We strolled slowly out of the venue and into the chilly deserted streets of Notting Hill and hailed a taxi as it drove down the road looking for customers leaving the small wine bars and cocktail lounges. The driver needed to make three stops to drop each of us home because there was no driving home tonight. The alcohol was acting as a temporary amnesia drug to help us forget about all the worries in our lives, all the things that we did not want to think about at this present time. The taxi ride took us over Battersea Bridge to the first drop off for Leyah in Streatham, then the short journey towards Thornton Heath to drop Janet off. As we pulled up to her house I could see the sadness in her face, the fact that she had to walk into an empty house. I remember that feeling, the notion of being alone, no one to tip toe into the house for in case you woke them up, no one to slip gently into the bed like a feather for just in case you disturbed their tender dreams. It was not a nice feeling, how I don't miss it at all. But I understood how she was feeling and to make it worse she was more than likely thinking about Marcus tucked up all snugly with that cow, holding her tightly in his strong muscular arms. I know those thoughts can hurt you like a knife wound to the back but us women just cant stop thinking about such hurtful things, wishing that it wasn't so, wishing that we were the ones being held at that moment. Janet slowly rose out of the taxi, we exchanged a brief goodbye and I ordered her to rest her head, telling her that I will call her tomorrow. She murmured the same, before hurriedly walking towards her house with her keys ready to push through the door. A chilly wind was blowing and the scattered leaves on the streets were dancing a circular motion as if they were reciting a short performance. I watched Janet disappear into her house safely, before the taxi drove off towards my destination through the quiet deserted streets of South London. I sat in the back of the car thinking about going home, thinking about how I actually felt about Bobby, how I felt about the relationship. Did I actually love him or was I afraid to be alone! I must love him to put up with all this drama but in contrast if I did I wouldn't be flirting all the time with other men. I would be satisfied with him and him alone. But I'm not, I need more but I'm not sure if I need it from him! We arrived at my flat and I paid the taxi driver the fare which had totalled £54. I took my keys out of my bag as I closed the taxi door, allowing the driver to search for his next customer. The sound of my heels echoed on the pavement as I walked towards the communal door. As I arrived the wind blew across my face and made me shudder quickly, forcing me to take shelter. I quickly shut the door behind me and climbed the stairs to my second floor flat, thinking about Kamarni and how he made me feel, briefly reliving the moment I stared in his eyes as he was playing and the gentle touch of his aloe vera hands, watching them move seductively over the strings as his head move in rhythm to the sounds. I opened my eyes forcing myself to gather my thoughts together and get in this house. I quickly looked at my watch, it was now 3:45. I wonder if Bobby is even at home, knowing him he is out with his 'boys'. Oh well at least I don't have to worry about being quiet, not that he ever does when he comes in late.

I pushed the key into the door. Well here it goes …

Chapter 13.

Janet

I looked over my shoulder and watched my phone ringing again on the armchair. I sighed. I had successfully avoided all incoming calls from Marcus for the past two weeks by fobbing him off and telling him that I was busy, promising to call him back. Now his name was flashing on my caller I.D. again. I took a deep breath before reaching for the handset holding it in my hand, watching it ring.

Should I answer it?

No. I just can't face talking to him at the moment. I put the phone back down on the chair, rubbing my hands through my hair. I had such a long stressful day at the office today and I was not in any mood to try and pretend that I was not hurting, that I was not suffering inside. All I could think about was Marcus walking down the aisle with that woman and the two of them sitting cosy in their living room with the baby bouncing happily in its bouncer. Shit, why was I feeling like this! It's not like we have been close lately. It's just that he has this weird effect on me. He was like a drug, which I had previously detoxed from and now it was in front of my face here again, more powerful than ever. I couldn't get him out of my mind.

I held the phone in the palm of my hand once again as it continued to ring, I lounged back in my large cream sofa with the dim ceiling lights casting a slight shadow across the room. Marcus had left eight missed calls and three voice messages and yes I felt bad that I hadn't answered not one of them. It's just that I can't bring myself to it! I know he must be worried, but I did say that I would call him back and he knows that sometimes I have these busy periods where I don't answer my phone! Actually that was a lie! I almost always answered the phone, even if it was to say I will call the person back, especially if it was him. A few more unanswered calls and he would get the message that I am just too busy to talk to him at the moment. It was now eight thirty and I was sat comfortably on the sofa watching Waiting to Exhale on my plasma screen hung on the centre of my huge coffee coloured wall. My living room was surrounded by various decorative wall mounts which I had accumulated from my trips to Africa, giving the room some culture. My house was well decorated. I was a bit of a perfectionist and very house-proud. I liked having nice things and being surrounded by order but it was lonely sometimes. I had three bedrooms, one which I used as an office and the other one a guest room, not that I had many overnight visitors. My well sized dining room opened up the adjoining conservatory and I had a huge garden which I recently had a landscaper design to include decking, beautiful floral arrangements and a little pond. I loved my great outdoors, it was my sanctuary, somewhere I could go and gather my thoughts. Well that was only when the weather was actually nice enough to do so, which was very rare these days, just like my happy days!

Suddenly there was a knock at my door… who could that be? I slowly rose up, suspicious like I was a TV licence avoider. No one had said that they were coming by, only my mother would stop by unannounced, but it was a weekday so I quickly eradicated that possibility from my mind. I was all out of possibilities and my query was left blank. I cautiously proceeded towards the door, trying to look at the silhouette through the frosted glass pane but I failed to recognise the tall slender shadow. Maybe it was Frank from next door returning the car hoover I had lent him last week. Nah, doubt it, not at this time of night. I had given up guessing and asked who it was. As I awaited the reply patiently I heard a familiar voice which made my body freeze in astonishment…

"Jay, it's me" Came the recognizable husky voice.

What was he doing here knocking at my door? I was puzzled. I awoke from my temporary shock and hurriedly turned to look in the mirror next to the door to fix my hair and make sure the rest of my attire was in order.

"Marcus… what are you doing here?" I said with a slightly shocked sound in my voice as I opened the door.

He looked at me with a sincere look on his cute face as he was exposed to the warmth escaping from my house. "Well, I was worried and you haven't answered my calls or returned my messages, so I thought I better come over and check that you were okay"

"Oh!… well…." I had nothing to say in my defence, but before I could concoct a story in my head, he cut me off…

"Look are you going to leave me out on your doorstep in this cold or let me come in?"

"Sorry, of course come in. It's just that I wasn't expecting you so I'm a bit stunned that you're here"

He smiled at me suspiciously while I opened the door wider and motioned him to come in, slowly shutting the heavy oak door behind him as he walked past me and into the corridor. He suddenly stopped and automatically slid off his shoes placing them neatly alongside the skirting. Damn, he looked so nice. How dare he come into my house unannounced looking all sexy still wearing his suit. I looked on in admiration at his slender body in his well tailored grey suit with a crisp light blue shirt underneath and a complimentary silver striped tie. Wow. Marcus sure knew how to dress and how to make a suit look good. I escorted him into the living room, trying to shake the tiredness out of my system. He entered and sat down on the two-seater sofa, his eyes looking around in amazement.

"Wow girl, you have done so well. Your house is remarkable. I knew my girl would do well, but damn!"

"Oh, stop Marcus" I laughed. "You know your house is ten times better than mine"

"Babes, you have done so well, I'm so proud of you"

"Thanks. It was not easy as you know, but I've made it. I've finally managed to get the house which I have always dreamed about"

"You sure have girl"

I could see the admiration in his eyes and I thought back to when we were in college, how we always used to speak about our lives in the future and how we would like to be living comfortably by the time we were thirty. I smiled remembering the conversation. We both had done well having almost everything which we had desired back then and before our desired age limit. It was all because we stuck to our dreams, we did not let anyone tells us that we could not achieve what our hearts desired. Marcus found it harder than myself, having come across a lot of discrimination and negativity within his chosen field and mostly from his peers but he did not let it deter him and now he was one of the top Barristers in England. We had each others backs and would always be inseparable.

"Jay, so where have you been? How comes you haven't called me back?" He asked lounging back into the soft leather.

"Marcus, to be honest I have been so busy trying to get this new contract sorted out. Everyday I get home, I'm just so tired. I was going to call you at the weekend anyway".

"Jay, you don't need to lie to me, I know you better than I know myself remember!"

It was true, I was lying and Marcus knew it, but I could not tell him the truth about how I felt. But why not? Let me just get it out in the open...

"Jay, I know you're shocked and upset about Jasmine. Fuck it, I am too. But I need your support right now. I need to know that I can come and talk to you babes. I don't know what I'm doing anymore, I don't know if I can make this work!"

I could see the worry in his face as he spoke and yet his words were not making any sense to me.

"Marcus, what do you mean? You've totally lost me"

"I don't know myself Jay. It's like I'm trapped in the twilight zone. I don't think I want this anymore. Jasmine's moved in to my house now and it's been a nightmare! And to be honest I think it's because I do not really love her yet. I'm just pretending to myself that this is the right thing to do. She's talking about the wedding and stuff and showing me all these wedding books. It's just all so real now and I'm not sure if I can actually do it!"

Yes, realisation! Marcus was actually thinking straight now, the cloud had disappeared and he was peering through trying to find the light. This all happened so fast, I don't think he even had enough time to consider the consequences and the lifetime commitment he was signing up for. He knows Jasmine is not 'wifey' material, she is just a trophy girl. Someone who's beauty will dazzle everyone everywhere they go, but she is all looks and nothing else. Shallow. Very shallow.

"Marcus I'm not sure what to say. A couple weeks ago you sounded so sure that you were doing the right thing"

"I know, but how can I marry someone who I do not love? Jay, *I don't love her*".

The way Marcus stressed the last four words I felt like he was trying to convince me, but why would he be?

"So why are you marrying her? Marriage is something you cannot rush into, you cannot go into it hoping that one day you will wake up and everything is different, that you love her. It doesn't work that way Marcus and that way someone will get hurt! Don't let her pressure you into it if you're having doubts"

My response actually came from my heart. No I didn't want him to marry her but I did not want him to make a huge mistake and regret it later after it was too late. Marrying her was defiantly a huge mistake and he knew it would be, but he was fighting with his morals and trying to do what would be right for the baby. Marcus was sitting looking all stressed, with his head clasped in his hands. His sensual eyes which

79

normally glowed were sunken in its sockets. I looked on feeling sorry for his predicament, but feeling sorrier for myself that I had lost the best man in my life. I need to divert my thoughts before I talk myself into exposing my true feelings. I took the opportunity to offer him a drink as the conversation was becoming too deep. I rose up gently acknowledging his sorrow by lightly touching his shoulders before walking towards the kitchen leaving him sitting on the sofa in deep thought. When I entered back into the room, with the two glasses in my hand Marcus was standing up looking through my CD collection. I couldn't help admiring him standing there. I was mesmerised by him, lusting after him, yet he was here to hear words of comfort, to help sooth him out of his confused state. I couldn't lie to him I had to tell him exactly what I felt about the situation. I walked towards him and handed him the glass of Guinness. He sniggered, expressing his recognition that I remembered his choice of alcohol. Since he had been in town I had gone and bought four, just in case he ever ended up at my house, no sexual intentions but I just wanted to be prepared! He took a sip of his brown beverage which left a small amount of froth on his upper lip before he skilfully removed it instantly as I secretly watched.

"Jay, you still got that CD which I made for you back in college! I can't believe you still have it" Marcus said excited, taking the CD out of its case and admiring the little message which he had wrote on it: *'To my girl for life. I will always be a true man'.*

I smiled as well, remembering the reason why he made the CD, which was to try and prove that he was not like the other guys at college, adopting Jagged Edge's tune *'True Man'* as his theme song. "Of course I have. Why wouldn't I?"

"You got all these old school songs that I haven't heard in ages babes. Damn, I got to put this on..." He said excited as he walked towards my stereo throwing his jacket to one side.

"What you putting on?"

"Wait and listen babes, I haven't heard this for the longest!"

He opened the CD drive and placed the disk in. As soon as it loaded he pressed play on the system selecting track number nine. I listened carefully, sitting in the sofa anticipating the song to start. Then I heard the tune begin…

"Oh my gosh, Bootsy Collins babes! I remember we used to try and sing this song whilst trying to revise" We both laughed reminiscing on those times.

"Jay, get up. Come dance with me" He said walking over to me offering his left hand as support. I had to laugh at the thought of it, but he looked so funny lightly moving by himself to the music twisting his hips and his shoulders to the sounds of the lyrics in front of me, humorously.

"Dance, where! You're funny" I giggled. Marcus reached over and pulled me out of my slumber as I tried to hold back.

"Come on, this was our song!"

It was true, we loved this track. The lyrics were so inappropriate right now, because I would rather him be with me instead of Jasmine. Pushing the thoughts into the back of my head, I got up reluctantly and joined him in the middle of the living room. His hands were as soft as I remember. He placed them strategically around my waist and we rocked to the sound of the music coming from the stereo. His touch made my body melt. I was trying to keep my mind focused, trying not to imagine the night we shared and how good he made me feel. But I gave into the feeling, closing my eyes and squeezing a little tighter. We danced to the entire song and into the next song which was another one of our other favourites; 'Tender Love'. As the song began he held me tighter and pulled me nearer, so close that I could feel the beating of his heart as I rested my head on his comforting shoulders. The moment felt so beautiful and I was trying my hardest not to feel every moment of it. Trying to hold back the feelings which I felt at that moment in time. To make the battle worse Marcus began singing in my ears. I don't think he realised what it was doing to me, it was just a natural reaction for him. He always used to sing this song every time it came on. But now the soft sound of his voice and the feel of his warm breath on my ears were making me tingle all over. We danced passionately, with my head buried

81

deep in his chest, caught up in the moment. He was rubbing my upper arms as we danced, our hips locked together. I could tell that he didn't want this moment to end, just like myself. But it was all too much and I had to do what was best for me and interrupt the rising heat. My heart could not take anymore because the moment felt so right, but it was wrong. I wanted him to be mine, all mine. I stepped away deceivingly reaching for my glass. Marcus picked up on my uncomfortable vibe and thoughtfully tried to change the awkward moment.

"Jay, these tunes make me feel so young again. They make me feel like I have no problems at all. It's funny"

"I know what you mean. If only that was the case" I turned and looked away, staring at the muted TV. If only he knew what I was really feeling. How much I yearned for him.

Marcus lowered the volume on the stereo and reached for his glass to quench his thirst. I tried to do the same but to help cool down the heat which had surfaced through that dance. We sat back down on the sofa sipping on our drinks, bathing in the chilled atmosphere. It was nice to sit and chill with Marcus, we hadn't done this in such a long time. We were relaxed talking and laughing about the old days. It was getting late, yet we were not worried about the time even though we both had work in the morning. A few hours later and we had gone through two bottles of wine and two Guinness and we were feeling very tipsy. I was laughing at everything. I knew the wine had gone to my head! I just hoped Marcus had not driven over here, because there is no way he could drive home now with the amount of alcohol that was in his system. No I'm not suggesting that he should stay, all I know is that he shouldn't drive. We lounged on the sofa talking, listening to Angie Stone playing in the background. I listened attentively as Marcus began telling me about his experiences in Luton. All the country girls that tried to bed him and the amount of people that asked him if he lived in Brixton. I had to tease him on a few occasions because I know he must have slept with at least one blonde bimbo! Although he continues to deny it, I don't believe him. Come on now, what man would reject a girl throwing themselves at them everywhere they go! That's impossible for them and Marcus is H.O.T.T, so I know that they must have been hounding him down constantly. It was funny listening to him talking because all his words were lethargic, he was in his 'chilled out' mood which the effects of alcohol had taken him to. I loved the way which he switched out of his work mode, leaving all the elocution lessons at the office door and then shifting into his 'normal' mode.

I got up and dished up the left over dinner from earlier for him. I had cooked flying fish and macaroni pie with salad and roast potatoes. It was such a coincidence because this was one of his favourite meals. It made it look like it was destined to be tonight! Destiny had brought him here. Oh shut up Jay, what was I thinking! Marcus sat and ate the plate of dinner on my frosted glass table as I sat and watched him wolf all the food down. Damn he even looked sexy as he ate, his small dimples sat on his cheeks and moved in time with every chew he made. It made him look so seductive. It was amazing how you notice every little thing about someone when your feelings for them change. After he had finished, I washed up the dishes and we sat and watched a comedy DVD which I had recently purchased from my trip to New York. We were positioned across from each other, he was lying stretched out across the three-seater and I was sitting in the armchair opposite, my legs hanging over the sides. We sat there laughing at the comedians and their fresh jokes. I loved stand up comedies; they always made me laugh my heart out. There were the brief moments when Marcus would stare in my direction inquisitively, checking if I had caught the humorous moment. At times I dared not return the stare, I had to avoid his glance, turn my face like a shy schoolgirl and laugh. It was a nice feeling; we were unconsciously flirting with each other and loving the subtleness of it.

"Jay, thanks for the food it was lovely. I miss your cooking"

"What! Does your missus not cook for you then or she just can't cook like me!"

He laughed "Yeah something like that... Jasmine doesn't cook at all babes. We live on pure take away if I don't cook! That's one thing I would like to change about her"

"Rah, poor you! Now that's funny because you are a man that loves his food. How are you going to cope when you get married and the baby needs a healthy meal? You're going to have to hire a chef!" I laughed at this because Marcus loved his food more than he loved fast cars!

"Well, I've told her already that she is going to have to learn. I can't live with no woman for the rest of my life who does not know how to boil an egg and Jay, she doesn't know how to boil an egg, literally!"

"That's funny babes" I shook my head in disgust.

"Imagine! And she's going to have my baby. Trust my luck Jay! Don't get me wrong she is very sexy, beautiful, and stunning! But she lacks the skills which make a wife! Well she doesn't even have potential in that area. I'm worried about how she will actually cope being a mother Jay!"

Wow, I knew she was a 'high maintenance chick', but damn! Sometimes beauty is not enough. I could hear it in his voice that he was actually pissed at the situation he was in. Here he was going to make this chick, and yes I will continuously call her that because she does not have the qualities of a woman! He was going to make this chick his wife. The mother of his children!

"Well, look. You have to teach her. Do something babes"

"All the guys say to me, *'Rah Marcus, your woman's criss'. 'Your woman is so beautiful'. 'How you lock down a woman like that?' 'Has she got a sister?'* But Jay I'm telling you, it's not all good as people think. Trust me! You're my best mate Jay and I can tell you everything cant I?" Before I could answer he carried on. "Jay, the woman is nasty, she can't keep the house tidy. It's driving me nuts! She don't like hip-hop, she don't like Tupac, can you believe that! You know how much I love his music! She doesn't eat fish, doesn't eat meat! I used to think that was cute, but damn it's not anymore, its bloody annoying. I take her to mums for dinner and mum is looking at me like Jasmines sick or something. You know mum takes pride in her cooking, especially when she's got visitors. The first time I took Jasmine there mum cooked lamb, curried chicken, fried dumpling, festival, grilled fish and rice and peas. You know the girl didn't eat any of it, not even the rice, because she don't like peas! Babes I was so embarrassed, Mums face was so push up…"

"I would have loved to have seen that! I can just picture the look on your mums face!"

"Jay, Mum was just looking at me, like *'A wah kind of gal this you bring inna me home!'* All she ate was the potatoes and salad. She didn't eat anything else because it was too fatty, and not cooked with olive oil! Jay I'm serious, if I was white I would have been red like a beetroot!"

"Its true, how you go pick up a gal like that?" I humoured.

"I don't know, trust me it must be Karma for something I done back in the day, because I'm telling you its just nuts babes"

Marcus continued talking, while I was laughing at the stories he was telling me about Jasmines weird habits and faults. It was kind of strange listening to him talk about the woman who was having his baby and who he was planning to marry. But at least he knew what he did not like about her. I knew if it wasn't for his morals and the pressure from his mother about not being like his worthless father he would not even be considering trading his players card for this woman!

"Jay, Thanks for letting me chill at your house for a while babes. Its always nice chilling with you. We used to do it often back in college. You know my mum loved you, even now she is always like *'How's my girl Janet, she such a lovely girl'*"

"Aww, I love your mum too, she makes me laugh. You know it was actually her who taught me how to cook fish!"

"Oh, okay. I thought that no one else could have taught you how to cook that good!" We both laughed.

We sat for the next twenty minutes talking and joking, until Marcus glimpsed at his watch and realised the time was actually minutes to one. Without making a fuss he lay there in the same position and asked me to call him a cab. He knew he was in no fit state to drive after he came staggering back from the guest toilet. There was no way that he would consider taking the chance of risking his career. A part of me didn't want him to leave. I was kind of hoping that he would ask to stay here, in the guest room of course! But I knew he had to return home. Back to her!

Ten minutes later and we heard the cab pull up outside. The driver pressed the doorbell to alert us that he had arrived. Marcus rose up from his relaxed position, rubbed his face and stretched before walking over to the dining chair to retrieve his suit jacket. He had placed it on the back of the chair earlier while we were dancing in an attempt to make a statement that it may just get hot up in here. As he reached out his arms and placed one through the sleeve and then the other I looked at him as the jacket slid up his tall slender back in what seemed like slow motion, resting on his broad shoulders, the lust taking over me, wishing that I could rub that long back into the early hours of the morning. I walked behind him as he strolled towards the front door, stopping in the corridor to put on his shoes and check himself in the mirror, fixing his shirt collar.

"It's been a nice evening, Jay. I'm glad to see that you're alright, although you have been ducking my calls for the past few weeks!"

"Oh my gosh! I haven't, like I said I was busy and I apologise. I should have returned your call sooner"

"Whatever Jay. It's cool. Well I hope we can do this again sometime. I miss chilling with you"

"Yeah, it was nice. Well you better get home and get some rest. I'm sure you have to get up early in the morning"

"Yeah, six o'clock babes. I will come and collect my car tomorrow. I can't believe you had me here drinking so much. Good thing I catch the train to work."

I looked up at him and laughed. Marcus casually leaned over and gave me a huge hug, my face buried in his chest. I loved the way he held me so tight. Every time he hugged me I didn't want him to let me go. I just felt so safe and secure in his arms. I responded by holding him just as tight, inhaling his scent. Eventually he loosened his grip and opened the front door exposing the moonlight and the brisk draft. I gave him a tender kiss on the cheek and a smile that said *'I need you'*, but all I could murmur was "Get home safe".

"I will. Tomorrow Jay, muwah"

I watched him walk to the cab and climb in the back seat, talking to the driver to give him directions. Then the silver Peugeot drove away, leaving me at the door looking on. I slowly shut the door behind me, thinking to myself how much I had enjoyed the evening. Spending time with Marcus was invigorating. I felt so awake right now. He had filled my body with a feeling which I could not explain. I never realised how important our friendship was to me and how much I missed having him around. I mean we could joke and chill together so naturally, without feeling shy or intimidated. We could sit and talk about anything with each other and as much as I loved him right now and was upset about his decision to marry that 'chick' I was glad for the friendship we had. I slowly walked through the corridor and back into the front room to tidy up before I retired upstairs to my bed. As I picked up the empty glasses I could smell the scent of Marcus's cologne in the air. Mmm the lingering smell of Jean- Paul Gaultier, how I loved the scent so much. As soon as I finished tidying up the living room and kitchen I turned off the lights and walked up the stairs to the bathroom. I stood in the mirror talking to myself as I wrapped my hair, took out my contact lenses and undressed into my lingerie. Marcus put a smile on my face this evening and I'm glad that he came down, although it was unexpected considering that I was avoiding him. I froze thinking about us dancing in the living room and his hand placed on my lower back. My body shuddered as I remembered the moment, the feeling. Shit! My best friend was taking over my mind! I was losing all control of my thoughts. I hated that feeling, yet I was embracing the feeling of being in love. But it was difficult, it was hard. I tried to suppress the feelings for so long and here I am in love with my best friend who is expecting a baby and engaged to be married to another woman. I have to take control of my feelings and quick, before I get hurt!

Chapter 14.

Leyah

"Thanks for the lovely flowers, you really didn't have to"

"So when you going to let me take you out beautiful?"

I held the phone rolling my eyes as he spoke. I could not believe this man was hounding me like this. He would not take no for an answer! Does he think that he can send me flowers and I will jump to his every demand! Brian was a nice person to talk to, we were able to discuss everything from music to politics. Only problem was that he was not a very good looking man. No actually I won't say that, but he was not 'my' type. He wanted to be with me and he wanted to be with me bad. When we had conversations he would always mention his desire to have children and how he would be a good father and step father to my daughter. Wow, now that kind of talk freaked me out, he was going too far! He just would not take the subtle let downs to show him that I was not interested. Just because I have one child already he thought that maybe I was some kind of baby making machine, that I should be happy to roll over and have another one! Well I had some news for him; not only am I not interested in him, I am not interested in having any more children for now either. I mean I'm just getting my body back and it has not been easy. Dating was kind of hard for me because, I haven't really been with anyone since my trauma with Reese. He really scarred me for life! I can't trust another man, well I find it very hard to trust any man. I gave my everything to Reese and he just took my heart, chewed it up, spat on it and then stepped all over it again! I don't really want any man at the moment anyway! I'm fine by myself. I've got Asia to concentrate on. My friends don't understand my philosophy to survival without a man. Don't get me wrong I have urges, I'm only human. But I haven't slept with anyone in the past year! I've been utilising the platinum rabbit that Keshia bought me for my birthday. I was seeing this guy briefly; Ricky who worked on the floor above me. He was 5'6, caramel complexion and funny. We got along well and would meet up frequently for lunch. After a few months we started seeing each other. I wasn't really interested in anything long term so we had an 'understanding' where I would go around his house for a 'fix' when I needed it and we were free to date other people. It only lasted about four months, which was because he met somebody else, somebody who could give him more. I wasn't upset about it because at that time I didn't want to be in a committed relationship where I left myself open to be hurt. So good luck to him! I still talk to him now and he is happy. He's engaged and living in Slough with his woman. His relationship is all a big lie if you ask me because he is still phoning me asking to come round and I know what he meant by 'come round'. He wanted to come and ravish my body and make me hot and wet. It was tempting sometimes as he was able to fix my needs, but I always reminded him of his current relationship status. How dare he! How can he be putting such things on me, knowing that he has a fiancée who he shares a bed with every night! That is exactly one of the reasons why I am not in any hurry to be in a relationship. Your man could come home every night but still be playing out there. Living together does not mean anything; there is no guarantee to a monogamous relationship anymore. Men are all the same!

I glimpsed myself in the mirror as I continued to moisturize the cream into my silky skin, making sure that every spot was covered. Tonight I was going on a date with Lucas. He was this guy who I met while I was shopping at Tesco last month. I could feel him staring at me as I walked through the isles, then eventually we ended up in the same queue. When I turned and looked at him he plucked up the courage to ask me my name. I did not want to tell him, but I didn't want to embarrass him or myself in the busy supermarket that afternoon and I must admit he initially came across smooth so I told him. A short conversation pursued whist the middle aged Asian shop assistant rang up my items and I paid. As I continued to pack my shopping he felt more confident and bold and asked me for my number. At first I pretended like I didn't hear him, then he stepped closer and repeated it. I had to kindly let him down which did not deter him as he offered me his business card. I had kept the card with his number in my bag for two weeks, but after I mentioned it to the girls, they insisted that I called him and now here I am, about to embark on our first date. I don't even know why I am actually bothering. He did appear to be a nice guy though. He had gone out of his way in every conversation to try and prove to me that he was not one of those useless guys, telling me that he was currently trying to set up his own business. I don't know what in because I haven't really taken too much interest and his business card only provided his name and number. I sat down and pondered on the circumstances of the date. I'm only going out with him because Keshia and Janet keep on telling me that I need to get out more and that I need to give men a chance. But to be honest it is a waste of time. They are all just full of shit! They spit a load of lyrics which is in a manual or something and then get what they want and disappear back to their woman at home waiting! I stopped and thought about the overall situation, twirling a lock of hair between my fingers. Having spoken to Lucas on the phone over the past few weeks he seemed to be nice, polite, ambitious, comical and sweet. But that's how they trap you! You fall for them before you get to know the 'real' man underneath all the persona, only to find out that he is a fake! Everything was a lie! But this time I am going to try, I'm not going to take my old baggage on my new journey. I'm going to give Lucas a chance to prove me wrong. To prove that not all men are the same. They are not all lying, scandaless, cheating, deceiving dogs, but there are a very small percentage of men that are honest, trustworthy, dedicated and loving. I'm yet to be convinced!

I had driven the short journey through the traffic to drop Asia to my mothers earlier. I couldn't let Reese look after her because that would have just been too much headache. He would've asked me a series of questions; not that I have to answer to him or hide anything from him! I just did not want him snooping around for the next few weeks trying to see who the mystery man is, so I felt it was best to drop her to mums. She could keep her company for the night and mum was always happy to have her grand-daughter around, keeping her entertained. As the time passed on I stood in my mirror ensuring that my dress was hugging in all the right places. Tonight I was wearing the hell out of my black low cut dress which rested just below my knees and exposed my defined back. I looked through my messy jewellery box and decided to dress it up with some gold accessories. As I untangled my chain I spotted the Channel earrings which Reese had bought me one Valentines Day. Remembering the time I closed my eyes and smiled, deciding that they would be perfect for tonight. I stretched my arms under my bed and found the shoe box for my gold strappy shoes. I retouched my hair which I had let down as I normally wore my black and blonde twists up in a pony. This style gave me a wild mysterious look, which complimented my minimal make-up. I wasn't really into making an effort anymore but I still wanted to be desirable, I wanted to let the men out there know what they were actually missing with all their 'player' antics. It was now seven thirty and the night was getting a little chilly. Lucas was due any minute; I quickly sprayed myself with Channel Chance perfume and waited patiently downstairs. Ten minutes later there was a knock at my door and I went to answer it. I exposed Lucas who was standing there looking simple but smart, wearing a blue V- neck jumper with some black jeans. Okay, I thought, not bad but he could have made more of an effort. This must be the subtle look which he was trying to pull off, the look which said 'I'm laid back and don't really put a lot of effort into women because I get them a dime a dozen!' Look at me analysing his appearance, that one year course in Psychology is to blame. I stood back and watched him admire me, commenting that I looked beautiful, like a fallen angel. This looks like it is going to be a long night!

When I stepped outside my eyes eagerly looked for the car he was driving; a black Audi TT with a private plate which read SP33DY. Well that says a lot about him! I just know he does not think that he is going to get an easy ride with me! He looked like a typical undercover sweet boy. I wonder how many women he is actually sleeping with at the moment, thinking that it is okay because they are not 'exclusive', that he has not told any of them that they are 'together'! Well I am not going to be an addition to the countless hopeless women who he has fooled! He drove at a rushed pace to Fulham Broadway, the smooth twin turbo engine growling ferociously. Now I was definitely convinced he was a 'ladies man', his vehicle really said it all and the slow jams which he played the whole journey was definitely the give away. Eventually we arrived, finding a place to park we walked close together towards the Pink Hummingbird restaurant. He had booked us a lovely table which had full view of the exotic fish swimming in the huge fish tank positioned in the wall as a partition. We sat down and the waiter handed us our menus. I thanked him and opened up the interesting gold menu, my stomach was quietly growling. I just hope that their food tastes as good as the restaurant looks.

91

"So tell me more about yourself Leyah. All I know about you is that you're a very beautiful woman, and I don't understand why someone has not scooped you up already. What's your flaw then?"

"My flaw, why has it always got to be the woman's fault! Why do we have to be the ones with the flaws!" I answered slightly irritated as I peered over my menu.

"Okay. Well tell me why you're still single. Not that it's a bad thing, it is actually a good thing, especially for me!"

"Well… No I don't have any flaws for your information! And I'm single because there is a lack of decent men out there. And I have not met anyone worthy to be with me as yet"

"Oh wow, so you are telling me that I am not a decent man then?"

"No, I'm not saying that. I hardly know you. But I have not met any as yet. Well any that are single anyway!"

He stretched out his hand for me to shake. "Well hello Leyah, nice to meet you I'm Mr Decent Single Man!"

We both laughed. He had a habit of constantly looking directly into my eyes when he spoke, trying desperately to seduce me with his words. But I was not falling for his charm, I was immune. As we sat we fell into a debate while we ate about what constitutes a 'decent man' and a dispute followed as I tried to get my point across. I must admit he was funny. He made a joke about all the flaws which I brought up in men and found an excuse for almost every trick a man uses in the beginning to hide the fact that they are in a relationship. I don't know what it was but he kind of intrigued me but in contradiction to that his responses where making warning lights go off in my head. How could someone understand and interpret such behaviour and make it appear to be alright, that their actions are justified yet that person not practice that behaviour themselves? He must be like the rest of them!

We finished up our meal which I thoroughly enjoyed as it definitely lived up to expectations. I looked around admiring the happy diners as

Lucas paid the bill. Soon after we left and strolled back to his car discussing the things which we found irritating in the opposite sex, laughing at some of the things we brought up; such as un-manicured feet, dirty fingernails, body odour and hairy armpits. I observed that he had a thing about women being 'well kept'. His ideal for a woman was for her to spend her weekend getting beautiful for her man, making sure that her hair and nails were immaculate. That was definitely not me! The night was warm and still as we almost neared his car, which was now three cars ahead. Just as this old white lady walked past us with her walking stick Lucas turned and told me that he had a surprise for me. As I queried what it was, still questioning in my head why that old lady was out this time of night on her own. He hushed my thoughts, telling me that he was going to take me there now. I was a bit sceptical about going with him, he was taking me somewhere which could be in the middle of no where and could possible do anything to me! But my instincts said, 'what the heck'. Plus I had carried my can of mace in my handbag which was provided by my self-defence class I attended a few months back. As he drove through the dark streets I discreetly looked at him, looking at his every imperfection and trying to analyse him. Lucas was a good looking man, fair skin which I figured may be the result of his part Hispanic genes he talked about. He was about 5'6 and could have done with being a lot taller, but he had the personality which made up for it. He wasn't really my type but what was? Reese?!

After driving at speed for twenty five minutes we arrived the destination somewhere in Greenwich. He parked up near some newly built apartments over looking the river, in visual proximity of the O2 arena. I looked on taking in the amazing view. I hoped he was not taking me to his house or a hotel, because I certainly do not get down on the first date! I rolled my eyes as he got out and opened the heavy door for me, telling me that he wanted to take me somewhere beautiful to show me just how beautiful I was in comparison. I tried to hide my response as I blushed at his cheesy line. Catching me by surprise he slipped his hands into mine and led me down the pathway along the riverbank. I didn't pull away as I thought to myself, 'its not going to hurt, just enjoy the night!' Listening to my conscience I let him hold my palm as we strolled hand in hand admiring the lovely view of the moon reflecting on the water and the stars gleaming in the dark. It had been a long time since I had actually admired the stars. The weather was perfect, only a small summer breeze blew on the still waters and a few midnight clouds dressed the sky. I couldn't believe that I was actually enjoying myself. I was out here on a date, doing something different. We strolled for about an hour, not worrying about the time. Just walking and enjoying each other's company while he made me laugh. Okay, so maybe I was wrong about the majority of men, but I could not let this one night change my whole perspective and opinion of men. It was only our first date and this type of behaviour was expected. We neared the car and Lucas stopped and pulled my hand to turn me around to face him.

"Leyah, thank you for such a wonderful night. You're a really interesting woman and I like that"

"You're not too bad yourself " I replied, conscious of the awkward situation arising.

"Well I hope we can do this again sometime, maybe I can take you to another one of my favourite spots. There's this really nice restaurant on a boat in Docklands that you would love"

"Sounds nice"

I know he better not be expecting a kiss! I could tell by the way he was looking at me that he wanted to make a move, slowly edging himself closer. So before he could attempt to lean forward and lock with my lips I reached out my hand and opened the car door hastily getting inside while he stood for a few seconds in disbelief at how he lost the power in the situation. While he was driving me back home he had this grin on his face which made me feel like he felt he had achieved something here tonight. Like he had broken down my defences, but I knew the games men play all to well. He turned into my street and smoothly parked into a nearby space outside my house, careful not to scratch his twenty inch alloys. We both looked out the slightly tinted windows and watched a drunken man stagger down the road almost walking into a set of bins along his way.

"So Leyah. You want to do this again next Saturday?" He questioned, turning down the mellow sounds of H-Town playing on the car stereo.

"I don't think I can. I believe I've got something on next week"

"Oh okay, well what about Friday?"

"No, Fridays not a good day for me either. But I will phone you and let you know"

"Okay. Make sure you do. I will be waiting for your call. Look after yourself beautiful"

Now even though I am not doing anything next weekend I can't let him know this. I have to act less available, let him stew for a while. Keep him wanting more. Then I will see how interested he actually is. If you're too available the man knows that he can get you locked in a minute because you have no other potentials and a lot of free time on your hands which he can fill and then when it is time for him to move on, you're left depressed and lonely trying to forget all the memories you built together. No way, not me! I have already made that mistake in my life and I am not about to do it again! I was about to open the car door to exit when I turned and thanked him for the lovely evening and descended. As I put one foot out he looked at me as if I was doing something wrong, like he expected more. I kindly ignored his look and got out the car, taking my keys out my bag as I started walking up the path and to my front door. I turned around and gave him a quick wave as I reached my doorstep and unlocked the lock. I shut the door behind me looking through the peephole I noticed that Lucas was still outside. I know he could have never been waiting for me to invite him in for a 'cup of coffee'. Please! Why do men think that they can expect to come in after taking a lady out, like we are supposed to owe them something! Show them gratitude for the evening! Oh please! I'm fed up of men thinking this. I don't owe him anything and he surely was not coming into my abode after one date! He finally drove away, roaring his engine down the street. I turned and sluggishly walked towards my bedroom to undress and get ready for my bed. It was only ten past midnight but I was feeling tired. I must admit I had a nice night. Maybe, just maybe I will give him a call next week.

Chapter 15.

Keshia

This was all pretence. Here we were sitting around the large expensive marble dinning table having dinner with his family. Pretending we were happily in love. Yes I do love him, I love him with all my heart but I'm just not sure that I can trust him anymore. I mean once the trust has gone it's so hard to get it back. I want to get it back, but I don't know if I can. Things have changed. He has changed, I have changed and after last week's fiasco with that bitch Shanny I'm not sure if I can fight this fight anymore. But for now I'm just going to pretend that everything is okay with my pretend smile. Bobby has been trying to come straight home everyday this week and I must admit he has started to make more effort but it is not enough. I'm just worried that it may be a little too late. We were all sat finishing off the raspberry tart with ice cream, listening to Bobby's mother talking about the family and the recent family scandals. She was making me laugh, because she was a hard core Christian but she could cuss. She could not tame her tongue and told it how it was. Through his mothers gossiping I had learned that Bobby had this cousin who did not know who her son's father was. Now that was the talk of the year! Bobby's mum did not stop with that subject for about six months straight. It was frowned upon in his family, and rightfully so. She was a big woman at the age of forty four she should not be getting herself into such situations. Funny thing is Bobby's mum had this expression where she would turn up her nose and mouth in disgust, her scrawny face sour as if to say 'Well I'm going to leave them to it as long as it is not my child. The Lord will deal with her'. Bobby's sister Christina was lovely we got on well. She worked as a social worker and had the cutest two year old little boy who looked nothing like her. She knew that her brother was a dog and always reminded me that I was the best girlfriend that he had brought home, telling me that I had changed him for the better. Little did she know that things had not really changed at all! It was just all one big performance. Another one of Bobby's acting roles which he plays in his television dramas. But I opted to keep the peace, I could not tell her the truth. I don't like to involve other people in our relationship especially his family so I continued to let her think everything was rosy and played my character in the performance of the happy dedicated girlfriend. Bobby's mum had a large four bedroom house in Purley with her husband Mathew who was a successful banker. Bobby always used to throw this in my face, boasting that he had grown up in a stable environment and did not grow up on an estate. I hated when he spoke like this, sometimes it would make me feel really low because I had been that 'estate' girl. I grew up on poverty stricken North Peckham Estate and I did not know my father until I was in my teens. My mum got pregnant and had two other children with another man, who later also disappeared leaving her to raise us all on her own. Yes we were a stereotypical family from Peckham but I was determined to do something with my life, make better from the torn streets which I had grown up in. Unfortunately my younger brothers failed to think like me. They're mentalities are totally different, you could say that they are a bit 'hood'. Twenty one year old Kirk is currently serving time in Her Majesties Prison for gun and drug charges and Kyle was the biggest 'Shotta' on the estate, at his tender age of nineteen he did not want to hear anything from anyone. He did not even learn from the example of his older brother. Everyone thought that it would make him wake up and see that that lifestyle was not as glorious as some make it out to be, but Kyle just believes it was a 'set up', a scheme which the 'youngers' plotted to get 'Dripsy' as they called Kirk, off the street. Now he thinks that he has to guard his 'manor'! I just leave him to it now, I'm fed up of talking to him. He is fully aware of the consequences, he has seen it first hand. Even one of his close friends was shot and killed a few months ago but he still doesn't learn. It's so sad. I work with a lot of youths like him and I hear so many stories, but I can't help my own brothers. They have gone too far. I make time to visit Kirk every few months, send him money and other needed items. I hate to see him locked up like an animal and he knows that I'm disappointed in him. Everyday I pray that when he eventually gets out on parole he will turn his life around. Especially as he has two children out here, with two different mothers who need their father! Bobby's life was more stable, yes indeed it was but I had to remind him every so often that his family was far from perfect and he is the prime example of this.

I bent down and loaded the dirty dishes into the dishwasher with Bobby's reluctant assistance. He was standing humouring his sisters husband who thought he knew everything and was trying to explain to his mum and sister about Caribbean descendants being lost, not having any identity and blaming the increasing drugs and crime on us. My blood was boiling! That man could chat so much shit! I had to get out of that room, because being the only one in the house who was from Jamaican parentage I would have got ignorant up in there! I decided to hide out in the kitchen trying not to cause a scene due to the fact that I was becoming increasingly offended by the comments. Bobby could see it in my face that I was annoyed and had followed my exit. We had finished loading the dishes and I rinsed off my hands in the designer sink. I swear his parents were involved in some sort of scam. I don't know how they afforded such a state of the art house, when she was only a nurse. I knew all those trips to Nigeria were suspicious! I laughed to myself thinking of my stupidity. I saw Booby looking out the kitchen door, checking that no one was nearby, once he was sure that we were alone he decided to try and divert my frustration and anger by kissing my neck. Damn, he knew I loved that. He began working his way up to my ear lobes slowly. My tension slowly fading away.

"Stop. What are you doing?" I interrupted, moving my neck away.

"Nothing. It feels nice doesn't it?"

I mumbled in agreement, succumbing to the feeling as I gave him back my neck.

"Come follow me up stairs quickly" He whispered, taking hold of my left hand.

I looked up at him shocked. Oh my gosh, Bobby was playing with fire and I liked it. It was exciting. We sneaked up the back set of stairs and went into the large guest bathroom, locking the door behind us. We were acting like two naughty teens hiding from our parents. He was horny and I could feel his bulge through his jeans as he pressed me against his groin eagerly. We began kissing passionately. We haven't kissed like this for ages, the more he held me tighter the more I wanted him. He fondled with my dress attempting to take off my panties. As soon as he

98

succeeded I unzipped his zip and he spun me around and leaned me up against the clean white sink while he inserted me from behind with a huge thrust. He felt so good, I needed this. As he entered deeper, he began making a groaning noise. I think he forgot where we were. I tried to tell him to shush, which failed so I took my hand and placed it over his mouth. Through all the excitement he thrusted deeper and deeper until we both climaxed. Sometimes the quickies were the best sexual moments you have, sometimes it was well needed to bring the spark back into the relationship and today it had worked for us. He slowly pulled out while he kissed me all over my cheeks and neck, cleaning himself up with the wipes under the bathroom cabinet. After we both cleaned up we discreetly went back downstairs with a cheeky grin on our face holding hands, like nothing happened. When we entered the living room I saw his sister give me a smile which said *'Yeah, I know what you two were up to'*. Right now I didn't care, I was uplifted. I was satisfied. Bobby and I had not had sex since the first week he moved back in. The passion was dead, which was partly due to my anger with him and the decisions he had made. But now it was back!

We travelled the thirty-five minute drive back home with huge smiles on our faces; the ten minutes in his parent's bathroom had changed our feelings for the better. When we reached back into our house I began to tidy up while Bobby sat practicing the script for the new drama series he was scheduled to play. He had landed the role of an aspiring footballer who was torn between the streets and his dreams. I hated when Bobby took such stereotypical roles, but he always assured me that some recognition was better than none at all. I guess he was sort of right, it could lead to bigger roles. Hollywood as he had hoped. Since Bobby moved into the flat I had failed to give it the thorough attention it needed, it was in desperate need of a clean. It still looked disorganised no matter how many times I tried to organise his stuff, he still had bits all over the place. This cleaning venture was a way for me to find a home for all of them, well a corner or cupboard to squash them into. I dusted, polished and swept the flat, which took me two solid hours. The whole time Bobby did nothing but watch. He thought it was better that way because he would just get in my way. Once I finished wiping down the kitchen floors, I wiped my brow and decided that enough was enough. I needed a break. The first thought that sprung into my mind was to go to the gym and have a nice relaxing session in the sauna. As the vision of me relaxing played through my mind I escaped into the bedroom to change into my gym clothes.

"Babes, I'm going down to the gym. So, you can have some time to recite your lines. I will be back in a little while"

"Okay, baby. Be good" He said peering over his script.

"I should be telling you that babes!"

I gave Bobby a quick kiss on his succulent full lips and grabbed my gym bag out of the cupboard by the front door, which I had to pull out from under the many boxes of Bobby's crap. I picked up the car keys and walked out the door, onto the landing and down the steps of the flat, through the communal door. Once outside I felt refreshed. I took a breath of the fresh air, reached into the pocket of my tracksuit bottom and took out my mobile phone to give Janet a call hoping that she would join me. As I dialled her number I walked to the car parked in our allocated bay. We had allocated residents parking which was a joke sometimes, because you would come home to find someone had parked their car in your space. I was fed up with that happening so I adopted the routine that I would park my car in front of the culprit and block them in. Leaving them to beep their horn and wait for me to move my car. Equal inconvenience! I unlocked the car, opened the door and got in with my phone on my right ear waiting for an answer.

"Hey Kesh. What's up?"

"I'm just on my way to the gym. You fancy joining me?"

"Well, I'm not doing anything important at the moment, this can wait. So okay"

"Alright I'm going to come for you now"

I hated going to the gym by myself as it meant that I would have to engage in small talk with other regulars and discuss things that I was not really interested in. It did have its benefits though, for example you would hear about the staff members who were dating the members or having 'relations' with them and where. It was a raunchy world out there! My feet couldn't even touch the pedals because of Bobby's long legs. We often shared cars, but his BMW 3 series was currently at the garage receiving a service. It was nice to have the variety at times as it was noticeable difference from my 1999 Audi A3. I just thrived on the automatic/ triptronic gearbox, I loved being able to just put my foot down and go instead of fiddling with gears. It was a nice break. I started the engine and pushed the stick into reverse, slowly backing out of the parking space, past Mrs Wilmore's red Grand Cherokee and out onto the main road. Weaving through the back streets it only took me ten minutes to get to Janet's. I pulled up outside her house beeping my horn for her to come out, noticing her peer from the curtain. Her street was nice and quite, looking like a miniature suburb. Full of detached houses, with driveways and beautifully manicured gardens. A rare sight in this area nowadays. Two minutes later, Janet appeared at the front door with her gym bag on her shoulder wearing her black Nike tracksuit.

"Hey, lets go"

We took the short drive to the gym and parked up, finding a good space today. Normally finding parking was a nightmare, it seemed as though everyone came to this gym, although I rarely saw anyone whom I knew. We walked into the deserted foyer swiping our membership cards through the barriers. Once inside we proceeded to the female locker room and locked away our belongings. Placing our membership cards against the locker to secure its safety. We entered the busy gym and spotted two free machines so we decided to do a short cardio workout before hitting the sauna. Sweat dripped down Janet's face as she pushed herself on the rowing machine, while I ran at a steady pace on the running machine conscious of my aching bones following the extensive cleaning routine I previously conducted. I casually looked around, suddenly noticing a familiar reflection in the mirror in front of me. I turned around and looked to my far left absorbing the tall, muscled body which was dressed in a tight white vest and black tracksuit bottoms, his locks were all tied back in a ponytail. I could recognise the back of that frame any day! I gasped, what was he doing here? I swiftly turned away to look at my reflection to ensure that I was looking presentable, which was not the case. Sweat was dripping down my face, my black head tie holding my hair off my face and no make up! Damn, he may not even recognise me, let alone remember our convo. I continued working out on the machine, pretending not to notice him, glancing out of the corner of my eye every few seconds to see what he was doing. I wanted to alert Janet to the new wonder at the gym, but she had moved to a machine at the far end. Suddenly he stepped away from the weights, leaving it to the skinny underfed young white boy waiting and briskly started to walk towards the empty machines beside me, drying his sweat with his black towel. My eyes never left his sight as I secretly watched him through the mirror, hoping that he would come my way. I quickly turned, hoping that he didn't notice me staring. He stopped at the empty machine beside mine, failing to notice me while he preceded his work out, placing his water in the holder. Slowly he worked up his pace. Then came the glance, followed by a double take. Finally.

"Hey! I know you from somewhere, don't I?" He questioned, with his brow forming a confused state.

"Erm, I don't know. You do look kind of familiar" Yes I well and truly knew who he was, I just did not want to act like I was desperate out here, like he has been on my mind ever since we met. So I continued to play the guessing game for the next few minutes until he finally remembered where he knew me from.

"That's it. You were down at the Velvet Café the other week. Yeah, with a group of other beautiful women"

"Yes, I was...Oh yeah! You're... the musician" I said convincingly.

"Yeah. Funny to see you here. It must be fate!"

"Wow. It must be. What are the odds of this?" I said flirtatiously. "How have you been anyway?"

"I've been okay. And yourself?"

"Well, I've been good. I can't really complain" I was trying to act casual while pretending to concentrate on my workout and look sexy at the same time.

"You work out here a lot?" He asked.

"Yeah, I'm a regular here. Work out like three times per week. Surprised I haven't noticed you here before." I queried.

"Well I've been so busy lately. I haven't really had time to attend the gym. But today I decided I must make the time".

"Good thing you did or I may not have had the pleasure of seeing you again"

Wow, I can't believe Kamarni was here, at my gym! He was sure wearing the hell out of that tight white cotton vest. Like heck he hasn't been to the gym in ages. His body sure shows otherwise, it was so toned and defined. I released a breath, he looked like he did at least five hundred press up's a day!

I slowed down my machine. "So how's your music going? Have you performed anywhere recently?"

"Yeah. I have this regular spot down at Marshals on a Tuesday night, that's pretty good. I'm getting a lot of feedback from that"

"So you're a big star then. The ladies must surely love you"

"Nah. Not really. I just go and do my thing. I'm not interested in the groupies. I'm too old for that now. I just play because I love it. I love the feeling it gives to other people. You know!"

If only he knew what kind of feelings it had evoked in me that night and how I could listen to him all night long! "That's good. You know, you've really got talent. You can go really far. So have you got a recording contract?"

"Nah, not really. Don't really like the idea. I just like doing the little small things, you know. You get a recording contract, and they want to change you. They want to change your style and mould you into something commercial. I'm not really down for something like that!"

"I understand, a lot of musicians lose their roots when they go commercial"

We had a connection; I could feel it pulling from my body as we spoke. He was so sexy. I watched his lips as he told me about his inspiration for writing. Damn, he licked his lips just like Morris Chestnut. I loved talking with this man; he made me feel so relaxed, yet shy. Here we were working out together, talking like it was meant to be today. After a further ten minutes passed my body was becoming hot and my heart rate increasing, causing me to take frequent sips on my water. I don't know if it was the exercise or being next to Kamarni which was making me so hot. He was running like he was a pro at it. I could tell he had a lot of stamina and endurance! I caught myself staring at him in the mirror, looking too intensely at his body as he ran, his muscles in his arm flexing with every stride, his firm chest standing to attention with every pace. Wow! My observation was interrupted…

"Here you are girl"

"Hey Janet. Look who is here. You remember Kamarni don't you? From the Velvet Café the other week?"

"Yes I do. How are you?" She asked inquisitively, wearing her white towel around her neck.

"I'm… fine thanks… just trying to… keep fit and burn some calories"
"Well from here it doesn't look as though you should have such a hard time" Responded Janet.

We all laughed. I watched on as Janet secretly looked him up and down, discretely checking out his every asset under his loose tracksuit bottoms and tight white vest. And why not, he was one good looking man! She must have sensed that she was spoiling my vibes, deciding to retreat to the abs machine. Kamarni slowly reduced the pace of his machine, until it finally stopped. He reached to the drink holder and took a long sip of his Evian Water. How I wished that I were that bottle right now. I watched the condensation from the melted ice drip down his right arm, slowly running and enchantingly teasing me.

104

"I love the feeling after a long… *hard* workout. How about you?"

His emphasised words uttered passion and sensuality. I could hear the seduction in his tone, reading the innuendos between his words. Yes I would love to have a personal work out with you too! I thought.

"Yeah. It makes me feel so relaxed, you know… I'm able to let myself go and pay attention to the areas which haven't been worked on for a while"

"Yeah. I hear that! So… Keshia…"

He remembered my name!

"Tell me more about yourself, what do you do for a living?"

We walked over to the benches like two old friends reminiscing as I began to explain. "Well I work for a company called '*Urban Solutions*' where I help to arrange fundraising events for under privileged and socially excluded youths"

"Sounds interesting"

"Yeah it is. I enjoy it. You know, giving something back to the youths"

He nodded his head in agreement. "I hear that. They need some guidance out here"

"What about yourself, what else do you do for a living besides playing music to please others?"

"Well I am actually career hoping at the moment. By day I am a delivery driver, used to be a market researcher but got bored so here I am"

"You know. I'm actually working on this next project of mine. Called the '*Big Brother Sponsorship*' and you would make a great mentor for one of our young black boys"

Bingo! This was a way for me to slyly get his number. Please say yes. Please say yes! He laughed before answering my question.

"You know, you're good. I can see that you must be a prized possession for your company"

"Well, you know how it is. Come on you would be good at it. You will only need to spend a few hours per week with one of our boys. Let him see what it is like to have drive and ambition, to be somebody other than a drug dealer or a gun wielding rapper"

"Okay. As you put it like that. Sure. I will sign up"

"Great. I will get your number from you before you leave"

Yes. I had done it. I had successfully coached Kamarni into giving me his number. Well it wasn't actually all lies. I was actually planning on doing a mentoring programme, but the project had not yet been approved by senior management. But it will be. Definitely now! We continued to sit and talk on the exercise bikes, sharing small parts of our lives with one another as the rest of the sweaty gym worked out we laughed. We joked. We even doubled up as gym partners on the weights. I stood over his mahogany shimmering body encouraging him to do five more lifts of the 135kg weights. While he continued his sets I scanned the gym looking for Janet, conscious that I had been basically ignoring her for my own selfish reasons. I noticed her over in the corner talking to one of the other female regulars we normally see in here. Debbie was her name. She had a charcoal coloured complexion with a long pointy nose, which reminded me of my French teacher at school. Man, she was funny. She was wearing leopard print leggings and a tight black vest with her huge titties struggling not to jump out and say hello. I don't know how she can even think to attend the gym looking like that. What kind of workout can she actually do in that get up! You have to laugh! Kamarni, finished his last set and suggested that we go to the sauna. How would I cope in a hot steamy room with this man, controlling the tigress within, stopping her from leaping out at him! I need to bring Janet along. Yes she would be my restraint. He followed as we went over to get her, walking past the used gym equipment and towards the workout mats before spotting Janet doing squats with Debbie.

"Jay, you ready to go in the Sauna?"

"Hey Keshia girl. Who is this fine brother?" Debbie said in her loud fake American accent.

Wow she was quick on the mark. Her eyes were all over 'My' Kamarni.

"Well this is my friend Kamarni. Kamarni meet Debbie"

They shook hands. Debbie holding on as long as she could, caressing his soft firm hands. Okay bitch let go! I was being all territorial towards something which was not even mine yet! Calm down Kesh! She finally released her grip and let his hand slide out of her palm. Before Janet could answer Debbie jumped in and invited herself to the sauna with us. I looked at Janet, who looked back at me, then we both looked at Kamarni quickly. He had this puzzled expression on his face, like he had just seen the Prime Minister pumping weights. He clearly did not understand why we were hesitant about Debbie coming into the sauna with us. But he soon found out...

Janet grabbed her cotton towel, while Debbie picked up her water bottle desperately trying to seduce Kamarni's body with her large watermelons. I shot her a look, which stated 'don't even think about it'. I could see what she was thinking and what she was planning was not in my game plan. We all walked through the air conditioned corridor, past the swimming pool which was filled with swimmers performing various techniques in the warm, chlorine filled water. As we were walking Kamarni gestured with his head to two young guys casually walking through the complex. Debbie recognised the tall mixed race one sporting an old school high top. He looked like a washed out wannabe player. She exchanged a brief hello with him as he undressed her with his eyes which wasn't hard considering that she hardly had on any clothes. Err! We stopped at the changing room to strip off into our swimsuits. Debbie of course changed into the skimpiest zebra print swimsuit. She loved to show her best assets to the fullest. Her breast were double F's, all natural which she constantly reminded us of every time we saw her. I changed into a simple black swimsuit which was low cut at the front. Nothing special. I looked in the mirror quickly, conscious that my flesh would be on display to the sexy musician. Good no visible marks. Only the sight of my footprint tattoos on my right ankle. Janet wore an army green tankini, with her hair tied up in a towelled head wrap. Finally ready we walked out into the open, holding our towels, ready to go and steam all our aches and stresses away.

We reached the sauna and Kamarni was waiting outside. Damn… all three of us stopped in owe. I had to lick my lips. He had on blue Addidas shorts exposing his bare chest which was even better than I visioned. Where had this Black Pharaoh come from, he was beyond what I had ever imagined. He had a perfect toned complexion, not a blemish in sight. I had a thing for tattoos and he had a few, I looked on admiring his upper left breast with a Lion stretching out his claw. Following his sexiness I saw another one on his upper left arm of a Crucifix and the words- '*Only God can judge me*', decorating his right upper arm was Chinese writing. His muscles bulged making the tattoos appear larger. Breathe. He held open the heavy steamed glass door for us to enter. Thankfully it was not too packed, only two other ladies filled the room. They both looked like they were in a world of their own, minding their own business taking advantage of the steam, heat and blissful silence. The lady lying on the top deck was in her early 20's, reading the latest copy of Essence magazine. She was showing off her assets wearing a pink and white striped bikini. With her perfectly toned flat stomach on display, complimenting her cubic zirconia silver belly piercing. I caught Kamarni glancing over at her but quickly retreating remembering he had company. The other woman was older; her head was invaded by grey hair which was placed in a bun at the top of her head. Janet and I both had to laugh as she had her flowery towel wrapped around her, with a plastic steam cap on her head. She did not care about her presentation. Even in the company of a fine brotha like Kamarni. Why should she, she was sporting a very heavy diamond cut ring on her wedding finger. Only the three of us looked like desperate potential girlfriends, admiring Gods finest creation. Even the young girl had to look twice and push out her chest a little further, hoping to draw some attention. She looked as though she was used to receiving daily compliments. We occupied seats on the nearest benches we could find, Debbie rushing past me to grab a seat near to Kamarni. This was like a fight for the last snatch of Zebra in an African Jungle. She was out to capture my prey. Janet and I shared a glance and shook our heads. We took our towels and placed them on our space on the wooden benches, lying down on them casually. Debbie got up and poured more water on the hot stones which occupied the left corner of the medium wooden based room. Hot steam rose instantly. She sat back down, complimenting Kamarni's physique trying desperately for a compliment in return. Ignoring her desperations we passed time discussing the latest song by R. Kelly and the sexual accusations he was facing. Debbie was all in Kamarni's face and you could see that he felt uncomfortable. The young girl got up and left the room, unsatisfied that she did not get any formal recognition. Kamarni took his cue and rose up, adjusting his composure he walked over to the corner of the room and relocated himself beside me, changing the conversation swiftly. Being all hot and sweaty next to Kamarni was heavenly. Although we were not in the type of situation I would have liked us to be in, it was nice. I wanted this man. He was intriguing and sexy. I wanted to know more.

We all sat there for the next ten minutes laughing and joking. He had a wicked sense of humour. Everyone was laughing, even the older lady was engrossed in our conversation and was laughing along with us. Time had passed and Janet made the first move to get up and out. The heat was becoming unbearable. So we all took that as our cue and decided to finally exit as the room became occupied with a few other members. Once outside the sauna, we said our goodbyes knowing that the time we had shared had come to an end. We would all go and shower, change and return back to our lives outside of the gym. Back to normality. As we stood outside of the sauna I was subconsciously waiting on Kamarni to make the first move. He looked at me, discreetly giving me the once up and down while doing his Morris Chestnut impression. Yes, this was my moment. I felt the mutual attraction. The sparks which flew between us. Janet and Debbie had already retuned to the lockers. It was just the two of us in the corridor. He lent forward, I could feel his warm breath touch my cheek and he whispered in my ear...

"So how are we going to do this then?"

My heart stopped. Was he offering me an indecent proposal, here in the gym or was I imagining it. Reading too much into his words? "Do what?" I stuttered, feeling all flustered.

"How are you going to get my number? You're going to have to wait for me to get changed"

"Oh...yeah... I nearly forgot, my mind was elsewhere." Somewhere wrapped up in silk sheets with you! "Meet me by the front desk after you change"

"Sure"

I watched as he walked off into the men's changing area. I can't get over how sexy he was. Where has he been all my life! Why didn't I meet him before I met Bobby! Twenty minutes later and I was waiting outside at the front desk. I had to give Janet a quick briefing why we were waiting for Kamarni and as expected she gave me the first degree, trying to plug me for more information. I told her how it was. He was helping me with my latest project and wanted to be a mentor for the youths. Of course she didn't believe that was my main motive. Janet could read me like a book sometimes. She knew that I was gaming for Kamarni and knew that I was looking him and looking him hard! She turned and looked at me seriously, warning me that I should be careful, before it ended in tears. Please! It wont, well at least it will not be me shedding the tears. Kamarni came walking out of the distance and through the barriers. He had put on dark denim jeans and a stone coloured Timberland jumper, his platinum chain hanging down his chest complementing a custom made diamond studded guitar pendant. He walked up to us with a smile on his face, apologising for keeping us waiting, explaining that one of the guys were talking to him about training together which he dismissed. He looked at his Armarni watch and moved his bag on his right shoulder a little higher. He reached into his pocket and pulled out a piece of paper, placed it in my hand and then made a very impressive attempt at the seductive biting of the lip. He looked dead into my eye, ensuring that our gaze was engaged and spoke to me with the softest sound of an Angel.

"Make sure you call me... Right sorry but I've got to rush. You ladies drive safe, and take care of yourselves. We should do it again sometime."

Yes we should and sooner than later, I thought! We exchanged kisses on the cheek and quick goodbyes before he rushed out of the gym leaving me and Janet conferring to ourselves. We picked our bags off the floor, said goodbye to the reception staff and walked out the automatic doors to the car. As we began to walk I caught a glimpse of Kamarni driving out of the parking lot in a black Volkswagen Golf. As he saw me, he slanted his head and gave me a wink as he sped by. Janet turned and looked at me suspiciously.

"Okay. Now give me the real low-down"

She looked at me with her intrigued brown eyes, ready to hear what I had planned for Kamarni. I wanted to tell her but there was nothing much really to say at this moment. I mean all we did was have a little work out together. Yeah I got his number, but that was on a business basis not yet pleasure! While we drove to Janet's, I explained the attraction which I had towards Kamarni. The sparks which I felt and the sexual tension which was obvious as we worked out together.

"Wow. Kesh you are such trouble. I must admit he is one fine brother, but you got Bobby. I thought you two were working things out?"

"Yeah we are. But Jay, it just doesn't feel right anymore. I mean I know he's still doing the same shit. Still talking with that bitch Shanny, and believe me I am not NO fool!"

"Yeah, but Kesh two wrongs don't make a right. Think about it first"

"I have. Look nothing is going to happen. I've just got mad lust for Kamarni, like every other woman with eyes. Come on, he is so sexy. You can't blame me"

"Yeah I can't blame you. But just be careful. Don't get yourself into anything you can't easily get out of "

Here she goes with her 'better than thou' reasoning. I'm a grown woman. I've got to keep my options open. I dropped Janet off at her house and gave her an excuse for not coming in for a drink. I had enough of her talking me out of Kamarni. As she climbed out the car and shut the door behind her, I reached into my pocket and took out the piece of newspaper Kamarni had written his number on. I looked at it, smiled to myself and then put the number back into my tracksuit pocket, patting it to ensure its safety and proud of myself that I had managed to obtain it. I gathered my thoughts, pushed my foot down on the clutch, slipped into first gear and drove off home.

Chapter 16.

Leyah

"Look you need to stop calling me. Why are you checking up on me anyway? Have you nothing better to do?" I shouted down the phone, whilst trying to make a cup of tea.

"I'm not checking up on you, I'm checking how my baby girl is"

I gritted my teeth. "She is fine now, just like half an hour ago when you called and the hour before that! Look I do have things to sort out! Your constant phoning is disturbing me now Reese I am trying to be polite!"

I was getting very irritated now. Asia only had a little temperature and runny nose and Reese was treating it like she had been diagnosed with Meningitis! I knew that this was just an excuse, he was acting more anxious than usual, like he was so concerned that he should come around to make sure that she was okay. Anything to try and come down in order for him to try and persuade me that he has changed! Anything to make my blood boil! Rub the situation in my face!

"Leyah I'm just concerned about my baby's health. I'm here to make sure she is okay. I'm worried"

"Please Reese! Are you trying to say that I am incapable of looking after my daughter and nursing her back to health?"

"Correction 'our' daughter! And I'm not saying that and you know it. But I just want to ensure that she is okay. Did you give her the night dose of her medicine?"

"Look I'm going now Reese!"

I hung up the phone. He was calling too much now. Not only was it infuriating but I was also becoming to be suspicious at his real motive! He had been the one to collect her from school yesterday, because they could not get hold of me and now he was not letting me forget it! He was everywhere, every minute, every second and he is not even physically here! At first it was nice of him to check on her after he dropped her home, but as soon as he collected her from school he had taken her to the doctors and collected her medicine from the pharmacy before I was able to do it. He was proving to me that he is capable and that he would drop everything for our daughter. I know he really enjoys being a part of her life. But I know this already, he did not have to reinforce it like this! Maybe he had heard that I was on a date last weekend. But who would have told him? Nah, I'm just being paranoid! I know Reese, this type of behaviour has always been instigated by something or someone!

After he had finally vacated my phone line I went and tucked Asia safely into her princess sheets, reading her favourite Barbie story until she fell asleep. She was so beautiful. Although she looked so much like her father she had the odd little features from me. Her cute button nose, that Reese always admired on me and she also inherited my full size ears. Other than that she was the perfect clone of her father. I always resented Reese for that. Every time I looked at her she reminded me of him. How he use to make me feel when he used to compliment me every time he saw me or walked into a room. He made me feel like a princess and now he was making Asia feel like one too. He devoted everything to his little girl. She was the apple of his eye. He would do anything for her, even put his relationship at risk for her; which he has done on more than one occasion. Reese did not care. He was the type of man that would cheat, get caught and blame it all on his woman for not giving him enough attention and neglecting his needs! He was an arrogant bastard at times. But he was not my problem. Like I said good luck to Shantel! My priority is Asia, and as long as he makes sure that he looks after her and does not let any woman affect this, then it is okay with me!

I hadn't called Lucas as yet as I was still sceptical about our date. Why would he want to take me on such a romantic walk on our first date? He was definitely trying to make me fall into his web fast and furious! I did have fun though, he did seem genuine but things are never as good as they seem. I should just give him a call and see what he is up to. I rushed downstairs to look for my mobile phone which I had on charge since Reese had killed the battery calling every hour on the hour! I contemplated on the move which I was about to do, but quickly resorted to continuing the act before I talked myself out of it. I searched through the phone book and stopped at L. There it was, Lucas. Right here it goes…

"Hello…"

"Hi this is Lucas Banton Speaking"

"Wow, are you always this formal on the phone?"

"Yes I am." He laughed. "Who am I speaking to?"

"Do you not have my name stored in your phone?"

"Sorry, but I have my bluetooth in and it answered automatically"

"It's Leyah"

"Oh… hi stranger. Didn't think that you would call"

"Well of course I would, why wouldn't I?"

"One second…"

I listened carefully as I heard him close a door, entering somewhere more quite.

"Sorry… Well it has been two weeks since our date and every time I offer to take you out again you provide a new excuse!"

"They were not excuses. I have just been busy with all this studying I'm doing at the moment"

"Okay. Well I will let you off. But you have to make it up to me!"

Look at him. Make what up? He is lucky that I even phoned him at all.

"Make what up? What for?"

"Make up for the two weeks which you have been denying me your wonderful company and grace"

I had to laugh, this man's charm is so cheesy! "Well I will let you take me out to the Musiq Soulchild concert in a couple of weeks"

"Wow, you're very demanding aren't you? Okay. I guess it's a date then!"

I thought to myself, I'm not going to give this man the pleasure of my company again so easy. I better do it right and let him work for this! Musiq Soulchild tickets were just the answer. I wanted to go to this for the longest, but I didn't want to be there with my girls looking like a lonely hearts column displayed for all to see. Most people would be there with their partners, holding hands, hugging each other and singing to the words. That was my mistake when I went to the Joe concert last year. I felt so pathetic standing there with Keshia by my side. Don't get me wrong I was glad for the company and it was one hell of a concert, but I needed to be there with someone from the opposite sex. Now Lucas taking me to this concert was a test to see how much he really wanted to go on another date with me, the tickets were almost sold out so he would have to act fast.

"Okay, well I'm going to get onto the tickets, the best seats in the house" He paused for a brief moment and the phone went all muffled.

"Leyah, I got to go. We'll talk soon. Bye"

Lucas hung up the phone suddenly without even waiting for my reply. That was strange. Why did he run so quick? I could hear voices in the background of a woman I think, it wouldn't surprise me if he was a married man! Men are all the same. Well I'm going to remain positive like Janet always advises. I'm not going to think the worst just because Reese had been a bastard as well as all the other countless guys we

116

seemed to come across. Faith is not one of my strong points at the moment, but I will give it a go. We had just made arrangements to go to see Musiq Soulchild and that was fine with me. Just as long as he keeps his promise then I won't have much to moan about and part of my faith will be restored. I turned and looked at the clock on the mantle, it was only quarter past eight, this evening was dragging. I sat and flicked through the Sky channels, of course there was nothing worth watching. I settled and watched Desperate Housewives. As my mind drifted I sat and thought about where my life was at the moment. Was I happy? No I was not. I was content. I was at the stage in my life where you just get on with it. Adjust to the situation. Here I was a beautiful young single mother, working as a housing officer trying to make ends meet, whilst also studying with the ambition to hopefully own my own business, trying to do it on my own. Reese was always offering to help me financially for 'Asia's sake', but I refused. I am not some poor helpless woman, I have my pride. I'm not going to live out of the hand of the man who broke my heart, who cheated on his fiancée with me, who lied and deceived me until he could not lie anymore! No way. He is there for his daughter and his daughter only. Asia never goes without. But I do. I go without the touch of a man, the feeling of being loved, being adored and being held delicately. Sometimes I feel jealous of Keshia's relationship, she doesn't deserve to be in one at the moment. Don't get me wrong I love her to bits, she is like a sister to me but her and Bobby are taking this whole relationship thing as a joke. They don't take it seriously; they fail to love each other endlessly. They abuse the fact that they are together. Although most of it has been Bobby's fault, Keshia is not making it any better. She has turned and done exactly the same thing which he done to her. When will this end. It's all the deceit and deception in relationships now which frightens me from entering one. Reese hurt me but looking around at the men that are out there and considering what he put me through, it doesn't look like there is anything better left. They are all the same or worse. He is one of many men who commit adultery or fail to remain monogamous. Is this what my Asia has to look forward to? A lifetime of hurt and deception in relationships?

I reached towards the table stand grabbing my book. Since my unfortunate singlehood I had consumed my evenings with reading romance novels. Dreaming of being the one in love with the perfect man

117

trying to please and satisfy my every desires. The one I was reading at the moment was similar to my life at the moment, the main character Chelsea was embarking on numerous unsuccessful dates. Looking for her prince charming and the man who ends up being her everything is the man who she least expected. The man who she confided all her disastrous dates in. He who listened attentively to her likes & dislikes, her fears and inhabitations. She didn't know it, but he was so into her. I was up to the chapter where he was trying to win her over. He was going out of his way to indirectly show her that he was perfect for her. He had found the precious love in her. Why could my life not plan out like that? Why couldn't my prince charming be waiting? Since my departure from Reese I haven't met another man like him. No one could match up to the way he treated me and although he had a woman at the time, he managed to make me feel special. He made me feel like I was number one in his life, like I was the one who he shared his every breath with. I must admit, he was the perfect gentleman when we were together. He made me happy. I do miss that feeling and I resent him for making me feel that way. It made it so much harder to forget about the good times we shared because his deception clouded the bad times. But I try to keep it in the horizon that he lied, he cheated, he deceived me and his fiancée. He had his cake and bwoy was he enjoying it. What made it worst was the fact that Reese was still with Shantel. She had stuck by him like a woman who had already taken her vows and was living it '*until death do we part*'. I really don't understand why they haven't walked down the aisle as yet. I mean she has proved herself as a fool for her man and they have been together for a while now, it must be over six years at least. I rolled my eyes, how would I handle it if he came and told me that they were finally tying the knot? Would I be bothered? Hell no! I can't stand that Bastard! What he did to me was wrong. He hurt me. He has made my daughter a statistic. I can never forgive him for that. What if he wants Asia to be in the procession? Could I really say no? It would be such a shot in the heart if he marries her. He couldn't tell me. But I know he would, he wouldn't miss the opportunity to rub it in my face. This is why I need to hurry up and find someone. Show him that I have moved on. That I'm not mourning over him, not holding on to what used to be. I need to find me a relationship!

I was woken out of my daze when my mobile went off. I was convinced that it was Reese again so I took my time reaching across the sofa grabbing the handset; to my amazement it was not him. I looked at the screen and saw Keshia's name flashing with her contact picture of us in the Grand Canaries the previous year. I pressed the answer button and heard the excited husky voice down my line.

"Hey girl, what's up?"

"Nah, nothing I'm just here. Had a long day and Asia's not well"

"Aww, my poor princess. I'm gonna come round tomorrow and bring her some ice-cream or something"

"Err, she needs soup not ice cream" I joked.

"Please, ice-cream helps everything. Leyah, we're going out to this little spot down Ealing on Saturday so make sure Reese takes Asia"

"What. How can you just tell me, you're supposed to ask!"

"Oh come on, you need to get out anyway"

"Why so far?"

"Well... we've been invited by Kamarni to come and watch him play. Sounds like it's going to be really good"

"Oh, so you mean he has invited you and you're just dragging us out to be your tag alongs?"

"No nothing like that. He said to bring you guys. Come on it will be fun"

"Okay, well I will see how Asia is by then and let you know"

"Oh please. Come on she has a father and you know he wouldn't mind"

"Yeah, but I don't want to just abandon her whilst she is sick"

119

"I hear you, but baby girl will be alright with her dad. So I will pick you up Saturday about ten. Okay love ya, bye"

Just like that she was gone. Keshia made me laugh, she was like a black panther, gone in seconds. She never really waited for a response when she wanted her own way. Well at least she was keeping me at high spirits- keeping me up to date on the scene. She was the one who helped me the most through my depression stage after Reese. Finding out about his fiancée and then the confirmation that I was pregnant, I thought my life was over but Keshia helped me to see sense, well through her 'logic'. It wasn't the end of the world. I had to do what was best for me and my life would not stop because of a man and a baby. It was his loss and I would show him. Although I have yet to 'show him', I was doing well at this moment in time. Just as I made a move to get up and turn off the television, my mobile went off; a text message. I pressed the retrieval button and went into my mailbox. Yep, right on cue. It was Reese asking me to give Asia a kiss from him and he would pass by tomorrow. He is so conniving, does he really think he can pull the wool over my eyes again. The end of the text read: *Love you loads. Big Hugs and Kisses X.* Now correct me if I'm wrong but I believe that is a subliminal message directed at myself. There was no Love Daddy or tell Asia that he loves her loads. This man is still trying to play games!

Chapter 17.

Janet

We walked through the smokers outside enjoying their nicotine and into the packed bar on Ealing Broadway, scanning the large dimly lit room to find the bar. It seemed like there was a good crowd in here tonight. I looked to my left as we moved carefully between people swaying to the music. I spotted Kamarni across the dark room talking to a large framed white man in a white shirt, looking like age and stress had taken its toll on his wrinkled skin. You could tell by the sight of him that he was trying as hard as he could to hold on to the little remaining youth he still had. Within seconds Keshia noticed Kamarni with the aged man and began walking over to him with no hesitation, swinging her hips to the rhythm of the tune which was playing, abandoning me and Leyah to continue our path towards the bar. At the same time as we continued to slip through the crowd a hard faced man pulled on Leyah's arm hoping that she would take him up on his advances. He stood holding his bottle of Dom Perignon Champagne on full display in her vision, looking her up and down thinking she was one of those shallow girls who followed the smell of money. A pretentious woman. Well he was sure wrong, because she shocked him by shrugging him off not even acknowledging his rudeness and continuing beside me on our route. We finally made it to the bar, squeezing our way towards the counter and waited to order our drinks. I scanned the room and noticed that there sure were some fine men in here tonight. There were the *'Pretty boys'*, with their perfectly lined haircuts, slick suits with not a crease in sight. Drinking brandy and talking to either the blonde haired white girls or the black Barbie dolls, both of which wore less clothes then Pamela Anderson and matched her with their cosmetically modified breasts on full display. Then there were the *'Nigerian posse'*, they were there flossing with their drinks and ordering everything at the bar. Trying to expose that they had money to burn, attracting all the Gold diggers. The girls that wanted to

121

have a good time and did not care at the cost. Wanting to be the centre of someone's attraction tonight no matter how unattractive their taker was. They are the girls who were unwilling to put their hand in their purses at any point tonight, they were the willing takers and the Nigerian guys made sure that they would floss as much money as they could to try and bed them. Across the other side of the room were the *'Geeks'*, the guys that came out trying their luck at finding a nice pretty lady. Ones who didn't care that they could not hold a general conversation or approach women, but hoping that they would find one who would be interested in quantum physics and technical terminology for the most simplest things. And of course you had the *'Shottas'* the *'Flossers'* the *'Thugs'* sporting huge heavy platinum chains, fat chops, diamond cut earrings and numerous gold teeth. Wearing the latest clothes and trousers half way down the backside, exposing the colour of their designer boxers to all! Observing the different types of people was comical. It was interesting but scary to see the lack of quality which men possess out here for us unfortunate single women. I collected my thoughts which were now plagued with the thought of ending up with one of these useless 'playing' men for the rest of my life, then I caught view of a nice group of four guys standing over at the other corner of the bar, engrossed in conversation, not worrying about the girls that were dancing in front of them to the sounds of Dwele. One of the guys caught my eye and was looking over at me, well I thought he was, but it could have been the girl behind me wearing the shortest dress I had ever seen and a head full of curly long weave. I turned my head subtly as I noticed him definitely smiling in my direction as the lights from the bar lit up his face. I pretended that I didn't notice him as Keshia came towards me walking through a group of young women doing a two step, eventually blocking eye contact between us, unknowingly rescuing me from this uncomfortable situation. She weaved her way through the masses of people to get closer to us and accidentally bumped into a girl wearing a blonde weave that had just paid for her drinks, spilling a few drops of her beverage onto the floor. The young girl turned around angry wearing a little pink frilly frock which clashed with her hair. Clearly unhappy that her drink had spilt she gave Keshia a menacing look, acting like she wanted to start a war right there, ready to cause a scene. Keshia politely ignored by uttering sorry and continued to join us as blondie stood there cursing to her friend. I was glad for Keshia's reaction as I was not able for a cat fight tonight!

"Kamarni said hi. He's reserved us a table in the VIP area" Keshia said all hyped.

"Oh lovely, where is he?" I shouted over the loud music.

"He is just over there talking to a few people. He should be starting soon. Look at him he looks so fine tonight"

As Keshia spoke her words betrayed her relationship which she had with Bobby. The lust in her voice exposing her true desire for Kamarni and the look in her eyes blatantly undressed him as he stood unsuspectingly.

"Behave. I thought you were just friends?"

"Yeah, we are. Can't I look and imagine?"

"Well as long as that's all that you are doing!"

I looked up as one of the bar staff finally came towards me awaiting our order. I was temporarily mesmerized as he had a glowing golden Mediterranean complexion, with a full head of curly dark hair and large well kept hands. He looked like he should be a model not a bar tender. Leyah ordered a bottle of Rosé wine, waking me out of my daze. I reached into my handbag and took out a twenty pound note to pay as it was my turn to buy the first round. Leaving a generous tip the bar man thanked me with his wide pearly white smile, if only I was a little younger he would have my number right now! We weaved our way back through the crowd and towards Kamarni who was waiting for us in the small V.I.P section. He was stood looking uncomfortable talking to a middle-aged woman wearing a pair of denim shorts and a little cream top which showed her heavy boobs. He looked relieved when he spotted us in the distance walking in his direction, like he was waiting for the conversation to be interrupted. It was evident that the lady was trying her luck at getting his number, unfortunately she retreated unsuccessful and to the scornful glare of Keshia. I laughed as Kamarni uttered thank you and ushered us to sit down on the soft brown leather seats. As we passed him Leyah and I said hello and gave him a friendly greeting of a kiss on the cheek, captured by his sweet smelling aftershave that stole the surrounding air.

We had ventured down to West London tonight to hear Kamarni perform at the Priory as it was their special soulful sound night and he was the headlining act. I observed the packed venue which was filled with all types of people. It was nice to see people sharing a different environment away from the sweaty stuffy raves where you were guaranteed to see the usual suspects. We placed our drinks on the table as the soulful sound of Jill Scott came through the speakers. Keshia had grabbed Kamarni onto the dance floor and was teasing him seductively with her dance moves. Jealous eyes were piercing through the dimmed lighting but I was in full view of one group of women who were focusing on her, watching closely with daggers. They must have been real loyal fans because if looks could kill Keshia would be dead three times over! I nudged Leyah and pointed it out to her and watched her giggle remembering the old days when it used to be us giving out the dagger looks for fun. We turned away and continued to sway and enjoy the music in the company of one another, feeling the lyrics echo through the room and the people feeding off the mellow sounds. The music faded and Kamarni let loose of Keshia's waist whispering something into her ear before disappearing into the crowd towards the backstage area. Shortly after, bright spotlights beamed on the stage, exposing a pretty dark skinned woman wearing a tight green and white flower wrap dress and an afro hairstyle, she stood with a microphone in her hand. As she familiarised herself with the stage she silenced the crowd and began to introduce the night, thanking people for their continued support. Once she had got full attention of the crowd she proceeded to introduce Kamarni, the introduction was overwhelmed with excited cheers and applause from the lively audience. It was like he was Jay-Z getting ready to perform his biggest hits. It was amazing. You could see Kamarni was feeding off the crowd, happy to witness the response. I looked over at Keshia and could see that she was doing the same, like she was Beyoncé watching her man go out on the stage and please the crowd. Kamarni started by performing a remixed acapella version for the cover of 'Sweet Lady' with his guitar in his hand. He continued by playing some more soulful songs which he had written. The crowd loved him. His voice was soothing, like a southern humming bird. Throughout his performance he was looking over at Keshia, making sure that she felt his every word.

124

Trapping her in his web of fantasies and romance. Leaving her bathing in the seduction. Feeling like she was the only one who mattered. Every woman dreamed of having a romantic attentive man and Kamarni was executing that with precision tonight, like he was sculpting a perfect ice sculpture. Moulding it to how he wanted it to be, watching the ice melt in his hands, dripping in the basking heat.

He had finished his performance, leaving the stage enduring loud applauses and screams. We stroked his ego even more by telling him how good he was and hugging him. Thing is that he was really, exceptionally good. He had been blessed with an amazing talent and he was using it to his advantage. The women loved him and the guys looked on with blank expressions wanting to be him. Slowly the music came back on and I surrendered back to dancing wanting to make sure that I fully enjoyed my night. I let the lyrics take me to another place allowing my body to sway to the rhythm. Suddenly I felt this hand touch me, I turned around thinking that it must be Leyah but to my surprise I was greeted face to face by a tall medium built man, recognising him as the guy who was looking over at me by bar earlier. He was about six foot, wearing a white shirt with the two top buttons undone and black jeans.

"Hi there princess, how you doing? You're looking really nice tonight. You must be complimenting your man nuff tonight"

I expressed my slight amusement. "Actually I'm here with my girls"

"Okay, so your husband is at home I take it?"

"Not exactly"

"So therefore I take it its okay for me to offer you a drink, as a platonic gesture of course?"

Wow, this guy was forward at getting the answers he needed and he was making me smile. That was a first. "Errm, well..."

He turned and looked at our table. "Can I offer your friends a drink also, because you all looking stunning tonight"

"Well actually… errrm…" Before I could answer Keshia stepped in and answered for us.

"Yes, we will have a bottle of Rosé please"

"A bottle of Rosé, that's fine. Is that for all of you or would anyone like anything different?"

"That's fine thank you" I rushed, before Keshia could make any more orders.

He directed his words at me, while stretching out his hand for me to shake. "Sorry for being rude, and your name is?"

I smiled and answered, as I did he held my hand in his soft palms which complimented him as someone who was well groomed.

"And I am Michael Mensa"

I smiled. "Hi Michael, this is Leyah and Keshia"

"Hi, nice to meet you ladies. I hope that you are all having a nice evening. Hold on I'll be back, let me go and get your drinks"

He walked off towards the bar while we all watched him move his slender body through the crowd. I must admit that he looked good and smelt even better. We stood there and conferred amongst ourselves about our first impressions of him.

"Oohh, he's cute"

"Nah, to tall for me"

"What are you talking about, too tall? He dresses well though!"

"At least he has manners. How many men do you know these days that offer to buy you and your friends drinks?"

"That's true. I must admit he has some lyrics on him"

"We need to come down to West London more often. South brothers don't have it going on like this!"

We all laughed, knowing that it was true. These days you're lucky if a man even offered to hold your glass when you went to the ladies! I spotted Michael walking back towards us, stopping to talk to a guy who he appeared to know who looked very simple in a green T-shirt and a pair of stone washed jeans. I frowned as it did not look like he had made much of an effort to come out tonight. Must have a woman waiting for him at home! Michael walked towards us with the simple guy in tow. As he reached our table he introduced him.

"Ladies this is Jermaine, he is one of the resident DJ's here, DJ Skeelo and this is Janet... Keshia and... Leyah" We all smiled and waved politely.

I thought to myself, wow how did he remember all our names so quick. This guy was smooth.

"Oh okay. So was that you playing earlier?" Leyah questioned.

"Yeah. Did you enjoy it?"

"Yeah. You played some really good songs, you don't really hear them out in clubs anymore"

Leyah knew a lot about music, that was her favourite past time. She knew every form of genre, every artist and every song. All she had to do was hear the first five seconds of a tune and she would be able to name it. For the next twenty minutes she engaged in a short conversation with DJ Skeelo and got a few names of the artists which he played exclusively earlier tonight. He handed her a business card and promised that he would send her an exclusive mix CD. I know that must have made Leyah's night. DJ Skeelo approached Michael and informed him that he had to disperse to go and do his set. As he did he said goodbye and directed a dazzling smile at Leyah exposing his perfectly straight teeth, he touched Michael with fists then made his exit.

127

"Alright Ladies, I'm going to have to join my friends as I'm being unsociable. I will catch up with you later during the night."

Micheal finished his sentence and looked at me, focusing his words at me he seductively whispered in my ear as his hot breath shot down my neck as he spoke.

"I will speak to you soon, okay"

He gave me a smile from the corner of his mouth as I nodded my head in a silent agreement. Although he was a little corny he made my stomach flutter. Michael retreated back to the corner where I first noticed his presence and rejoined his friends. We all looked at each other, smiling at the outcome of our evening so far. We continued dancing and enjoying ourselves to the soulful music DJ Skeelo played, when the next song was interrupted by an announcement…

"Yeah. This song has been dedicated to the lovely lady Janet, coming from someone in here who likes your style. Go there girl! "

I turned to Leyah in shock upon hearing my name as I did I felt the touch of warm breath whisper in my ear "Can I have this dance?"

As I swung around to my left I saw Michael standing behind me. He had this innocent look on his face which made me smile. I held no resistance and politely accepted his proposal, but before I could finish my words he had turned me around to hold my waist delicately. He held me so close to him that I could smell the familiar scent of Issey Mayaki. I recognised this smell because it was one of my preferred fragrances for men, not as good as the captivating smell of One Million but it was making the whole scenario so real and sensual as we swayed to the sounds of Raheem Devaughn.

"Are you enjoying yourself tonight?" He questioned.

"Yeah, it's quite a nice place here. I don't normally come to places up West London"

"So what brought you out tonight?"

"My girl Keshia. Her friend was the guy singing on stage with the guitar, he invited us"

"Oh, okay. Well, I can always show you a few more nice places around here"

"We will see…I take it you live in West London then?"

"Yeah, I just bought a place in Chiswick"

"Oh okay. Nice area. So what do you do for a living?"

"I'm an accountant for a firm up in the City"

"Oh nice."

"And yourself?"

"I'm actually a HR Manager for a Media Company"

"So you're a professional. Where are you based?"

"Our main office is by Chelsea Bridge"

"Nice. So, gathering from your fine figure I take it you're in the gym often and you have no kids… It's just an observation."

I looked up at him puzzled but having to laugh at his comment, where was this guy going with this? He had a cheeky devious smile on his face. What an assumption. A correct one I must add.

"Actually… I try to get to the gym when I can. I'm not there often, my figure just comes naturally" He had a shocked expression on his face. "And for your information I do not have any children as yet. I'm looking the right man to settle down with"

"That's good, I'm looking for the right woman also"

We both sniggered at his cheesy line and started dancing even closer. He put both of his arms around my waist. I thought to myself, this guy can move but not as good as Marcus. He is cute though and there is something about his persona which intrigues me. I like the way in which he is making an effort and it is a positive that he also makes me laugh. The song faded and the mellow sounds of Anthony Hamilton began to play. I could feel him getting lost in the soft beat. Although I was enjoying dancing with him, I couldn't stop my mind drifting. I was thinking about Marcus. He had been the last person who had touched me so intimately and we had danced close that very night when he was at my house the other week. As Michael held me in his arms, I felt like I had betrayed him. I was thinking about another man, while close with another. I couldn't help it my mind was consumed by thoughts of Marcus. I had hoped this night would help me to shake off the feelings which I felt for him, help me to forget what I held in my heart but I had failed. Damn it! Let me just get my mind together and concentrate on now! Michael seemed like a nice guy, he was a dark chocolate complexion, dressed nice, made me laugh, and was confident but suave. I liked this about him, I deliberated in my head and concluded that I wouldn't mind knowing a bit more about him.

The music changed and I slowly let go of Michael, allowing myself to get some air as my hair had definitely sweated out a little and my little black dress was getting creased. I looked around the nearby people dancing, looking out for my girls. I shortly spotted Kamarni and Keshia. They were slow grinding to the music over on the wall, concealed by the dark. I could swear they were tearing off the paintwork, I could see the beads of sweat on Kamarni's face and Keshia's hairstyle had fallen from all the heat. Their bodies conjoined like Siamese twins. Watching them made me remember the parties my parents used to attend when I was little, where all the parents would be slow, slow dancing to the point where it looked like they wasn't even moving! I spotted Leyah swaying with a chocolate brown guy, wearing a nice black suit. His look reminded me of Reese for some reason, but I was glad that she was coming out of her shell. Since her date last week she was letting herself go. Letting go of the animosity and contempt which she held towards men and she was smiling more which was a good sign. It was getting late and the bar was due to shut in ten minutes. The remaining few people took the opportunity to get in their last dances to the slow jams and the geeks tried their last attempts at getting a dance before the night ended.

"So baby girl can I get the pleasure of gracing your company again and fulfilling my promise to show you a few more nice spots in West London?" Micheal stated, holding the small of my frame close so that I could hear him over the music.

I looked up into the dark brown pools of his eyes and analysed his request. I casually replied "Sure, why not"

Michael reached into his jean pocket and took out his iPhone. I looked at it doubtfully and wondered if I should actually give him my number or take his. I decided against my normal procedure and tapped my number into his phone discreetly. I didn't want on lookers to think that I had purposely come out to find a man in a bar tonight, like the lonely heart I was. I finished typing my number and handed him back the phone, he looked at it and then back at me testing that I had given him the correct number then he typed in my name and pressed save. He leaned closer and gave me a light peck on my cheek with his wet lips, before vowing the night goodbye. I responded by giving him a slight smile as he stepped back.

"Goodnight princess. I will call you"

"Okay. Night"

Michael walked towards the exit to catch up with his friends. He looked back as he neared the door not wanting to leave me behind, but knowing that he had to. Leyah was gathering our jackets and bags from our VIP area while Keshia and Kamarni were acting like there was no one else in the room. They were still grinding against the wall to the last song. I could see the intensity of the dance. The way which they held each other tight revealed the desire they had for each other. Kamarni looked lost in the sounds of the music and the scent of Keshia's perfume, his head buried deep in her neck. I witnessed him giving her light kisses in that exact place as Keshia squeezed him tighter. They began whining lower and lower, Keshia swaying her bottom from left to right, lower and lower, tantalising the onlookers as Kamarni's muscular hands exposed

131

what her movements was doing to him by chasing her back in an intense grip. Finally the music stopped and the lights came on. It took Keshia and Kamarni a few seconds to realise that it was closing time and there was no music coming through the speakers. They released each other's grip and looked around, flustered. Upon witnessing that they had finally separated, we rose and watched as Keshia noticed us waiting patiently leading Kamarni over to us by the hand.

"Oh my gosh. Sorry girls"

"It's my fault. I couldn't let go of her" Kamarni confessed lightly drying his face from the masses of sweat which he had developed during the intense dance.

"Well, it doesn't matter. You did what you're supposed to do. Enjoy yourselves. Now let's get out of here before they escort us off the premises" I said jokingly.

While we walked towards the exit, Kamarni slowed us down by saying goodnight to a few staff members and the old white guy who he was talking with when we entered the club. We reached outside, which was still mild and warm, and was bombarded by the flyer touts, handing out invites to their next rave. Most of which landed on the floor a few yards up except for one which was complimented with a CD. Trying to rush to the car Leyah and I struggled to walk as our feet had given up to the suffering from the heels. As expected Keshia and Kamarni lagged behind arm in arm. While we led the way reflecting on the night, Leyah told me all about her Reese look-alike. I was disappointed that she decided not to exchange numbers with him, because he was one sexy fine man but she explained that she did not need another Reese in her life anytime soon and we both knew that she had a radar for men like him! We arrived at my car and I unlocked the doors and jumped onto the cold leather seats, rushing to start the engine in an attempt to rush Keshia.

"Hey girls, I'm going to get a lift with Kamarni"

Leyah and I looked at each other suspiciously. Yeah we knew this was going to happen. Keshia had hoped it would go down like this from the

132

beginning. We knew exactly what was on her mind and to be honest neither one of us could really blame her. Kamarni was a fine male specimen and Keshia was right, he looked damn good tonight! Well she is a grown woman, she can do as she likes, who are we to remind her of her morals and commitments which she had consented to with Bobby. I for sure was fed up of reminding her, but Leyah on the other hand was not. Her heart still ached with the pain which Reese had put her through and although Keshia was reversing the perpetrator role, it was still the same wrong in Leyah's eyes.

"Kesh, I don't think you should be going anywhere with Kamarni tonight. Don't forget Bobby is waiting for you at home" She whispered trying not to trigger Kamarni's hearing. "And you need to go home, you look like you have had too much too drink, it may effect your sense of judgement"

"Look. I'm fine. Don't worry about me and definitely don't worry about B. Nothing is going to happen. Were just going to talk on the way back"

We both sat there unconvinced, but allowed her to make her own decision.

"Well call me as soon as you get back home or send a text. I will be waiting" Demanded Leyah as she scrutinised the situation.

Keshia nodded to Leyah as she turned and waved goodbye to us. She shut the passenger door and walked towards Kamarni who was waiting patiently nearby on the curb. They both watched as we pulled off, driving down the busy streets to make our journey back towards the south of the river.

Chapter 18.

Marcus

I angrily slammed the phone down on the table. Why did Janet have to go out tonight? I could do with her company right now. Jasmine is driving me bloody mad. This loss of freedom is not working for me, I feel like a prisoner in my own home. It is not good for my health. Yeah it is nice to have someone to be my companion, someone to lay on the sofa with, someone who I can laugh and joke with, the one person who I see before I go to bed and the first beautiful face I wake up to in the morning. But damn it, I need my space! I can't breathe without her saying something. I'm spending as much time at the office just so I can avoid her. She blames it on her hormones but I'm not convinced at all. I mean even when she used to stay overnight at my old place in Luton she would display some questionable behaviour. I would debate this in my mind but then dismiss it moments later when she would come in the room wearing some sexy lingerie making me forget what I was annoyed about in the first place. She sure knew how to take my mind off the problem at hand. I remember this time shortly after we had met where I had taken her with me to a company dinner, damn she embarrassed me. I was so mad at her for flirting with one of my co-workers, after witnessing her behaviour I was determined to end the relationship that very night. I was so humiliated. Jasmine was unable to control herself and had got drunk on the free alcohol throwing herself all over my boss son Wilson, flashing her long chocolate coloured legs in her little red dress while he told her about his boat and his country house. I mean she was acting like a straight up hoe. Acting like I had hired her for the night to accompany me there. It was embarrassing; my colleagues were looking at me like I had brought one of the skanks from the city centre to join the banquet of partners and their elegant wives to this ritzy dinner. I could not believe her. As soon as we left there I took her straight home, she knew I was mad and knew that I was going to end it that night. So yes, she put on her best gaming shoes and went for the kill, like her life depended on it. I guess she knew she had a heck of a good man and did not want to lose it. She took out her glossed silky lips and caressed my neck with every ounce of seduction she had in her body. She knew that was my spot. Just below the left ear. Kissing and biting it gently. Then she took her moist lips and pleased my manhood for thirty five minutes straight! Right outside her house, in the driveway. Licking and tasting, pleasing and teasing. Damn! Just thinking about it gets me hard every time! That night she had me tingling all over, like it was my first time receiving pleasures of that kind. I mean she was an expert at it. My hands were holding on to the steering wheel so tight that I thought I was going to burst a blood vessel in my veins! Yeah, she had my blood racing that night. Gasping for breath!

Now here I am a year later, still with her, carrying my baby and engaged to be married. How did it ever get to this? She jedied me. She had me doubting myself, questioning if I was the one being unreasonable, irrational and selfish. I knew I should have gone with my instincts. But the lust got the better of me. The sex was off the chain! She was a freak and every man loves a freak in the bedroom. But looking on it now she is not the type of woman a decent man like myself would marry, settle down with and have kids. She was only really good for one thing. Yes, she is stunning, smart and she has a mean walk where her ass just rolls with every stride she takes, even women can't help but to turn and look. She had that down to perfection. She even heightened my male fantasies by telling me about a few lesbian encounters that she had in the past. That was all exciting and a turn on at first, but that is not wifey material. I don't want everyone looking at my 'wife' thinking. "*Yeah I used to hit that*" or "*she used to suck me off until my eyes rolled back*". I need someone who is more discrete. I know I told her what happened in the past, stays in the past and not to carry any baggage like that into the relationship, but shit! She's got a truck full of luggage. Every time we go out, there's some revelation that she's got to tell me! I mean, are the surprises ever going to stop coming. Are there any more things to pull out the closet!

I wish Janet wasn't out tonight. I need to off load on her right now, she is the only one who understands me. My office has become my haven.

My safety net to get away from it all. The mountain of paperwork on my desk mask the regret which I felt right now. Only the walls understood my pain and turmoil. Why didn't I pursue Janet a little more? I should have never given her, her space. All this would have never happened if it was not for her. Her rejection pushed me into the arms of many women. I was searching for that feeling again. That feeling that Janet always made me feel. That total tranquillity. The feeling you get after winning your first medal after working so hard. That feeling of owning your first home. She was my everything and she just tore me in two. Turned ice box on me. Now look, I'm trapped in a life which I don't want, one which I wished was someone else's right now. Many guys want what I have. Jasmine is a gorgeous woman but she is just not for me. Look at this picture; her in that shiny silver sequined dress and me in that brown Paul Smith shirt which I loved so much until she decided to try and operate the washing machine. I don't know why I have this on my desk, pretending to the world that we are okay. That we are happy. She may be but I'm far from it right now, I'm only doing what is best for my unborn child. I made my bed, so I guess I have to lie in it!

I felt the vibrations of my blackberry on my desk frightening me out of my thoughts. I rushed to answer it hoping that it would be a stress reliever on the other end of the line, but it was quarter to midnight.

"Hello can I speak with Mr Walters please"

"Yes. Speaking"

"Hi, this is PC Ingleton from Brixton Police station. We have your brother Mr Jamal Walters in custody and he is requesting that you are present"

"What! Okay I'm on my way!"

I finally left the police station after two hours and my neck was aching me with tension. I thought for a minute about phoning mum to let her know about Jamal but I decided against it because it was too late, it was two in the morning. She definitely did not need disturbing this time of night, especially for this bloody brother of mine, she had suffered enough. Jamal was my younger brother. He was only twenty-seven and had unfortunately fallen victim to the drugs world. He was an addict, addicted to crack and heroin. Everyone used to love him, he was the family favourite. Funny and cute with his large hazel puppy dog eyes a throw back from our great grandfather, what a waste! And to top it off he was also a frequent patient at the psychiatric hospital suffering from drug-induced psychosis, which they did suggest was schizophrenia but could not put a clear diagnosis on it because of his illicit drug use. Now here he was once again, arrested for theft of a mobile phone. I was getting fed up with bailing him out and representing him every other week. Since I had been back in London this was his third arrest. Luckily for him I knew my profession like the back of my hand. I knew they could not charge him, they didn't have enough evidence against him. But the charging officers bailed him to return pending an identification parade. They were getting as fed up with this as I was, he was well known at their station. The drugs had robbed my younger brother of all his inherited good looks, his face was now plagued with spots, bad skin and over grown dusty hair. He looked malnourished and filthy. Baby Jammy! It was a sad sight.

"Bro, thanks for coming down for me, blood! Them boy dem, they just arrest me for no reason"

"Come on Jamal. I know and you know you have done some wrong things in your life. And I want you to be honest with me this time… did you steal the phone?"

"Bro, how can you ask me this?"

"Look, I'm no fool. We have been through this enough times already. Did you smoke the phone?"

"Bro" He broke down and put his face in his grubby hands, rubbing his long dirty fingers through his hair "I didn't do it bro. Not this time. I know I have disappointed you in the past. But I'm trying bro. I'm trying"

I wanted to believe him, but I knew this scenario all too well. It was like groundhog day. He did it, he knows he did it and he knows he had already exchanged it for a quick hit before he was arrested. The officer had told me that he was high and tested positive for the drugs already. But they found nothing on him, no weed, no crack or heroin and no phone. Sometimes I gave in to the thought of him actually being charged and put in prison for one of these offences, hoping that the prison environment would do him good and would force him to detox. But I knew the prison system too well. Yes, you could get drugs on the inside too, any drug you wanted you could get it behind bars. I've heard all the stories first hand. It is a shame how our prison system fails offenders. You can go in fine and come out an addict.

"Bro, can you lend me twenty pounds, I have no electric?"

Please! I am not falling for that again. He had pulled this trick on me and mum a number of times and he had taken the money to get a rock. I looked over at him in the passenger seat.

"Look, come to my house and clean yourself up"

I knew Jamal's flat would be uninhabitable, he very rarely cleaned and drug paraphernalia would be everywhere. I would have to go there tomorrow and clean up for him. I made a mental note to buy some bleach and cleaning products in the morning. When I suggested that Jamal come round, I had forgot that I no longer lived alone and Jasmine highly detests my brother. She lifts her nose up at him like he's a common street rat, even if I mention his name! I hate that about her. Her thinking that she was better than everyone else. She doesn't have a squeaky clean past! She previously slipped up and disclosed that she had experimented with coke for a while, so she was actually no better than him! I didn't really care, Jamal was my brother and my brother comes first. I was my brother's keeper and he needed me. I remember clearly when I first got the call… I was still at college, no older than eighteen. Jammy must have been sixteen. Mum had called me at Janet's house and I knew straight away that something was wrong, she was all distressed and jittery on the phone. Eventually the rushed words escaped from her mouth and she told me that Jamal was in the psychiatric hospital following a psychotic episode. I felt beleaguered and confused with the revelation. It was too much for me to handle. My baby brother, Jammy, a mad man! Luckily for me Janet was my sunshine in the horizon, she comforted me and kept me grounded. That same chilly windy winter evening, she followed me down to the cold hospital to meet mum and Auntie Pat. I remember stepping inside and having an uneasy feeling, like I was entering a prison. Janet never left my side. She was my rock all through this and has constantly been the one to help me accept all this and deal with it. I stared out the window into the blank deserted streets and thought about her, she was a good woman, none of these women I have been with can ever be like her. She was definitely one of Gods fallen Angels. Someone to touch peoples hearts in a magnificent way and she had definitely touched mine, over and over again.

I pulled up in my drive, turning off the headlights and looked at the clock on the dash. It was ten to three. Shit, I just hope Jasmine doesn't wake up, I can't deal with her noise this early. I turned to Jammy in the front passenger seat and warned him that Jasmine was in the house sleeping, pleading with him to keep his noise to a minimum. He looked back at me un-phased, agreeing to my request before jumping off the leather heated seat and opening the door. When he got out he comically shut the door carefully to reduce the slamming sound, mocking my request. I shook my head trying to mask my amusement. As we stepped towards the front door, the porch light came on. I unlocked the door and turned on the lights to the living room. Jamal, looked around amazed, this was the second time he had been to my house since I had finished the decorating.

"It looks nice Bro. I love it. Rah you must be rolling in it now!"

"Thanks, but no I'm not. I had the help of a friend who is an interior decorator since you have been a bit scarce"

Before Jamal had been held captive by the drugs, he wanted to be an interior designer and electrician. He used to have an eye for detail, now that was all wasted, a distant dream. He had turned into a common thief. A drug fiend. I watched him in awe looking at the decorating; I just knew he was thinking that he could have done that, if only his life was different. I showed him to the bathroom upstairs and gave him a fresh towel from the cupboard. He thanked me then entered the tiled bathroom, locking the door behind him. I looked at my bedroom door, thankful that Jasmine hadn't awoken and gently walked to the spare room to find Jammy some of my clothes to put on. I was in the kitchen

139

fixing some coffee and grilled bagels with creamed cheese and salmon, when ten minutes later Jamal came downstairs wearing my old basketball top and some jeans. He smelt much better. He sat straight down at the breakfast bar to eat what I had quickly prepared, wolfing it down like he hadn't eaten for days. I watched the darkness get brighter as we sat for the next thirty minutes talking. I tried desperately to convince Jammy to get into a rehab but it was all in vain and I knew it, he wasn't ready. I looked at him disappointed as he openly admitted that he liked the feeling that the drugs gave him too much to go clean. He liked being in that neurotic state, enjoying the temporary high which it gave him. Talking to him was a waste of time, but I always held onto the little glimmer of hope that he would one day see sense and have enough courage to make the decision to change his life. His mental health was suffering as a result and he knew this. I wanted my little brother back. I wanted Jammy back, he was going to be an uncle. Guilt came over me and tears welled up in the ducts of my eyes. I felt so hopeless, like I had failed. Just as I forced the tears from flowing from my eyes, Jasmine came down the stairs wearing her pink satin robe and fluffy slippers.

"Oh, nice of you to think of me when you decided to bring your brother home for a late night party!" She snapped, looking Jammy up and down with her false eyelashes.

"Jasmine, sorry to wake you. Were we making too much noise?" I questioned, not really wanting to know the answer.

"Oh no. I can actually sleep through the sounds of laughter and high pitch voices." She spat with sarcasm in her voice.

What was wrong with this woman! This is my house and I can sit and talk with my brother if I wanted! Is that a crime?

"Look, Jammy is staying over tonight"

"Oh, nice of you to inform me of that too! I'm only your pregnant fiancée"

She was talking at me like Jamal didn't even exist, like he wasn't even in the room. Hands on her hip and her mouth all screwed up which made her look like she had a lemon in her mouth. She was unbelievable.

"Look. I don't have to consult you on everything, especially when it comes to my brother. So sorry for waking you! Come Jammy, let me show you to the guest room!"

Jammy ignored her, gazing at her to get her more annoyed. I got up and walked out the kitchen leaving Jasmine standing there in disbelief. I really can't believe the behaviour of this woman. This was my brother we were talking about. No matter what, you cannot put family out. She was being illogical; it must be her hormones! I turned the light on in the guest room, which was down the hall to the master bedroom. Jammy dived straight onto the double bed, clearly tired, his innocence vividly appearing, reminding me of when we were younger. I wished him goodnight and retreated to my bedroom. As I entered, Jasmine was sitting on the bed with a cup of tea in her hand looking at me scornfully. I ignored her stare; I wasn't going to argue about this tonight, I was too tired. Walking over to the en-suite bathroom I jumped into the shower for a quick clean, exited and grabbed the robe from the back of the door. The frosty atmosphere hit me as I maliciously walked straight up to the chest of drawers and dug in the bottom to retrieve my pyjamas. I haven't worn these in ages but tonight was definitely one of those nights fit for purpose. I put them on and climbed into the bed, intentionally facing the opposite way ignoring Jasmines grunts and heavy sighs trying desperately to evoke a reaction and I drifted off to sleep.

A few hours later I was awoken by the sound of the door shutting. I looked at my digital clock on the side displaying ten past six. I looked over at Jasmine, thank God she was still in deep slumber. I quietly slipped out the bed tiptoeing down the hall to check on Jamal. Of course I knew he would not be there an empty green room greeted me with the bed made up. I proceeded with my investigation downstairs and he was gone. As I scanned the room I noticed my wallet on the kitchen table, I opened it and instantly recognised that fifty pounds was also gone. Yep, he had stolen from me to go and get another hit. Jammy!

I cannot let Jasmine know about this, she would just enjoy throwing it back in my face. I really need Janet right now.

Chapter 19.

Keshia

It was early hours of the morning and the birds were chirping outside yet we were sitting in his Volkswagen sharing our life experiences, watching each other deeply like we were trying to touch souls. We hadn't moved since we arrived at his car after watching Janet and Leyah drive off. I listened attentively as I learned that he grew up in North West London. Surprisingly, he told me that he was quite well known in that part of town but unfortunately it was not for all the right reasons, which was no fault of his own, but by association. As he spoke I could see the pain and hurt which he had witnessed, which eventually led him to move out of the area and settle in South London. He explained that he had been living here for the past eight years. He lightly touched my hand and my heart pounded deep in my chest and made me realise that I want this man in my life. He was quite a deep person, someone who wanted a lot but appeared to be held back by his past but now he had finally severed those chains and was focusing on his future. One which I was hoping would include me!

We drove at leisurely pace back to the south side. He was purposely trying to delay the time which we had remaining together as neither of us wanted the moment to end. We were getting to know each other better without forcing it. Everything just slipped out naturally, there was no script, just the willingness to share ourselves with each other. I didn't want this to be the last time. I wanted more. I was lost in his eyes as he turned to me when he spoke of his passion; his music. Seeing his arms on the steering wheel was exciting my senses. The way which he gripped the leather made his muscles flex with every motion. His locks hung lose out of his ponytail, making him look like a rugged movie star attending the Grammy's. It gave him such a sensual look, one which begged for attention. I couldn't believe the intensity of the dance which we shared tonight. I had felt his every move, every inch of his body and I mean 'every' inch. Now I was definitely determined to make this man yearn for me as much I as I wanted him tonight. Whilst he sang on that stage, I felt like everything revolved around me. Like he sang every word to me, leaving my heart dancing in my chest having me panting like he had just made sweet love to me over and over again. I watched intensely as his lips sang the lyrics into the chrome microphone, noticing the way which he licked them after every verse, gently moistening them. His deep eyes telling a tale of seduction and sensuality. Wow, this man had stolen all my senses for real. I want him and tonight he made me realise just how much I wanted to test his other talents. I directed him towards my deserted street and indicated for him to pull up some distance from my block. He undid his seatbelt and looked me straight in my eyes. His stare burning an even further hole deeper into my heart.

"Keshia" He licked his lips before resting his head back into the headrest.

"Yes"

"Thank you so much for coming tonight. I'm really glad that you came"

"So am I. You really amaze me with the way you perform and sing so well. I mean your really, really good" I stuttered.

He leaned in closer, closing the gap between the arising lust. "Thank you. I'm blessed. You know I wrote a song for you"

"You did?"

"Yeah, I was just mesmerized by your beauty inside and out. You blew me away. One day soon I'm gonna sing it to you"

"Kamarni. Thanks" I blushed.

I wanted to hear it now. I wanted to let the words tease me and make me feel for him like no other. No one had ever written me a song, let alone a poem before. This was definitely a first and a plus. Gosh I love this man.

"Keshia, you know the first time that I met you, I was attracted to you instantly. Your beauty captured my attention from when you walked into the room... I was trapped from then... I tried to fight it but I couldn't. Your presence was too strong. That's why I had to come to you when you signalled for me to come over, but I didn't know what to say. You had me tongue tied"

"Wow, I didn't know... Sorry" I smiled.

Yes. He felt the same way I did, I couldn't confess that he had the same effect on me though. I wanted all the attention right now, the feeling of being the object of someone's affections again. It was a wonderful feeling that rushed across my body. Bobby's lyrics were all played out now. I needed something fresh. I closed my eyes as the sound of Aaliyah's rendition of 'At your best' played in the background making the moment magical.

"You know I had to call you over, your voice was too beautiful not to compliment"

"I must confess Keshia you had a real effect on me tonight... and don't think that this happens to me all the time... I don't really fall for fans...but..."

Fans! Come on why was he taking it to that level! Fortunately for him I could tell he was struggling with his words and that was the only reason why I didn't jump down his throat after calling me a 'fan'! He continued to struggle with his words and I could see that he wanted to reveal something to me. He was rubbing his short well lined stubble with a confused look on his agitated face, so I intervened and took control of the situation the best way I knew how. I leaned closer to him and kissed his juicy lips that had been calling me all night. He responded eagerly, the passion stealing the moment. Gliding his strong tongue through my parted lips he held the back of my head forcing our mouths closer and his tongue deeper. His touch felt so good. So natural. We tongue wrestled in the car for the next thirty minutes not caring about the outside world. I forgot everything about Bobby, not even considering the fact that he could actually drive past and witness my betrayal. I was wide open. Even though we struggled to breathe it didn't bother either

145

one of us, we just enjoyed the moment. Sitting in the front seat of his car with our tongues dancing together passionately. Unexpectedly the banana cake we had bought on the way home at the bagel shop fell to the floor, crushed by our bodies. Slowly he interrupted the ripple of sensations that were passing through my body and looked me in my eyes...

"Keshia...you taste so nice..." He licked the moisture from his lips.

"Look...I need to confess something to you"

I looked at him with an intrigued expression and silently gestured for him to continue.

"Babes, I don't want you to hate me for this... But I enjoy your company and talking to you. We are so alike..."

I listened eagerly as he continued, worried about what he was getting at! But I became distracted staring into his beautiful eyes with his perfectly shaped eyebrows which were slick and showed me that he had some sort of mixed origins.

"... But Kesh, I feel for you like no other at the moment and I have never felt like this. I mean...I just wish things were different at the moment...Everyday I speak to you I want to tell you, but I just can't get the words out" He took a deep breath before continuing. "I'm not single Keshia... I have a woman"

My mouth dropped, this cannot be happening to me. My sexy musician is already taken. What was all his intense kissing about!

"What? How long have you been together?" I said clearly shocked as I pushed his hand off my thigh.

"Well, we have been together for the past ten years"

"What? How could you not tell me this? You two have been together for a decade! What am I some bit of fun on the side to spice up your relationship? Giving the groupies some love?"

146

How dare I get so angry. I was in a similar position. I had a partner too, but he had been with her for ten years! Ten bloody years! My palms began to get sweaty.

"Babes, look it's not as you think. I did not plan for this to happen."

"Plan what? Because you have been flirting with me as much as I have with you. We talk on the phone for hours nearly every day!" I said clearly annoyed. Kamarni looked on trying desperately to control the situation.

"Yeah, I know…it's just…"

"Well it doesn't matter, because I have something to confess as well"

He looked at me reluctantly with curiosity in his eyes, searching me suspiciously for what I was about to disclose...

"Yeah. Go on then"

"Well… I've got a partner as well. I live with him too, but I'm only with him for convenience at the moment. I thought I still love him but since he moved back into my place I have realised that I don't!"

There was a long pause, the type of silence for reflection. The type where you think of something careful to come back with and he did just that!

"Wow. So we're both deceivers here and you have the cheek to go off at me" He sniggered uncomfortably resting his head back onto the headrest, trying to analyse the situation we just evolved.

"Look, I'm not the one who has been with my partner for ten years, okay!"

"You're right. But it does not interfere with the way I'm feeling for you! It's weird… So where do we go from here?"

I looked at him slightly disgusted, but weak for how I felt about him too. I looked out the window into the dark searching for an answer, but I knew what the answer should be!...

"I can't answer that. It appears you have more to lose than me"

"I know. Keshia, I like spending time with you. I haven't experienced anything like this before. I have never cheated on my woman either. This is a first for me."

"So you're trying to say that I'm the serpent in this? That I came into your secret garden and forced you to eat the forbidden fruit?"

"Yeah. Something like that" He chuckled.

This was unbelievable. Where do we actually go from here? A decade! Never cheated! I don't know if I believe that one, because a man as sexy as him must get offers as often as LL licks his lips and how does his woman let him come out all the time alone. She should be beside him at every gig, supporting her man. That's what I would do, because a man like that would definitely have a train of women queuing up behind him. In desperation and reading my thoughts he pleaded...

"Keshia. Don't say you don't want to see me again. Don't say that. We get on too well to depart now"

"Babe, you have been with your misses for ten years. Ten years is a heck of a long time. I can't fuck with that and I won't even try..."

"I'm not asking you too"

"So what are you asking me to do?" I said, throwing my hands up dramatically in the filtered air.

I cut my eye at him as he placed his hand back onto my thigh, slightly rubbing it and awakening my suppressed feelings.

"I don't know. I can't deny how I feel about you babes"

"Look, we'll just have to be friends. Nothing more! Platonic friends, that's it!"

The words, exited my mouth strong and powerful, but I knew I didn't really mean it. Kamarni looked at me intensely with stressed eyes, contemplating my request. There was nothing else I could do at this moment. I had to make him want me. Make him crave me. I want him to suffer and realise what he could have here. Obviously, the length of time he has been with his woman, he must be bored. He needs something different now. Something to make him feel young again, regain his sexiness, be daring, take chances, have fun and live on the wild side. I bet she doesn't even wear sexy undies for him anymore. I'm sure after being together for that length of time you must get complacent. You have nothing more to learn about the other. He must be with her out of loyalty. The way we connect is just too deep. When we are in each others presence I can feel him, his desire and need for me. The thirst which he has, like a vampire draining its victim it's not lust, it's something deeper than that. We connect on a spiritual and emotional level. That's exactly what I will do. Make him realise that he needs to be here with me. Beside me, holding me, stroking me. We looked on deeply at each other comprehending the contemplation. This was the best way to handle the situation but Kamarni was unaware of my real motive. Finally agreeing we made a verbal agreement that we would try and remain friends, nothing more just friends. Although we both knew it would be hard, being friends was the best thing to do right now. We were both in situations. His was worse than mine but nether the less we both were in the same predicament.

As I composed myself to get out the car, straightening my clothes and fixing my hair I could see the look on his face which silently whispered for me to stay... to follow him to somewhere intimate, where we could continue this night in the privacy of each other. I ignored the request and vowed goodbye, giving him a tender kiss on his forehead. He looked at me confused and questioned if that was all he was going to get. Before I could answer he took my head and forced my lips onto his. Our mouths connecting like they were made to be together... joining perfectly like two pieces of carved shapes. I gave in to the fight and responded like this was goodbye making sure that I gave my all into this kiss... proceeding with my plan but fully enjoying the moment. I could feel his

149

hands wondering over my toned stomach, up towards my breast arousing me. Not wanting him to have an easy ride I broke the kiss. Gasping for breath I completed my goodnight and grabbed the door handle, rushing out of the car into the crisp early morning air which woke me up instantly. I looked back and watched Kamarni watch me with desire burning in his eyes. I gave him a sympathetic smile and continued on my path towards my flat hoping he didn't see exactly where I was going. It was the early hours of the morning, Bobby will be wondering where I am. I neared my front door noticing the lights of Kamarni's car turn out the road and off into the rising sunlight. I reached into my handbag and took out some chewing gum, checking myself in my little cosmetic mirror which I fondled out in the process. My hair was all over the place. I looked like I had been sleeping rough! I ran my fingers through my hair being unable to find my brush trying to ensure that I didn't look suspicious. Although it was very unlikely that Bobby would be sitting up waiting for me I had to do it, just in case. I opened the front door slowly, looking around the room as I proceeded, listening out for any noises which would alert me to his status. He was asleep. I put my handbag down and took off my heels. These new Office shoes, sure did some stepping tonight. Kamarni had danced me into the moonlight. I entered into the dark of the bedroom quietly and took off my clothes, gently placing them on the chair in the corner of the room. Bobby was laying on the bed with the sheets all twisted over his semi naked body, exposing his hard firm torso which was not as toned as Kamarni's but a close match. I slipped back out and into the bathroom taking off my make-up, tying my hair back in one before brushing all traces of Kamarni's DNA out of my mouth with the aid of Aquafresh toothpaste and mouthwash. I closed my eyes and reminisced about the way which he held me and the softness and attentiveness of his kisses which he planted on my lips. His thoughts made me want more, wishing that it was him lying in my bed not Bobby. Snap out of it! I grabbed my black night dress and placed it over my hot naked body, the fabric brushing over my skin as I stood and imagined it were Kamarni. How I wondered what he would feel like, what our bodies would feel like together. Shit, stop! I gathered my thoughts and went back into the bedroom. What was my life becoming?

Who was I?

Where was I?

What do I want? I couldn't answer those questions.

I slipped into the warm bed trying not to disturb Bobby's dreams, which failed. As soon as my body eased in he turned and flung his arms around my frame.

"Baby your home"

"Yeah"

"Did you have a good time?"

"Yeah…it was okay" I lied…It was more than okay. I had taken off wallpaper with the *'Sexy Musician'* and I had felt his every bone in his body. My senses had been awakened in every place tonight. Everyway possible and yet I had not been sexually intimate.

"That's good. I missed you"

Yeah right, I thought. You didn't miss me. I bet you just got home not too long ago yourself. The only response I could summons was…"I missed you too baby" I could feel his nature beginning to rise. Oh please don't get horny on me now and steal my thoughts of Kamarni. My silent request was ignored. Bobby was awoken by the sexual demon within him. He turned me to the side and began to rub his shaft on my opening, desperate to get it moist. As soon as it responded he pushed his love inside of me, aiming to please himself more than me. He worked up his rhythm as my mind drifted and I allowed thoughts of Kamarni to enter and steal the feeling that Bobby was trying to rise within my rosebush. I smiled to myself; Kamarni would make me climax tonight.

"Morning beautiful. I made you some breakfast"

I was totally bewildered. Have I woken up into a dream? Was this reality? Was I waking up to breakfast in bed! Wow. This had to be a dream. Bobby hasn't made me breakfast in bed since we began dating. I rubbed the sleep out of my eyes in disbelief as he came towards me with

151

a tray prepared with the full nines; scrambled eggs, French toast, grilled tomatoes, chicken sausages, waffles, beans and fresh orange juice. I stared at the tray thinking what I had done to deserve this or better still what has Bobby done that he needed to conceal!

"Thanks baby. What's this for?" I asked confused as I sat up in the white sheets.

"Can't a man make his wifey breakfast anymore? Nah it's just to show my appreciation. To show you how much I love you"

"Aww, thank you baby. I love you too" I lied. Well I did love him it's just that I wasn't *in love* with him anymore. Waking up to him in the mornings used to make my skin hot and tingly, just watching him get ready in the morning made me smile with satisfaction. I used to love the way he always completed his little exercise routine in the morning of fifty press ups and fifty sit ups followed by various stretches. Now it was irritating. Actually it was infuriating. When he climbed out of bed these days I was glad for the space. I didn't even turn over to watch his body flex to the morning air which he filled with his motions. I was no longer his number one fan. No longer madly in love with my '*beau*'. He no longer filled my world with the happiness and craving of being in a relationship. I was bored.

"Baby, I was thinking that we could go for a riverboat cruise down the Thames this afternoon and then stop for some lunch at one of those little places you like down Covent Garden"

"Bobby, I'm tired. I got in too late"

"Okay we can skip lunch. What about one of those early evening comedy shows that you love?"

"Hmmm, not sure. I would rather stay at home and relax to be honest"

"What! My pumpkin doesn't want to go out. Are you sick baby?"

He touched my head comically like a junior doctor at the hospital taking care of their first patient. Truth was I was broken by the revelation Kamarni told me last night. Ten years!

"I'm fine. Just a little tired"

"Well, look you better get up. Baby, you know I'm going to be away in the next two weeks filming. So I want to spend some time with you before I have to leave you… all alone… without smelling you next to me"

He looked at me with his sad almond shaped light brown eyes. His mouth turned upside down in a pout. Why was I resisting him so much? I wanted to go, but my body just wanted to retreat in a lazy harmony today with thoughts of 'what if 's'. But he was right, he wouldn't be here in two weeks, he would be gone for three whole months. I need to act like I am going to miss him, although half of me actually would, I didn't want to fully admit it. I wanted to forget about my feelings for him and concentrate on how I would get Kamarni. But truth is Bobby's eyes had me weak. His strong masculine voice had me weak. He still had something over me that something which made me want to try again. Kamarni was just a vision out of my reach. The forbidden fruit.

"Okay" I retreated. "Can you let me eat this wonderful breakfast in peace first?"

"Only if you promise to get up afterwards and accompany me to wherever I want to take you"

"Bobby, you're killing me here… Okay! Now can I eat?"

"Of course you can precious. I'm gonna go take a shower"

He rose up off the bed and teased me with his nakedness as he stepped out of his boxers, leaving them on the middle of the floor walking into the all white bathroom. I sat there and began to eat the food he had prepared, swallowing a fork full of beans and toast. I lifted the glass of orange juice and noticed a little yellow post it note on the bottom. Imprinted were the words 'I love you'. I smiled to myself. Bobby had a

153

way of doing this. When I felt that I no longer wanted him and he no longer made me tingle, he had a way to do just that. To slither his way back into my heart with little gestures. This is what made me fall for him in the first place, the little thoughtful things. He had failed to do anything like this in months. Why now? Why all the sudden attention? What was he guilty of? Curiosity plagued my mind as I digested my food. So many thoughts entered my box of memories and warnings which I had collected within my mind throughout our relationship, but nothing made sense at the moment. I finished my plate of breakfast and watched Bobby come out of the shower with a black towel draped around his waist. He was a handsome, sexy man, that was for sure. He had this small little waist and heavy broad shoulders which made me laugh but he was complimented with a well toned upper body. One which made his clothes hang with debonair. He was still my man and my man was sure working that towel. He walked over to the dresser and squeezed out some cream, rubbing it all over his upper body. The rays of the sun sneaked through the curtains and bounced off his glistening body.

"Baby, I was thinking that we should invite Danny and his new girlfriend over for dinner this weekend"

"Why?"

"Just so that we can spend some time together. You two need to get over this little beef you have with each other"

"I don't have a problem with him! It's him that has a problem with me!"

"Yeah, but baby. You don't make it any easier for him. You hardly say two words to him when he is about"

"I have nothing to say to him"

"Yeah, well let's just do this. For me, please"

"Yeah, sure. Whatever you want. So who's the unlucky lady this time?"

He laughed. "Some posh brunette girl who is training to be a doctor"

154

"Oooh, nice. I don't know how he gets them"

"I know. He has the lyrics"

"Hmm, the lyrics don't last. Sooner or later they realise that he is a fraud. All talk and no action!"

Bobby took off his towel and proceeded to massage the coco butter into his thighs. My body started to heat up. He was having a strange effect on me this morning. I was horny for his love right now but I tried to fight the feeling, not wanting to fall for the expected.

"Okay, but lets just try and be nice to him. Okay?"

"Yes baby"

"Come and cream my back for me"

I thought he would never ask. My hands slowly caressed his shoulders working their way down his spine and across his lower back. The shape of it reminded me of Kamarni. Strong and defined. Shit, look at me comparing the two. I need to stop this. Kamarni has a woman and I have a man and my man is trying to make this relationship work. I must try as well. I worked the cream deeper into his joints, letting the motions flow seductively. Kissing his back then slowly working my way down his spine. He let out a small moan of approval as I continued on my path back up to his neck. All these thoughts entered my head, wondering if Kamarni made similar noises. Did he like his neck gently teased? Bobby relaxed his neck and let it fall to the side. I bit gently into his flesh as he winced in enjoyment. I slid from behind him and onto his lap, forcing his love inside of me. My juices were ready for him. He was ready for me. My mind was thinking of Kamarni; how would he feel if it were him I was on top of right now. We rocked and built up a steady rhythm. I moaned as my walls were stimulated, bringing me to ecstasy. A few minutes later he managed to do the same. This was not good that I had to think of Kamarni in order to make me climax. My head was a mess right now. His kiss had done something to me. It had me enchanted with his scent. His touch. His feel. I opened my eyes as Bobby disturbed my thoughts by whispering into my ear.

155

"Thank you baby"

He rose walking into the bathroom to clean up, content with the union we shared. I laid back onto the ruffled sheets and made a decision… Today would be the day that I forget about Kamarni and my desire to feel him up close and personal. Today would be the start to me and Bobby, again!

I have to make this work.

It's the right thing to do.

Chapter 20.

Leyah

The doorbell woke me out of my dream and startled me. Forgetting to grab my robe I rushed downstairs to open the door failing to check myself in the mirror. I stood at the doorway annoyed that Reese was the disturbance.

"Reese your early" I cussed opening the door wider, exposing my night clothes and my hair hanging messily over my face.

"Sorry for waking you. It's just that I had an extra ticket to go and see the Tweenies on ice this afternoon and Shantel can't make it. The show starts at one…"

I looked up at him irritated for his disturbance knowing that it was an attempt of another cheap move but before I could show my disapproval he continued.

"…And Asia suggested that you come instead of Mum. So here we are"

Asia looked up at me from her fathers arms displaying a wide smile which pleaded with me to say yes. I just couldn't turn my baby girl down.

"What time is it now?" I questioned, running my hands through my messy hair.

"Its ten thirty"

"Why did you come so early then? Why didn't you just call?"

"We have to get there on time and Asia was so excited. We wanted to make sure that we caught you in time and ask you together"

Reese was pulling out all stocks. What was he playing at? How dare he come to my house this time of morning!

"You look nice by the way" He said looking at me in my short olive silk nightie.

I had forgotten that I was standing here all exposed. I noticed his eyes wander towards my chest. My nipples had hardened to the feel of the cold morning air. Feeling uncomfortable I crossed my hands over my chest and instructed him to wait in the living room. He let Asia down, and she raced upstairs to retrieve a drawing she had done at nursery. As he walked in and sat down on my sofa I realised that he looked too comfortable! I didn't like him in my house and he knew this. I knew his tricks he came here this early to see if I had company. To catch me in the act! He was using Asia as a ploy, a way to worm his way into my home and snoop. Right now he was unsupervised in my house! I shook my head back to reality. I will not have this, he will not control me or my space anymore!

"Look Reese. You have to go and come back in about an hour. I have to get showered and dressed"

"That's okay. I will just wait down here with Asia"

"Err, I don't think so"

"Are you kicking me out of your house? Don't you trust me?" He had a devious smile on his face. I raised my eyebrows

"Is that a rhetorical question?"

Reese knew I was serious, the look on my face hadn't changed from the menacing one I had given him at the door.

"Okay. Okay. I'll go, but I will be back in exactly one hour"

He rose his tall body from the sofa where he had made himself a bit too comfortable. Just as he was about to walk out the room Asia's little legs came running down the stairs with a few drawings in her hands. Noticing her dad getting up ready to leave she panicked.

"Daddy, where you going?"

"Oh…" He looked at me "Well Mummy needs a few things from the shop, so I'm just going to go and get it for her"

Why does he choose to use me as his source for his lie? He always had a way of getting out of things on top.

"Oh! Can I come?" She asked looking up at him with her big eyes and thick lashes.

"Of course you can baby" She rose her hands and handed her father the pictures. He slowly flicked through the selection and stopped at one, examining it carefully.

"Have you seen this?" He handed me the picture with a huge grin on his face and looked at Asia. "This is beautiful baby. Did you draw that all by yourself?"

"Yep" She said, delighted with herself.

I looked at the picture and my heart sank. She had drawn a portrait of herself, me and Reese all holding hands with what looked like a rainbow behind. Although it was very childlike I could still make the figures out.

"That's you, that's mummy and that's me"

Reese and I both looked at each other. He had a huge smirk on his face. This is exactly what he wanted, more ammunition to fire his plan. Asia was old enough now to notice that she was living within a separated family. She knew that it was not normal. She had a daddy that loved her very much but did not live with us like other dads. She wanted both her parents together and Reese used this to his advantage. Instead of explaining the situation to her in a way which she would understand, he

159

decided to plant ideas into her head that maybe one day we will be a proper family again. He made it look like I was the one who was keeping her from having a proper family network. He was such a master manipulator, I hate him! I leaned forward and reached out for the rest of the drawings from him and watched scornfully as he went back out the front door with Asia in tow.

"See you in a bit Leyah, and try and be ready"

"Don't rush me!" Cheek! I shut the door behind me and slowly strolled back upstairs to get ready.

An hour later and Reese was back knocking at the door. This time I was ready. I had showered and changed into a grey dress, pinned my hair up and put on some mascara.

"Wow, you scrub up well" He joked with I hint of sarcasm in his tone.

"Shut up" I snapped, forgetting where I was.

"Mummy, don't say that!

"Oh yeah, Sorry baby" I looked at Reese with contempt as he handed me two Asda bags.

I reached out my hand and received them confused. I opened them up and looked inside to notice a few bits for Asia and a bottle of wine with a box of Swiss selection chocolates. He knew this was my favourite. He looked at me content with my reaction and put on his smug voice.

"Just an apology for waking you up so early. It was Asia's idea"

"Thank you. But I suggest you take it home for you fiancée" I said as I tried to hand him back the bag.

Reese looked at me and shook his head. "You're impossible. I'm trying to call a truce here"

"Truce for what? For all the hurt and pain you put me through or all the stress you put my baby through?"

"Our baby..." He corrected. "Look, I know you hate me and you have every right to but I'm trying to make amends now. I'm trying to be the best father I can be and I know you think I'm doing this for other reasons but I love Asia and I want what is best for her and that means us getting along with each other. Asia really enjoyed herself the other week and she would not stop going on about it. To be honest Shantel got fed up with hearing it again this weekend and so we decided it was best to retreat early"

I laughed. The truth had finally found its way out. He had made Shantel jealous and she was fed up of playing happy families with his daughter. I keep telling him about this, it was not fair on her. Not like I was bothered about how she was feeling because she has put me through enough stress to last a lifetime when she should have been taking it out on Reese, but solely directing all her anger at me instead. Like I was the one who was lying and cheating on her behind her back. She just better not distress my baby or she will have hell to pay!

"Well. That's charming isn't it! You just make sure she doesn't upset Asia or I will have to minimise the amount of time she stays over at yours"

"Don't be silly. It's nothing to worry about"

"Reese, don't bother and let me tell you something, don't ever pull a stunt like this again. I don't appreciate you coming to my house this time of the morning without a phone call or anything!"

"Why, were you hiding someone upstairs?" He questioned while looking at me sceptically.

I looked back at him offended as he stared at me anticipating my answer. "What I choose to do in my own time is up to me. You have no right to question what I do. All you do have is the right to question things about your daughter!"

161

"Yeah, but if you decide to have any man around *our* daughter. Then I believe I have the right to know about it"

"Oh like I had the right to know about you fiancée when you chose to serenade me with your words and I love you's. Please! Do me a favour and change the record. You have no control over me Reese. I am not your woman or your bit on the side. So concentrate on your fiancées whereabouts"

"Leyah, you know what I'm saying. If you decide to bring another man in Asia's life I deserve the right to know. There are too many peado's out there to take risks"

"Reese, stop being foolish now. I don't think I will bring home a paedophile and who said that I will introduce anyone I choose to date to Asia anyway?"

"That's good. I hope not"

How dare he! I am old enough to live my life the way I want to. I hate the way which he manages to hear what he wants when we argue about things. I should have just told his lying arse to keep his nose out of my business. My roof is my own. I am the only person who pushes keys through this door and when the time comes and I find a special man who can love me for me and not lie or hurt me like the way he did, then it would be my choice and I would have every right to introduce him to our daughter. I was not going to be a nun for the rest of my life. I wanted to be married one day and have the family life that I always dreamed of. He was okay, he was living his life and although we had Asia he still had his freedom. He still had room to manoeuvre and do what he pleased. He had Shantel, and when Asia wasn't there I'm sure that they would play the happy loving couple. Why should I be left at home bitter and resentful of their relationship; if you could call it that! I want to be loved one day.

I stood at the kitchen door and continued the dispute with him as he looked on at me from the passage way.

162

"Look don't expect me to forget what you have done to me. I'm coming out with you today, because you used Asia once again to make me agree to this and as she enjoyed herself so much the last time we all went out I've decided to do it again for her! Not for you!"

"That's fine with me. It works every time" He grinned to himself as he looked down at his Rolex on his wrist. "Right time to go baby girl" He shouted as he turned and walked towards the door.

Asia came running out of the front room with her Barbie doll and waited impatiently by the door. I picked up my bag and ushered Reese and Asia out the door, before checking myself in the mirror. Yes I looked fine, wearing my grey casual dress and black leather boots. I was not happy about this arrangement. Reese appeared to be getting too comfortable with the three of us together. I must admit though, it was nice being in a family unit doing things together, even if it was a lie. I wonder how Shantel must feel. It is not easy to digest that your fiancée has fathered a child while engaged to you and now that child is imposed on you as a constant reminder of his infidelity. Now he wants to play happy families with his daughter's mother on occasional weekends. I know I wouldn't be able to cope with it. She is one tough skinned woman.

Chapter 21.

Reese

"Where have you been? I've been calling your phone all day?" She stood with her hands on her hips wearing a short designer black dress with big gold accessories making noise with her every move, demanding an answer from him. Her long slender legs bare and her long brown hair resting on her back exposing her strong European features.

"I told you I was going to take Asia to see Tweenies on ice" Reese confessed.

"That was over ten hours ago! Where have you been up until now?" She screamed, standing with her arms crossed. Looking at him with menacing eyes, Reese quickly tried to think of an excuse in his head.

"I passed by mums and had some dinner. Further more stop questioning me!"

"Stop questioning you! Stop questioning you! You have been gone since ten o'clock this morning. I haven't heard from you since and then you walk into the house and expect me not to ask you where you've been. You should have dropped your child home since six o'clock, that leaves two hours!"

He swiftly turned his head towards her and stormed up to her heated. She stepped back, knowing that she had angered him, unsure of what he would do next.

"Look her name is Asia and I told you I went to mums and ate some food" He shouted up and close to her face until she could feel his breath on her pale skin.

She put on a brave front and shouted back at him. "You mean to tell me, you watched Tweenies for eight hours?"

"Don't be silly Shantel" He said walking back towards the cabinet to grab the bottle of Brandy and a glass.

"So what did you do for eight hours?" Shantel's voice became angry as she stopped his path and gazed intensely into his eyes, looking for a glint of a lie.

He took a large gulp of the Brandy, letting the burn glide down his throat, easing the tension that was building in his body. "Baby. I told you. The weekend is the only time I really get to spend with my daughter and I like to maximise that time as much as possible. You had plans today, so you couldn't come and enjoy the day with us, that's not my fault!"

"So you choose to spend the day doing what with Asia, she's three years old!"

"Yes she is! We went toy shopping and got some ice cream before the show started"

"Oh" Shantel's voice lowered as she stretched her arms out towards Reese to hold him in an embrace. "I'm just wondering, that's all baby. I know Asia doesn't like me and I know her mother is a conniving little liar. She uses Asia against me. You don't see it" Water welled up in her eyes as she desperately tried to make Reese feel sorry for her.

"Don't be silly. Asia loves you and I am not going to leave you for Leyah" He played her game and held her close, stroking her face to keep the peace.

"Then why won't you give me a baby?" She snapped, stepping back abruptly. Her plump face reddening with emotion.

"I've told you already. Now is not the time. We haven't got time for a baby at the moment. We need to improve our financial status first"

This was a lie. His financial status was more than capable to deal with another baby. Truth was he did not want a baby with Shantel. Yes she was a good homemaker, but she lacked what he would call motherly instincts. She was not the type of person who he would want to raise his children. She was weak. Her views could be moved with the slightest push. She was only a good business link. A gateway to increased profits. She was creditable in the property business... well her father was- *Taylor Properties*, this is what Reese needed. He needed to build his empire and so what if it was on the back of a well known property investor. He was willing to succeed by any means necessary.

"You gave her a baby. You brought your illegitimate child into our sanctuary. Into our harmonious relationship!" She continued shouting as her voice echoed throughout the empty house.

"Look, don't you dare call her that. She is my daughter and I love her. I have told you a hundred times I am sorry for cheating on you. It was a stupid mistake and I regret hurting you to this day. I love you and I'm sorry. But I am not ready for any more children right now. One day when the time is right. I promise baby"

His promise and his declaration of love rolled so freely off his tongue. He knew he did not mean it, but his words made Shantel believe it. She stepped back towards him and kissed his lips, happy that he had convinced her. He slipped his warm hands up her skirt feeling the back of her naked thighs and up to her flat cheeks, squeezing them gently. He knew how he could take her mind off his whereabouts and this baby idea... He led her upstairs, kissing her deeply trying to transfer the memories out of her mind, hoping that she would just forget everything. He had been making sure he wore a condom with Shantel every time. She had pleaded with him on many occasions that she was on contraceptives but he knew how much she wanted a baby and knew that she would lie to get it. No, he could not let Shantel get pregnant ever. Well not for him. He did feel for her but he didn't love her. She was not what he wanted in a woman. She was not ambitious, smart, strong minded, sexy or interesting. She was none of those things. Although, she loved to shop and could put together a mean outfit, he did not desire her like he had Leyah. The day Leyah walked into his life, was the day he lost all feelings for Shantel. He set about getting Leyah from day one

166

and was determined to make her his. He struggled to get her vision out of his head since he laid eyes on her. Her tall dark skinned tone had attracted him instantly. She was a perfect size ten, her long sleek jet black hair made her look like an exotic beauty. Reese could not take his eyes off her and he did not stop at anything to get her. Even when that meant him lying about his relationship, putting aside the fact he was engaged to Shantel. His loyalty to Shantel became purely an investment. He estimated that he had to keep her sweet and happy for the next six months to a year. Then he would have built up his company enough to leave her. He would no longer need to ride on the back of the Taylor train... to deceive her any longer... she deserved better. She deserved someone who would love her. Reese didn't. He couldn't.

Chapter 22.

Janet

The past few weeks had been interesting. It had actually been a whirlwind experience. I was being swept off my feet by Michael. He was such an exciting romantic guy. After the night at the Priory, he had called me the next day and we had talked for hours discussing everything about ourselves. A few days later and we met up for lunch and that was the start to my new beginning. He sent me roses at work, sweet little text and email messages, took me to nice tasteful restaurants and would call me every night when we were not together. He ensured that I was catered to at every opportunity. My head was sprung! I enjoyed his company, he never bored me, he always had me interested and longing for more. His life was a big soap opera but it was nice to hear him be so honest and forthcoming with information about himself. Unfortunately I couldn't do the same. He had asked me one night while we were sitting in each others arms watching Brown Sugar if I had ever been in love with a close friend. Of course initially I froze. I didn't know what to say, so I thought it was best to lie… or to distort the truth. I mean Marcus was engaged and expecting a baby. My feelings for him had to be suppressed. It was my own fault, I was the cause of all this. Marcus getting married was because I had let him go. I failed to show him the love which grew within me from the first time we met until the perfect night we spent together which changed our course for ever.

I gazed out the window and watched the trees blowing in the wind which brought back all the memories. I have never been able to get rid of the feeling I had for him and it was not just sexual feelings I had for him. It was much deeper than that. We had an inner connection. We knew each other intimately and professionally. He was the object of my every desire but I had lost it all. I had given him away to the arms of Jasmine. Now, I can't keep pondering on the thoughts of me and him one day being together. How could I even think that? That was now out of my reach forever. All the hopes and wishes I may have had were gone. Fallen into a deep opening, never to resurface again. Now I had to get on with my life, move on, he sure had! He was engaged to be married and expecting a child. Here I was with none of the above, not even in a serious relationship. I hadn't been able to commit to one since Marcus and I gave ourselves to each other. I concentrated on my career and that had been the focus of all my attention. Yeah I had relations in-between, but nothing too serious. I ensured that I did not have time for that by keeping myself busy. But now was my opportunity to make myself happy. Michael was a good man, a hard working man and he could make me happy. It was just for me to accept him in my life. Tonight he was taking me to a small theatre in Stratford to watch an African play. I was excited, Michael was so cultural I loved this about him. He was of Ghanaian parentage and he knew a lot about his cultural roots which was unwillingly imposed on him while spending five years during his early teens living there. We often discussed my travels to the Motherland and shared our experiences. It was truly a beautiful place. It was refreshing hearing him speak so passionately about his roots, our roots, the black roots. He even offered to take me with him next time he travelled back. I hastily agreed before thinking about the implications of my answer, what it actually meant... he was making future plans which included me! I'm not even sure if I am ready for all this. I thought about it carefully, and the situation which was before me... I only gave him my number that night because I needed help to get over Marcus, to help me deal with the pain I was experiencing. Michael just happened to be the unsuspecting victim. Although I am having fun, I hope he doesn't expect this to go too far too soon. I'm still in the healing process.

I looked in the full length mirror, after trying on numerous outfits, was ready. I had finally decided on my pleated Zara grey skirt and baby blue blouse with my dark blue designer boots which I had paid an arm and a leg for. I grabbed my brush off my bed and tied my hair up in a ponytail, making my face look petite. I admired my reflection, the style actually made me look younger than I was by at least ten years people would say. That was okay for me, I wanted to be ten years younger... step into a time machine and travel back to college. There would sure be a lot of things I would do differently!

169

Three hours later and we had left the small Stratford Theatre and entered back onto the mean traffic filled streets of London. I relaxed into the warmth of the car and watched as we drove past all the people at the bus stops freezing, standing with their thick scarves on and hands in their pockets. I was glad that he hadn't decided to take public transport or else that would have been me out there! The drive back was invigorating as we engaged in talks about the performance, the expertise of the dancers and precision of the script. We fell into huge laughter as Michael joked that he could do some of the moves we saw tonight, wanting to experience a laugh I challenged him to do just that later on. Half way through the conversation we were interrupted by the sounds of my phone ringing. I grabbed my bag off the floor and fiddled through it searching for my phone. Eventually I found it after tossing out my make-up bag and umbrella. Michael looked on at me with a smirk! It was only earlier that he questioned me about carrying such a large bag. I just couldn't help it, I loved large bags as I could carry everything in them, it didn't matter if I lost anything in the process. I looked at the flashing screen. It was Marcus... what did he want so late? It's past eleven o'clock! I reluctantly answered the call...

"Hello"

"Hey babe. How are you?" Came the familiar husky tone down the phone.

"I'm okay, you?"

"Jay. I need to see you. I've got so much going on at the moment. You're the only one I can talk to... Sorry are you out at the moment?"

"Yeah, I'm actually on my way home from the theatre" I replied, kind of bragging that I was actually out and not at my house, lonely as he expected me to be.

"Theatre? With who?"

I could hear the hint of jealousy in his tone. I liked it. "Excuse you, sorry I didn't realise I had to report my every move to you!"

Michael looked over at me weary about who was on the other end of the conversation, but I was not concerned with him right now.

"I'm just looking out for you babe"

"Well thanks, but when you decided to up and move to Luton, I had to look after myself " I stopped myself in my tracks realising that I had exposed too much, wanting to take it all back but I couldn't. Before I could retract my statement he responded...

His voice was quiet and sincere. "Jay. Sorry. I didn't know my moving affected you back then"

"It's fine. You had to follow your career. I didn't expect you to stay in London..."

"Actually, you abandoned me first. You up and went to Coventry babe! You was the one who left me"

I had to laugh at that, he was right. "Yeah, but I came back after the three years. Anyway, why are we discussing this now it has no relevance. What did you want to talk to me about?"

"I need to talk to you in person. I hate discussing my personal business over the phone. Can we do lunch Monday?"

"Urm, well I haven't got my diary in front of me but I guess that would be okay. I will pencil you in. I'll let you know if anything changes"

"Pencil me in, wow! So I'm only worth a pencil confirmation?" He joked. "Please don't forget Jay"

The sincerity was stronger in his voice this time, which let me know that something was seriously troubling him. I shuffled in my seat conscious of the piercing eyes which were staring at me.

"I won't. How's your brother by the way? Have you heard from him?"

"Nah. He hasn't surfaced his head as yet"

"Try not to worry about him he will make the right decision one day. Stop blaming yourself. There is nothing more you can do for him at the moment"

"I know, but I can't help trying Jay. I can't help it, he's my brother"

"I know, but he is also old enough to make his own decisions. You have done your best hun"

"I'm trying Jay. Thanks. Look let me let you go, your '*date*' must be thinking that your rude" He emphasised the word date with contempt. "Actually on the other hand…"

I knew exactly what he wanted to say. I laughed, cutting him off before he could finish and quickly ended the conversation. "I will call you in the morning. Have a good night. Bye"

Michael continued looking at me with curious eyes as he drove towards the Blackwall Tunnel.

"Who was that?" He questioned with authority in his tone.

"Sorry?" I had to check if I was hearing right. Was this man questioning who I was talking to? Who did he think he was? We are not an item! Damn we haven't even slept together as yet. Yes, he had tried many times but I felt it was too soon. I hadn't known him long enough. He had even tried to get me tipsy so that I would loosen up to him, lose all my inhibitions. But all his attempts were futile. Now he thought he had the right to ask me my business! I sucked my teeth. He was actually asking me the question as though I had a duty to answer.

"Why are you asking? I wasn't aware that you had any rights to me" I snapped.

"Sorry, I was just interested. You sounded engrossed in conversation"

"Well yeah. It was a close friend, my best friend actually"

"Okay"

172

We sat for the next ten minutes in silence. Trying to ignore the situation at hand I sat and flicked a piece of imaginary lint off my leg. I knew it wasn't his fault but I didn't like the way in which he questioned me. As the atmosphere grew frostier I felt I owed it to him to fill him in on all the important people in my life. The ones who meant a lot to me. That included Marcus. I turned to face him and explained that I was not happy at him questioning me. He apologised straight away without a justification which made me feel even more like a bitch! So I took a deep breath and told him about Marcus! Well the selective version about how we had been best friends since college and how he was special to me, something like a brother. Michael appeared to be a bit uncomfortable with my disclosure as I was bigging Marcus up constantly, but he seemed to understand that Marcus and I were very close. None of my past dates really understood our relationship, they always felt threatened and even though I always assured them that they shouldn't, really deep down they should. As much as I tried to deny my feelings for him externally, my love for him shone through which was mainly the reason for my short lived relationships even before we had slept together. I never really knew it back then and I didn't understand my feelings for him. But now I do. I have accepted that it is better for me to keep them locked away if I want to move on. Especially if I want to give myself a chance with romance.

It was ten past midnight and we had finally arrived at my house. Michael looked over at me through the dark shadows and thanked me for tonight. I looked at his sombre face and I could tell that he was still slightly annoyed with our discussion earlier. My whole demeanour had changed and I became defensive, like I had something to hide. I have to let go. I watched his expression and felt bad about the way I treated him, so I kind of felt obligated to invite him in. His face immediately lit up when I asked him! He walked in and casually sat down on my leather sofa. I walked straight into the kitchen and poured out a glass of wine for us both, downing half a glass in the process to boost my confidence. As I walked back into the living room I studied him, focusing on the positives of my attraction. No he wasn't Marcus but he was a good looking man. He had a round plump face but it made him look cute and it made his eyes light up. We sat down and watched a Denzel Washington film together while he held me close in his arms. I sat back and enjoyed the comfort it gave me. It was nice spending time with him, because he was so funny. I hadn't laughed like this with someone other than Marcus for years. We just seemed to gel together for some reason. Maybe I should think about him being more long term. Well at least give it some consideration. The room was silent as the film played in the background. I lay comfortable in his arms as he began stroking the back of my neck lightly with his strong soft hands. I could feel his touch making my body tingle sending hot flashes through my body. He began to kiss my shoulders while stroking my hair. It felt so nice. I could feel the tenderness melting into my body. I was nervous. I fought with myself trying to let go of my feelings. I wanted to prove to myself that I was over Marcus. I needed to force myself to lose those feelings, lose the power which he had over me…

I turned towards Michael and let his kisses trail across my neck and up towards my face. He kissed me gently, slowly reaching my lips. He pulled and tugged at them lightly before following the path towards my ears, then back down to my lips. My body was being slowly aroused by his touch. His hands glided over my body, my arms, my chest, my back as I moaned in agreement…

He whispered through his kisses. "Do you want me to stop?"

"No" I panted, giving him more access.

He continued to tease my body… slowly… gently. I gave release to the sensations and let my hands explore his body. I needed this feeling right now. I needed to feel him. He understood my urge and responded with eagerness. Forty minutes later and we were laying on my bed trying to regain our breath from the passionate moment we just shared. It felt as though we were both trying to prove something to one another, his being that he was the only man that I needed right now and mine being that I had let go of the past. He wove his hands through mine and looked deep into my confused eyes.

"I guess this means that we are an item now?"

I sat and thought about what he had just said. Hearing it come from his mouth made me feel positive. It made me feel special, wanted. I didn't have to convince him or hound him into the commitment. He welcomed it on his own. He initiated it.

"Well... let's just take our time with this, yeah?"

He sat up abruptly. "What do you mean?"

"I just don't want to rush into things. Just let it progress naturally"

Michael looked at me searching my eyes for a reason, failing to find any negative vibes he agreed. He kissed me on my lips to seal my decision and we remained in each other's arms until the morning. Michael was the first to wake up at six, anticipating his tiring journey back to West London in time to get to work. He found his clothes as I got up and made him a quick coffee. He quickly downed the caffeine awaking his senses. His eyes thanked me as he finished and we said our goodbyes before I watched him drive off into the cold morning air. I quickly closed back the door and retreated to rush around and get ready for work myself. I had a meeting at eight this morning so I needed to prepare my paperwork at the office. As I got ready I thought about last night. In the heat of passion I swore I had heard him say 'I love you', but he hadn't mentioned it this morning and maybe I was hearing things. He could have never said that ... maybe it was me just thinking I was the bomb! Yeah, that had to be it!

My heels clicked on the marble floors as I exited the lift and rushed towards the door to my office. Clara the receptionist was sitting at her desk applying her loud make-up as usual, barely glancing over her mirror to say good morning. I flung down my bag and opened my emails to gather the information for the meeting. As soon as it loaded I was bombarded with twenty five unread items. I scrolled down the list and saw that two were from Michael. I smiled and sat down on my chair to read them. He was so sweet, I clicked open the message and watched the animated online flowers he had sent me attached with a little poem about how much he enjoyed last night, thanking me. I blushed. He must be surprised that I had finally let him in, given him a part of me after holding back from all his previous attempts for so long. As I scrolled through the other messages there were the usual reminders from my manager and other employees and then I stumbled across one from Marcus. I opened the message and read:

Morning Babes,
I hope that you're wide awake! Don't forget that we are having lunch today. Let me know what time.
Jay, thanks for being there for me when I need you the most.
See you later X

I smiled, leaned back onto my chair and gathered my thoughts. It would be nice to see him, I actually couldn't wait. I was puzzled about what was on his mind, remembering that he sounded troubled on the phone last night. A thousand things went through my head but I failed to apply one to his current situation. I sent him a reply confirming that we would still meet up, suggesting that we meet at the little Italian bistro near my office for twelve thirty. As soon as I clicked send I sat back and retreated to my work, thinking about how I managed to indirectly get into this new relationship with Michael so soon. Was this what I needed?

It was twenty past twelve and I was sat at our table fixing my make-up, anticipating Marcus arrival. It was quiet at this time as people normally started packing o u t the venue at one o'clock. This was the reason why I suggested we get here this early, so that we would definitely get a good table. The food here was lovely, slightly over priced but worth it. All the staff knew me as I frequented here at least twice a week. Thankfully I had managed to get us a table over by the window which had a spectacular view of the Thames river. I smiled as I viewed a cute young couple walking hand in hand along the river front, marvelling in their love for one another. I glanced towards the entrance and laid eyes on this sexy tall slender figure walking towards me, wearing a spotless black suit. My heart stopped. He was too much to look at. All the ladies turned and stared in his direction, watching this sexy man take confident strides across the restaurant floor wearing his framed glasses. I loved this look on him, he looked so edible and professional. He was perfect. Exhale.

"Hey beautiful"

"Hey sexy. Can you not go everywhere looking like a model please!"

He laughed. "Why thank you for the compliment, kind miss"

We both laughed quietly as I rose up and held him in a tight embrace, closing my eyes as I felt our bodies close in together, inhaling the fragrance of his aftershave lifting from his skin.

"Thanks for taking some time out for me" He said, holding my hand and ushering me to sit back down.

"Don't be silly, that's not a problem babe. You know I have always got time for you"

He smiled exposing his beautifully lined teeth. We ordered our lunch from the pretty young dark haired Italian waitress and continued the conversation.

"So what's wrong? You sounded a bit distressed on the phone last night. Is everything okay?"

"Yeah, I just wanted an excuse to see you really!" He tried to laugh and mask his troubles, but I knew there was more to this meeting than just wanting to see me.

"Come on. I'm flattered and all but I know that something is up with you. I can sense it in your tone!"

"Jay your right, I hate that you know me so much!" He laughed. "Truth is I don't know. I don't know if I can do this anymore... I can't pretend anymore, I really can't..."

What was he talking about? Pretend about what? I looked on puzzled, waiting for him to continue. He made a huge sigh before he spoke, looking down at the table and re-smoothing the table cloth.

"...Jay, the other night I heard her talking to someone which sounded suspicious... don't get me wrong I wasn't snooping. But it didn't sound right. When I asked her who she was talking to, she lied. She said she was talking to her friend Carrie but the conversation did not sound like she was talking to no woman!"

177

"What? Are you sure? I mean she could have been!"

"Jay, I know what I heard and that was not Carrie. She was speaking in all hush tones and giggling like a school girl"

"That means nothing. She wouldn't lie would she? Come on she is pregnant with your child and engaged to one of the most handsome men in London!"

"I know Jay, but it just doesn't feel right. You know?... I don't trust her, something just doesn't feel right"

This was awkward. How do I try to convince him to stick it out and trust her when I love him. I need to be a real friend for him right now and tell him the truth! The truth is that he has no real evidence. He can't just accuse her or assume that she is cheating and I cannot just agree with his irrational decisions because I want him for myself. What am I to do? I composed my thoughts and pretended that I wasn't madly in love with him.

"Marcus, you have no proof do you? You have to trust her?"

"I've tried. Jay I always knew that she was a flirt and had a speculative past. But I put that all aside and tried to make the relationship work. Then she got pregnant and I had to deal with it! Now she is making me have serious doubts about her. I don't know if I can marry her Jay. She doesn't accept my family for one, she hates Jammy with a passion. She had the cheek to tell me that she does not want him back at the house. We had a big bust up about him coming that night I bailed him out of the police station"

"What? Why?"

"She can't stand him. She looks at him like he is the scum of the earth. I mean that's my brother, how dare she Jay!... I can't marry her. I just can't!"

I lightly touched his hand, watching the distress overshadow his brown eyes, turning them darker than usual, losing the sensual look that he walked in here with.

"Babe calm down. It will work its self out. I don't know how you managed to get yourself into this…" I said trying to comfort him.

My phone and the habit of ringing at the wrong time and today was no exception as it rang interrupting our discussion. I didn't want to answer but Marcus insisted that I did. As per usual it was Michael, annoyed at his timing I rushed him off the phone. I could tell by the disapproving tone in his voice that he was not too happy about being number two right now, but Marcus was my priority at this moment in time. He was venting out on me and I needed to be the friend that I was and listen attentively! He looked up through his confused eyes, having taken off his glasses and laid them on the table.

"Who was that?" He quizzed.

"Oh, that was… errm my date from last night… " I felt uncomfortable letting that information slip from my lips. Like I had betrayed Marcus or something.

"O-kay! So when did you hook yourself up with Mr Theatre?…You mean to tell me he stayed at yours? You didn't did you?"

He looked at me with his piercing eyes as I shuffled in my seat uncomfortably, feeling like I was cheating.

"What do you mean? I am a grown woman you know. I have needs too"

"But Jay, you hardly know him!"

"I know him well enough, to want to try and get to know him better. He is a good guy"

"The good guys are always the ones to watch out for! I want to meet him"

"What for?" I said shocked!

"To check him out. I can't have any riff raff with my girl"

Aww look at him all jealous, not even making an effort to disguise it at all. I felt bad about him finding out like this, just as he was telling me about his problems with Jasmine but it was good that it was out in the open. We continued to talk about Michael for the next twenty minutes completely forgetting about the reason why we were here in the first place.

"Jay, look just take it easy, take it slow with this guy. Promise me that you will be careful"

"Marcus, I'm a big girl. I know what I am doing"

"Yeah, I thought I knew what I was doing when I asked Jasmine to marry me!" He confessed, looking at me with his big doubtful eyes and humour in his voice.

"Yeah... so what are you going to do about that then? I mean are you going to call off the engagement?... Are you going to confront her again about the conversation?"

"Jay, I really don't know. I don't know what to do anymore. I'm no longer in control of my life... When did I lose control Jay?"

I couldn't answer it. But I knew the answer; it was exactly when he hooked up with that chick! Jasmine is no good for him. She never has been. Just look at him all tense and stressed, I can see the worry on his face. He has enough to deal with especially all this stuff with his brother. How can she be so inconsiderate! I can't stand her. Not only did she have what I wanted but she was a bitch with it! We sat and spoke for a while longer, enjoying our little lunch date until we both realised the time. It was already two o'clock. When we got together the time always flew by so quickly. Marcus won the race to pay the bill and smirked at me as he placed his black card on the tray. We both walked out into the fresh air as the sun beamed down on us. I put on my Dior shades, looking like a supermodel next to my Superman who had transformed back to sexy Clark Kent. He looked at me with admiration as the sun rays beamed off his flawless skin, taking my hand he vowed to meet with me again for lunch in the week as he was working at an office nearby. We exchanged our lingering goodbye and headed back to our offices. The scent of his cologne lingering on my blazer. As I made the short walk back to my building I reviewed the situation in my head. I had given Marcus my thoughts on the situation, but I was really not the best person for him to seek advice from. I'm in love with him and I don't want to be in love with him, I can't handle being in love with him! The revelations about Jasmine were partly soothing, purely because I did not want him to be with her, yet he can't just leave his pregnant fiancée and be with me! And what makes it worse is that it was all based on speculation, thoughts that she was lying to him over who she spoke to. What am I thinking? Were just friends and I have Michael now anyway.

Chapter 23.

Keshia

I sucked my teeth as I dragged my feet back into the living room and plonked myself down on the sofa with my mug of hot chocolate. I watched the marshmallows floating on the top exposing my unhealthy chocolate sin. This being friends malarkey was hard, although we vowed to do this I spoke to Kamarni daily and my feelings for him grew stronger and stronger with each day. We were having an emotional relationship and everything that he shared, left me more fulfilled each time. He was the water for my ocean, the sand for my beach and the sunshine through my cloudy days. He was the spark in my heart that ignited every time I saw his name light up on my phone. He definitely had me anticipating hearing his voice, I never had enough! Bobby had been away for three weeks now and I didn't have time to miss his company because Kamarni was keeping me occupied. Although Bobby phoned daily to check up on me and tell me how much he missed me, he had limited time to talk as most of his time was occupied filming. I was happy for him that he had finally gained a prospective role. This could open up a lot of doors for him. He was pursuing his dream. But my dream was still left untouched…

I sipped my drink and shook my head remembering the looks on Leyah and Janet's faces when they conveniently overheard my conversation with Kamarni on one occasion. They looked at me with cynical eyes, not knowing what to make of the situation. Yeah my girls disagreed with my behaviour, my close intense relationship with Kamarni but we had this circle of trust which we lived by. We would keep each others secrets until the end! No one would know outside of the circle. It was for the guilty party to come clean, to make the decision to take the stand for confession to their partner, in my case Bobby. But I would never confess to Bobby! Come on there is nothing to tell, I'm just 'friends' with Kamarni. Bobby has female friends, so therefore I can too!

It was another Friday night and I was sitting at home bored already in my pj's watching Love & Basketball for the third time this week. It was only seven o'clock, yet there was nothing to do. My head was restless and I just kept binging on food. My cupboards were full of snacks. I made a mental note to do an extra workout this week. I sat and painted my toenails, vex that Janet was out with her new guy and Leyah was at a family event. Without the two of them I was lost! I pondered on the thought of giving Clayton a call but quickly dismissed it remembering the last conversation which I had with him. He had me infuriated in an instant after telling me that he was going to come over to my place unannounced to surprise me. He tried to convince my mood by informing me that he was going to turn up with some wine, whipped cream and a bottle of massage oil. Shit! Imagine if Bobby was home, he just can't be doing that! That was my mistake bringing him into my home. But in my defence Bobby and I had broken up at this stage and I badly needed to satisfy my itch! I had to enlighten Clayton that he couldn't do things like that; turning up unexpected. No way. Unfortunately the only way which I could get through to him was by telling him that I was back with Bobby! And of course he did not take the news lightly. He even threatened to come down and tell Bobby of our brief fling but he soon changed his mind with some fake crying on my part. He knew if he ever did such a thing he would blow any chance of me and him ever having anything ever again, and believe, he held on to the thought of me someday being with him, in a committed full time relationship. Like that would ever happen! Just as I finished blowing my left foot with my mini fan, my phone rang…I looked at the caller display… yes my nightly dose of Kamarni…

"Hey baby"

"Hiya Kesh, you alright?"

"Not really just here at home bored out of my mind, watching a dvd"

"Don't tell me you're watching Love & Basketball again?"

Wow, he sure knows me. I think this is definitely an indication that maybe I've watched this film too much now, I need to buy a new flick.

"Errr… yeah I am" I confessed, laughing that he knew.

"Right, put on some clothes were going out. I'm coming to get you in an hour"

"Sorry?…"

"You heard! It's Friday night so get up, let's go out and enjoy. Soon come"

With that he hung up the phone. Well at least I have something to do now, I thought. I placed my mobile back where I had picked it up from on the sofa and dashed into the bedroom to find something to wear, but what would I put on. I have no idea where we are going. How could he spring this on me? Not that I really minded. I loved the way that he was spontaneous. He was exactly the kind of excitement which I needed in my life right now. I stepped out of my tracksuit and jumped into the shower, quickly washing away today's funk with my coconut body wash, making sure that there was not any unwanted body hair and getting rid of them if there was. As quick as I stepped in, I stepped out. Rummaging through my wardrobe trying to find something for the unknown occasion I selected my olive green Mango dress and thick black waist belt, exenterating my small waist and wide hips. I applied my make-up to perfection. Just as I finished putting on my cherry lip gloss I heard the Neyo melody on my phone. I raced into the front room to answer it, retrieving it just in time. As soon as I put it to my ear I heard the soft sound of Kamarni's voice telling me that he was on my road. I instructed him to pull over at the top by the corner shop, hesitant to let anybody know where I lived, Clayton was to blame for this. But I also couldn't disrespect Bobby like that. We lived here together like common-in-law partners bringing a next man to our door would be the ultimate sin. I rushed back into my room and sprayed on my Vera Wang perfume. Kamarni was five minutes early, luckily I was not one of those women who took hours to get ready. I had done well under pressure. I twirled around and gave myself the once over in the full length mirror I was satisfied with what I had managed to pull off. Damn, I sure was one sexy woman! Bobby didn't know what he had, how dare he venture else where, when he has everything right here! Oh well, his loss is another mans gain!

I held the collar of my leather jacket closer as I walked towards Kamarni's car. As soon as I was in vision he got out of the driver side and walked over towards the pavement, watching me, stripping me with his eyes. I could feel his stare burning through my body. The temperature rose as I strutted in my sexy black heels towards him.

"Wow, you look amazing" He looked at me in admiration.

"Thank you. I just threw something together quickly after you gave me such short notice"

"Well, believe me you done a *VERY* good job!"

He looked at me and smiled, giving me a kiss on the cheek. I closed my eyes feeling his lips touch my skin, sending goosebumps across my arms. Get a grip Kesh! I opened my eyes and repaid the compliment.

"You don't look too bad yourself"

He was wearing a grey Sean John jumper which left very little to the imagination. It hugged him snugly showing his defined torso and firm arms. He finished the look with a pair of dark grey trousers and matching grey leather shoes. His platinum chain hung down at his neck making him look so tasty. I wanted to grab him right there, drag him back upstairs into my flat and make sweet passionate love to him. But we were just friends. Two friends that were sexually attracted to each other…I exhaled. This is hard!

"Twinkle have you eaten yet?"

This was his new pet name for me, stating that it fit me because my eyes always sparkled.

Ohhh, how I would like to eat you right now!... "Err nah, I haven't"

"Good. I'm going to take you to get some food then we can go out for a little drink. I know the perfect spot. A friend of mine has just opened up a new restaurant. I hope you don't mind me taking you there?"

"That's fine" My eyes gave me away, he could tell how much I adored him. How much I wanted him but I would hold out. I am strong. I can do this!

We reached to our destination in busy Clapham. It was a lovely little romantic American soul food restaurant decorated with red and cream drapes and matching candles. Small tables decorated with beautiful oriental lilies complimented the room. As soon as we entered we were approached by an attractive Barbadian hostess who looked like an older Rhianna. Kamarni informed her that we had reservations and she quickly checked her book and escorted us to our table. To my surprise Kamarni ordered a bottle of champagne. I looked on surprised while the waitress walked off to fetch our order. Kamarni looked back at me, giving me his little devious smile which exposed his gold tooth in the back of his mouth.

"What are were celebrating?" He stared at me and laughed like I wasn't to ask for a reason, but since I had he answered me with his devious smile on his face. "We are celebrating our friendship"

Exhale again. I can't do this! I want this man too much. He was surely smooth. I was enjoying myself too much and my heart was heating u p like the Sahara dessert. Kamarni's friend had hooked us up with a platter full of samples of everything they had on the starters menu. The food was presented with perfection. There was not a piece of food out of place. Not only did it look good, it tasted even better. As much as I was trying to eat like a lady, the food was too nice to eat slowly. I was so comfortable with Kamarni that I actually didn't care what I looked like eating. Kamarni just smiled at me, happy that I was enjoying the food so much. I was shocked when the waiter came and cleared the table then came back over with another huge platter this time filled with a selection of main courses, which looked more delicious than the starters. Kamarni dished me out a generous portion then started on his own. We tried each selection of meat, before he urged me to try some of the spicy prawns from his fork which he raised towards my partially glossed lips... I looked deep into his eyes as he fed me some of his meal, being as erotic as possible, moistening my lips as he took the fork back. I could see him sensing my feeling, my response. His eyes were his let down but my advantage. The intensification of the flirting grew and it was mutual. We finished the meal over various topics of conversation as the Calypso music played in the background, talking like we had known each other for years. We were just so comfortable with each other. I knew every aspect of his life, well almost everything. I didn't ask for details about his relationship and at times I often forgot that he was actually in one, that he was committed to someone else. He was someone else's property. His rights were taken. But right now, right here, he was mine.

All mine!

We shared a dessert of warm cinnamon cookies with cream and mixed spice sauce. It was like we were on a first date at school. I didn't want this night to ever end.

"Twinkle. Shall we get out of here and go for some cocktails?"

"Yeah, sure. My stomach is full…"

"That's the plan. Well at least you won't get drunk and let me have my wicked way with you!"

I sniggered. "Oh so you believe you could have your wicked way with me when I'm drunk? And what would you do?"

"Now that would be telling… Let's go"

We rose, spotting his friend he gratefully thanked him for the meal. Kamarni made quick introductions as I shook his rough hand. His friend was dark and handsome. I scanned him, thinking that he would be good for Leyah, making a mental note to follow it up later with Kamarni. I can't believe he introduced me to his friend. Would he not have thought why is he bringing this strange woman tonight and not his fiancée. I was confused, but Kamarni didn't seem to care, so why should I!

We walked back to the car in the arctic cold with our arms linked. Everything just happened so naturally, our gestures were never forced. It was like it was meant to be. We drove the short journey to this little wine bar. When we entered the sounds of Black Eye Peas sung throughout the room, making me swing my hips to the beat. There was a mixture of all cultures in here having quiet drinks, chilling in the relaxing environment. We scanned the room finding a nice corner then deciding to take up residence before anyone else noticed the cosy spot. He picked up the red cocktail menu book and quickly scanned through the contents.

"Kesh. You need to try this drink. Let me order you one"

He quickly closed the recently viewed page containing the selected drink and rose to attend the bar.

"I want you to guess this drink Twinkle. I just hope you're not a light weight" He laughed as his toned body walked with swagger to place our order.

A few minutes later he returned with our drinks. He had two dark coloured liquids in a Martini glass and two small vodka shots.

"Right, lets take these two shots and guess what the flavour is"

I laughed, intrigued by his daring spirit. "Okay"

"One, two, three go"

We downed the small liquid which glided down my throat as I wished it were the touch of his tongue. It tasted nice and sweet like his lips did that night they joined forces to fight the long anticipated cause. We banged our glasses on the table once we were finished and I shook my head wildly as I felt the liquid warm up my insides then rush straight to my head.

"So what do you think it is?"

I wiped the excess moisture from my lips and thought about it for a few seconds, watching Kamarni await my answer.

"That has to be the Fruit Salad vodka"

"Your good! How did u know that?"

"Babes… come on you should know I have good taste!"

We both laughed understanding the innuendo behind my comment and then picked up the dark substance in the Martini glass. I looked on intensely at Kamarni as he demonstrated how best to drink it. Touching my hands softly he explained looking deep into my eyes. I could feel the passion reeling me in, holding me by the heart and drawing me closer, my blood was racing. No! I won't! I won't let it capture me! I broke of the intense moment by raising my glass and taking a long pull at the drink through the thin straw, which was the sweet mix of a pistachio and black cherry Daiquiri. From that first experience, I was hooked! We ordered three more and sat and enjoyed each other's company further. Kamarni continued to make me laugh as he told me about some of his olden days back in Trinidad. This man still intrigued me. I was intoxicated with him. It was fast approaching 3am and I didn't want to go home but the bar was closing. I could see the reluctance in Kamarni's walk that he felt the same. If only things were different…

Half an hour later and we had reached back to my road where the night had begun. I sat in the car not wanting to move. If only things were different. Kamarni turned to face me and lowered the music.

"Are you sure you wanna go home already?" He asked in his sad voice, creating an upset face.

"Why, where else is there for us to go?"

"Follow me somewhere quickly. I need to check on something"

I nodded my head in agreement and with that Kamarni put the car into first gear and turned the car around, driving towards Upper Norwood. We shortly pulled up outside of a small terraced house. I looked around sceptically, noticing the deserted street.

"Where are we?"

"This is my mums place. She's away at the moment I just need to make sure everything is okay. I promised I would keep an eye on it for her…come"

189

We got out of the car and Kamarni ushered me towards the front door. As I looked around my surroundings I noticed we were on a well presented cul-de-sac road with expensive cars in the driveways. I hadn't seen anything like this in South London before. I followed behind him as he opened the black metal gate to his mothers house, her front garden was amazing, decorated with roses and various other flowers which I couldn't name, it looked like something out of a garden show. Kamarni unlocked the door and escorted me into the unusual surroundings. As we entered I noticed that the inside was even more immaculate than outside. Kamarni rushed to switch off the alarm whilst telling me to go into the lounge and make myself at home. I looked around the hall as I slipped out of my heels conscious of the cleanliness of the house.

"Let me just look around and make sure that everything is in order. Do you want a drink?"

I looked at his smooth face and replied. "Yes please. Can I get a hot drink please, a mint tea if you have any" My head was tipsy but I was trying my hardest to disguise it, not wanting him to think that I couldn't handle my alcohol.

"Sure. This is a black woman's house babe. You know we always have mint tea!"

We both laughed as he retreated out of the room and into the back. He checked all the locks and windows while he put on the kettle. I sat in the living room looking around. There were very few pictures on the walls or anywhere in the room. Only one photo of Kamarni and his sister as teens decorated the bare walls. I rose up to take a closer look at Kamarni as a youth. It made me laugh because there was one with him posing like a 'rude boy' with his dry lips, coloured high top and braces. I burst out laughing admiring how much he had changed. Curling over in laughter I was startled by a gentle squeeze at my ribs from behind.

"Oi! Sit down and don't look at anything. I'm sure you've got some embarrassing pictures yourself!"

"Yeah, but this is a classic" I continued laughing. Kamarni pushed me playfully, tiggling me into submission. We collapsed on the sofa as he reduced the compression of his hands against my ribs. He was laying partly on top of me... suddenly becoming conscious of the compromising situation he rose up and reminded me of my tea. Quickly he exited the room to finish making it in the kitchen. Following his exit I straightened myself out and sat upright on the sofa waiting for him to enter back into the room. He smiled walking back into the room with two mugs in his hand.

"Here you go Twinkle"

"Thanks. So how long has your mum been away for?"

"Only two weeks. She is out there visiting my grandmother"

"Okay. So how comes you didn't go with her?"

"I was out there in the summer for my cousins wedding. I couldn't go again this year"

"Oh lovely. I love weddings. How was it?"

"I don't know. Okay I guess. Us men don't worry with all that stuff!"

He reached over for the remote beside me slightly brushing my legs as he did so. My body tingled with the feel of his touch. He began flicking through the channels not looking for anything in particular, trying to ease the mood. I looked at him from the corner of my eyes as we eased into each others arms, snuggling up on the sofa in front of the fire. Sleep was slightly taking over my eyes but I tried to fight it not wanting to let Kamarni notice that I was struggling to stay awake. I wanted to enjoy the time we were spending together, holding each other but he had already surrendered to the fight and was slowly dozing off. I smiled as I looked over at him, his chest moving to the rhythm of his breathing. His cute facial features enhanced. I turned to find a more comfortable position, making him stir. He awoke and looked at his watch.

"Baby it's late, can you stay here with me tonight?"

191

I was thrown off guard by the question put to me. "Sorry!... I don't think it's a good idea"

"Please. I won't trouble you. Trust me. We will just sleep in each other's arms. I can't drive right now, I'm tired"

I wanted to. I needed to feel wrapped up in his strong arms. I didn't want the moment to end and I was envious that he had woken up. But I was also plagued with the thoughts of his fiancée and Bobby seeing us wrapped up in each others arms, I soon shook those thoughts out of my conscious. I was tired, he was tired. All we would do is sleep right?... We slowly walked up the stairs and he showed me into his room. I was surprised to be greeted by his fully furnished and kept room at his mothers, he explained to me that he often stayed here to keep his mum company and get some peace to write his music. I admired the way in which he spoke about his mother. I could tell that he really loved and appreciated her. He handed me a black T-Shirt from his wardrobe as I observed the contents of his room, sneakily looking for evidence of his partner. Not a single picture was displayed. The room was neat and tidy; everything looked like it was in its rightful place. I gazed on in awe as he slipped out of his trousers and jumper, stripping down to his grey boxers. Exhale. He was total perfection. I inhaled his body, his firm thighs, his toned back, arms and chest, noticing a small birthmark on the back of his left thigh and a scar the size of a two pence coin on his right upper shoulder. He turned around noticing me absorbing his body. He grinned. I turned my face around embarrassed and slowly undressed, taking my manicured hands and undoing my belt trying not to look seductive or cause him to notice me. He tried to hide his frustration, the sexual tension was rising so blatantly. He offered to leave the room so that I could undress but a part of me wanted to tease him. I wanted him to see me in my sexy black underwear, I wanted him to fight with himself to contain the urge to pounce. What am I saying! I shouldn't be thinking like this, because we were just 'friends'. He cautiously entered back into the room just as I placed my clothes on the back of his leather chair, walking at a reluctant pace he proceeded towards the bed. I watched as his motions teased me. He bent down and pulled back the duvet before politely asking me which side I wanted to lay on tonight. It felt funny but nice that I was here. I felt so at home, I was totally comfortable with the fact that we would be sharing a bed together. I felt that I belonged here. But of course this was all a façade. It wasn't real. But it didn't matter, I was going to enjoy every moment of it. We wrapped up in the soft blue linen sheets cradling each other's bodies, basking in the body heat from one another. Kamarni held me around my waist tightly like I was his and only his. His body was so close that I could feel the hard thumps of his heart upon my chest. I closed my eyes as he placed a soft wet kiss upon my forehead, moving a strand of stray hair from my face.

"Goodnight Twinkle"

"Night"

"Thanks for staying" He whispered.

"That's okay. To be honest I was too comfortable to..."

Before I could finish my sentence he leaned closer and kissed me on my lips. He lingered there for a bit longer than he was supposed to but I didn't retreat. I didn't break off the intensity of the moment, the feeling of our lips pressed together in the passionate embrace. I could feel the passion racing as he fumbled with his tongue to part my lips. We shouldn't but I couldn't stop it. I wanted it. I introduced our tongues together, they reunited and got re-acquainted. His hands started to roam around my head gently pulling my hair and forcing our mouths closer, yet giving him more ease to have me how he pleased. As he pressed his body closer I could feel his stiffness, hard against my stomach, re-flexing to the touch. The soothing feeling woke me out of the moment. In an attempt to save regrets I pushed him away as he looked at me with horny mystified eyes.

"We can't do this...this is wrong"

"What? You want this as much as I do" He said, catching his breath back.

"Kamarni, we can't! You're engaged for crying out loud!... What am I thinking. What am I even doing here? "

I jumped out the bed, throwing the sheets to the side exposing Kamarni's bare chest and tattoos, which made my fight no more easier than it already was. He jumped up after me...

"Keshia, I'm sorry. Please forgive me. Come back to bed. I won't touch you. It's too late for you to go anywhere. It's my fault. Please"

I turned around and looked him in the eyes. I didn't want to leave but this man had me wide open. The feel of his hard erection was too much for me to handle, let alone the tender touches which he placed on my body with his huge soft musical hands. I wanted him as much as he wanted me and I couldn't control the feelings which he was evoking within me tonight. It was a struggle to fight from the release of his sweet kiss and I don't know if I'll have the strength to do it again, but where was I really going this time of morning?

"Look. Just promise me you won't touch me"

"Well I can't promise that, because I want to hold you in my arms and watch you sleep" He said with a hint of seduction in his tone, clearly not taking me seriously. However, he still made me blush.

"I'm serious. Don't kiss me like that again"

"Why? Didn't you like it?"

"That's beside the point. Look you sleep that side and I will sleep this side, with my back towards you!"

"Okay, whatever makes you happy... but I still get to cradle you right?"

"Kamarni..." He pulled me back onto the bed and tickled me playfully.

"Babes, I'm sorry. I got caught up. I won't do it again. We will just sleep, okay?"

"That's okay. Friends don't kiss like that! So we have to keep this in perspective!"

194

"I will if you can"

"Of course I can!"

He licked the moisture off his lips. "Well… that's not what you lips told me" He grinned. "But okay. I'm sure in the morning you won't be looking as sexy as you do now. So you won't have to worry"

We both sniggered and I gave him a playful push to show my disapproval of his little joke, while I snuggled back up in the warm feathered down duvet and glanced over his right shoulder. Why did I want this man so much? Why did I enjoy his company like no other? The feel of his hard heated body against mine was heavenly, we were a perfect fit…The last piece of a puzzle.

Kamarni sank deeper into his pillow before taking his strong arms from my petite body and covering our bodies fully with the duvet, blocking out the early morning cold. True to his word, he let me turn my body around so that my back was leaning against his chest, but he held me tighter and closer than before. He wrapped his arms around the wrinkled T-shirt across my stomach and I could feel him bury his stubble against my neck. His bare skin merging with the softness of my body. I closed my eyes and pretended that he was mine, all mine. Just as I began to lose myself I felt the warm scent of his breath place a path of gentle kisses along my head and neck... was I dreaming?... hopefully not… all my inhibitions began melting away, along with my fight with sleep…

I blinked the sleep out of my eyes and adjusted to the morning light. I looked down and noticed that we were still locked in a tight embrace. I smiled, holding onto the thoughts which I drifted off to sleep on. This was the best sleep that I had in ages. I loved being in his arms, feeling his touch, feeling his skin intimately pressed against mine. I turned around carefully, sliding my sexually frustrated body around and laid there admiring him. Taking in his every feature. I never noticed the little faint freckles on his cheeks until now. He looked so cute when he slept. His body was in total ecstasy, free and in total bliss. I couldn't help myself as I learned towards him and kissed his succulent smooth lips. He slowly began to stir, squeezing his face to adjust to the morning light as his arms squeezed my waist tighter to confirm that I was still beside him.

195

He looked over at me and grinned. "Morning beautiful. Well you sure proved me wrong"

"Why?" I questioned, confused.

"Because you look even more stunning in the morning than I thought"

I blushed. I couldn't imagine what my hair must have looked like. Normally I religiously tied it down with my silk headscarf every night unless I was due to receive some good romancing. Surely it must be all over the place, not even a hairpin had been used to flatten down the stray strands. He looked on at me in admiration and smiled before brushing away a stray strand of hair which I was hoping would not be there and seductively kissed the same spot. I looked up at him with my desirable eyes and watched him rise up out of the warmth and pull on a t-shirt which was lying on top of the sheets. The morning air was chilly, I thought the shudders I was experiencing was the response that Kamarni unintentionally gave me upon sight of his naked flesh but I was wrong, it was only the morning air and not the chills which he sent down my spine.

He licked his juicy lips. "Thanks babes for staying. I know it wasn't easy for you"

"It's fine hun. Thanks for keeping me company"

I looked at my Baby Phat watch reading the dial. It was eleven o'clock, we had slept most of the morning away. I squinted my eyes, feeling the after effects of last nights binge drinking.

"Kamarni, you need to drop me home. It's late"

"No problem, let me just jump into the shower"

"Okay"

"Do you want a drink?"

"Nah I'm fine"

Kamarni rose off the bed and exited to the bathroom. As he disappeared I quickly jumped up out the sheets into the cold air and examined myself in the mirror. There were stands of my long black hair misplaced everywhere, I quickly ran my hands through trying to fix up. How could he say that I looked stunning? I smiled to myself in the mirror and changed out of the t-shirt and back into my clothes. I sat on the edge of the bed twiddling my thumbs waiting for Kamarni to return. I looked at the ruffled sheets and thought about last night, making my body shudder. Shortly after the door opened and exposed Kamarni with a brown towel wrapped around his waist. I looked over in the corner of my eyes trying desperately not to concentrate on his firm body exposed to my eyes. I tried hard to suppress the thoughts that were going through my mind as he slowly selected his clothes from the wardrobe, getting changed. The material slowly caressed his skin as he covered his nakedness. I was drooling. I wish I could feel him pushed up against my body right now. But I have to fight it. I have to stick to my morals. It would be wrong for us to give into the lust, the temptation that haunted us whenever we were together.

"Right. Are you ready?"

I snapped out of my thoughts and jumped up. "Wait one minute"

I stepped up towards Kamarni and allowed him to lean forward and kiss my lips, holding my small waist. I closed my eyes revelling in the feeling. My hands grabbed his back, squeezing it firmly with desperation. Suddenly the room no longer felt so cold.

"Sorry I had to do that one last time before we left"

I was stunned for words; I had wanted him to do that since we woke. "It's okay. I wanted you to"

He looked at me with a smirk, happy with my confession.

"That's good, because Kesh I like you a lot and I know this is wrong on so many levels but I need you. I have never done this before but I just feel that I need you in my life"

"Kamarni. I feel the same, but... we have to fight it. We can't do this. You're engaged"

"And you're in a relationship!"

"I know, even more reason not to get carried away. Someone will get hurt. I'm not down for being the reason behind someone's failed relationship, someone's broken heart"

"So what are we going to do about it?"

"I don't know"

"I know that I need you Kesh"

"Don't say that. Let's just go"

I pushed him away. It was the most difficult thing I had to do, because my body wanted me to give in but my mind was saying no! Kamarni reluctantly turned and we retreated out into the deserted house down the stairs and out of his mother's house. He stopped and cautiously locked the doors behind us. This was getting heated. What were we doing? I walked behind his sexy shadow towards the car, proud that I hadn't given into the lust that would have consumed our bodies last night and taken us into total ecstasy! He walked with so much confidence as his jeans hung comfortably on his perfectly toned butt cheeks. Exhale... I convinced myself that if we had given in we would have been ridden with so much guilt this morning... well him more than me and he would have to go home and face that guilt... staring him in the face... carrying a bigger lie upon his shoulders. I couldn't let him do that! More importantly I didn't want to carry that guilt with me either.

The drive back took us longer than usual as the streets were filled with Saturday drivers out doing their weekly shopping, some relaxing in the local parks. Kamarni pulled into my road and pulled over where he had collected me. I scanned the streets, making sure none of my neighbours were about to witness me coming in at this hour wearing the same clothes as last night, looking like I had just returned from something unsavoury and not with Bobby! The coast was clear, so I leaned over and placed my un-glossed lips on Kamani's cleanly shaven cheek. He turned and looked over at me like he was carrying the world on his shoulders, thinking about the tangled web we had woven. I sympathised with his thoughts as we were both in the same situation. All we had to do was be careful, be strong enough to suppress our urges, our non-voluntary responses to the rising temperature between us and we would be fine.

My sin filled feet stepped into my warm flat as the heat jumped across my body. I threw my bag down on the floor, climbed out of my heels and headed straight for the bathroom instantly running the shower. I didn't want to wash off the scent of Kamarni on my skin but I had no option I needed to bathe. I quickly grabbed my towel and jumped out of the shower racing to answer the house phone which had been ringing constantly for the past few minutes. I grabbed the receiver and placed it to my wet ear…

"Where have you been all night? I tried the house phone fifty times and you're mobile. I was calling all night and this morning!!" Shouted the angry voice through my phone line.

I had forgotten that I had turned off my mobile. I couldn't risk Bobby phoning me while I was with Kamarni. Shit! What excuse could I use?

"Sorry baby my battery died and I went out drinking with Janet last night. Ended up crashing at hers"

"What! Could you not have phoned and let me know. You knew I would be worried"

"Sorry, I just forgot to send you a text beau"

"Hummm! Well where did you two go?"

"Some bar down Clapham"

"Some Bar?" He said with suspicion in his voice.

Damn what was with the Spanish inquisition! Why was he questioning me like this? I was beginning to feel like a terror suspect. I had to think fast. "Oh it was called the Black Butterfly, it's really nice I had this nice cocktail. Babe when you come back we have got to go there"

"Yeah sure. So you stayed at Janet's? How is she?"

"Yeah, she's fine. She has this new boyfriend now, Michael. Nice guy. We all must go out one day"

"So she's finally given up on the independent single black female role then?"

"Yep. Hopefully this might be the 'one'"

Bobby always used to tease Janet about her singlehood. Commenting that she was too career minded to settle down, he thought she would be a fifty year old mother with a good job, big house and reliant on a sperm donor. They never really got on. Janet detested the fact that I had decided to try again with Bobby. She always reminded me that I could do better. It was partly my fault because I used to confide in her about Bobby's antics. The girls, the pregnancies, the games and the various revelations. I couldn't really blame her for not liking him. If it was the other way round, I suppose I wouldn't like him either.

"Anyway baby. I miss you" He cried.

"I miss you too pumpkin. Cant wait until you get back"

"I should hope so, you know we got a lot of catching up to do now don't you?"

I heard a few voices in the background calling for the actors to get ready for scene eight.

"Baby, I gotta go. Take care of my body"

200

"Yes baby. Be good"

"I always am. Love you"

Now he didn't say that much, I was taken aback. I removed the phone from my ear and looked at it suspiciously like we had a cross line. "Love you too" With that admission the conversation ended. As soon as I pressed the end button a little knot twisted in my stomach and made me feel a little guilty about lying. That soon faded away as I thought to myself-' *Bobby does it all the time and it was only a little white lie right?*' I sat and dried off my skin reflecting back on the past conversations I had with Bobby. Something had been bothering my spirit, Bobby was acting a little strange the past few weeks. Something wasn't right. He was confessing his love for me a little too freely and that was unlike him. I walked around the room still shocked with myself for lying. The hardest part was actually trying to remember the lie which I had used, something in me set alarm bells ringing because I know that Bobby will be using it at a later date to test the honesty in my statement. I retreated to getting dressed into my black Nike tracksuit, the afternoon was mine. Mine to relax and ponder on my life as it was. I collapsed onto the sofa and let my thoughts get the better of me, the predicament that I had gotten myself into was my own doing. It had gone too far to turn back. I enjoyed Kamarni's company, yet I felt obligated to Bobby and I know Kamarni felt the same towards his fiancée. How was this going to work really? It could only end in tears.

Chapter 24.

Leyah

Over the past few months Reese and I had spoken a lot more than usual. We were being more amicable towards each other, well my behaviour towards him had improved. I must admit that it had a positive impact on Asia and she loved the fact that her parents were talking instead of bickering. Not that we did it often in her presence, but I would normally have a dig at him when the opportunity presented itself. Reese appeared to be trying harder with Asia, which was virtually impossible compared to the effort he put into her already, but he was helping me more. He was collecting her from nursery which meant that I didn't have to rush from work everyday, leaving me able to catch up on the paperwork I had built up over the past few months. He even offered to do my grocery shopping for me, now that freaked me out! Even though I could have done with the help I kept it in mind that he was not my favourite person or my best enemy. He was still number one on my hit list! Nothing he could ever do now would change the way he hurt me in the past.

I sat with Asia in the kitchen mixing dough in a large red plastic bowl to evidentially bake some cookies once she stopped licking the mix off the spoon. I laughed at her impatience, reminding me of myself when I used to cook with my mother. Eventually we placed the dough in the princess shaped holders with the excess mess landing all over my kitchen counters. There was flour everywhere even in Asia's hair! I shook my head as her little face looked up at me excitedly, then the sounds of Keyshia Cole rang from my mobile. Asia started to sing along, acting like a little diva until I answered.

"Hello"

"Hi Leyah, it's me. How are you and my little princess?"

"She is fine. Just helping me to bake some cookies. Asia daddy is on the phone" I said, wanting to keep our interaction to a minimum. I didn't even wait for his response, I just handed the phone to Asia at the soonest possible moment.

She wiped her hands on her pink top and took the handset, engaging in conversion with her father for the next ten minutes. After she had finished telling him about her new pony toy she passed the phone back to me, blowing him a kiss goodbye. I wiped the flour off my hands with the tea towel and took a deep breath before speaking, agitated at the fact that I had to.

"Yes Reese"

"Err, Leyah. I know your going to say no, but mum insisted"

What was he possibly going to tell me now!

"Look, mum is having her sixtieth birthday party on Saturday and she told me to invite you"

"What! You know I don't do family functions but Asia will gladly be there"

"Look,.."

"No Reese, how do you really expect me to sit in a room with you, your family and your fiancée? Come on, let's be serious!"

"I know but you know mum loves you, she wants you there"

"That's not the point. I'm the one who went and messed up your relationship in a lot of people's eyes..."

Although his mother was always sympathetic towards me, I couldn't attend. I loved his mum and she treated me like a daughter. She even frequently phoned to see how I was and would invite me around for dinner. She knew that her son was to blame for all this mess and would repeatedly express that she was not too fond of Shantel and how Reese could do a lot better... meaning me! I had often explained to Mummy Pearl, as she requested me to address her, that Reese and I were not meant to be and after what he had put me through, I don't know if I will ever be able to forgive him enough to get back with him. Mummy Pearl understood where I was coming from and often told me stories about her and Reese's father. The amount of times she had had to forgive him while they were dating and she would always end by saying that they persevered and made it through the rain. Forty five years of marriage before he passed and she would have never changed anything.

"Reese, sorry but I am not going. I just can't"

"Well at least think about it Leyah. Come on!"

"No, look. I'm sorry but that is one place I do not want to be. A room full of all your family, judging me. Then Shantel may cause a scene and mess up your mum's birthday. Sorry I would rather avoid that embarrassment."

"She wouldn't dare do that at mum's birthday, anyway she may not even attend"

"Shut up Reese!"

"No seriously! She may be going to Spain to see her grandmother that week"

"Oh... and so you want me to be the replacement trophy girlfriend? Go Jump Reese!"

"No, it is not like that babes..."

I cut him off mid sentence as I cringed at the sound of him calling me babes. "Don't call me that please!"

"Sorry, old habits don't die young. Anyway like I was saying, it's not like that don't misinterpret this, it is not me that wants you to come. It's mum. To be honest with you I do not want the embarrassment either. Not that I give a damn what my two face family thinks, I do not need the gossip. But if mum wants you there, it's not up to me. I'm just trying to make her happy"

"I hear what you are saying. But tell your mum something. Make up a lie if you have to, that's one thing you will win an Oscar for. I'm not coming!"

"Look, stop encouraging me to lie" I could hear the smirk in his voice.

"You know I will never lie to my mother. Just at least show your face"

"You know what; I will phone your mum and tell her myself, I just don't think that it is appropriate"

"Suit yourself. Anyway on another note, I have found this little ballet class for Asia. I could take her and pick her up. I think it would be nice for her"

"Since when did you start looking for ballet classes?"

"Look I only want the best for my little girl and want her to experience things while she is young. Expose her to new possibilities"

"I hear what you are saying Reese. Sounds good, but I haven't got the time to be racing her to ballet and then coming home to cook and get her ready for bed"

"Did, you not hear what I said? I will take her and wait with her. Listen I know that I have been a bit selfish in the past and left everything up to you during the week. But I want to make a change to that. I understand that it is hard for you and you're trying to study as well as raise our daughter and I can do a lot more to help. I just have to change my schedule around a bit"

Wow, now what was he up to. Why the sudden change? Asia is three years old and now he wants to help me more. I must admit it would help but I don't want him to think I can't cope and that I'm incapable to look after our daughter. I just can't trust Reese's motives, but I want the best for Asia too, she would love ballet.

"Look I don't know, I will have to think about it"

"That's cool, the next intake is not until summer so we have some time to decide. Don't worry about the fee's I will pay"

"I wasn't! Anyway Reese, we were in the middle of something"

"Oh, okay. Well think about mum's party and I will speak to you soon"

Before I could respond to his sly reminder to attend his mums sixtieth, he said bye and hung up. What is really going on with him at the moment? This behaviour was not like him. All this extended weekly contact was strange. I wonder if he has even run this by Shantel yet. Not that it is my concern, but I really do not need my baby exposed to her drama.

I left Asia sitting in front of the television watching cartoons, as I finished cleaning the rest of the kitchen. What really was Reese's game? For the past few months he had been acting strange. Something was not right, he was planning something. Something big! It wasn't new that he was always trying to be nice to me in order to worm his way back into my heart, but this was different. What's all this about helping me during the week? I hope he doesn't expect to be a frequent visitor to my house. Is he trying to crash any possibility of me having a relationship? This weekend was my date with Lucas and I just hope he is not thinking about messing it up! I need to let my hair down this weekend, all my essays were completed and I was glad to finally have some time for myself, well at least for the next few weeks before my exams started.

I sat drinking a glass of red wine listening to the sounds of Kelly Price, snuggled up in the sofa and pondered on Lucas. I hadn't heard from him all week. I reached over to my phone, let me just give him a call to confirm that we are still attending the concert Sunday. I flicked through the phonebook and located his number, pressing call...

"Hello Lucas?"

"Hi, who's this?"

"Okay now this is the second time that you don't have a clue who is calling!"

"Nah, it's not that. Who is it?"

"It's Leyah" I said sceptical of the reason why he did not recognise my voice. Did he really have so much women calling his phone?

"Oh hi. Sorry I've been meaning to call you. How are you?"

"Well I'm good actually, just finished some essays for my course"

"Good"

"So we still on for Sunday night?"

"Sunday? Errr.. yeah… sure"

"Don't tell me you forgot?"

"No, don't be silly. Sunday it's on"

"Good. Is everything okay with you?"

"Yeah, yeah everything is all good babes. Look, let me call you back in a bit"

"Okay"

This was typical behaviour of his, he would always tell me that he would phone me back and low and behold I would be waiting for days for the return call. There was something which didn't make two with Lucas. Something suspicious about him, I mean he seemed to be so sincere on our date and shortly after but now it was like he couldn't be bothered to make any effort to sustain contact with me. I don't even know why I am amazed at this type of behaviour; this was normal behaviour for a man. I know this behaviour all too well. The man would limit his contact because he was either not interested anymore, because you have not given him what he wanted which was to free up your goods or he was busy entertaining other women, having them on a frequent rotation! Well I'm glad that I have previous training for this under my belt, there is no way my head is going to get lost in his lies and deception. Not this time and not ever. I am just going to enjoy this concert and then he can do what ever he pleases in his spare time. I don't deserve to be treated like this, I can do better all by myself. I don't need any man to complete me. This is what they fail to realise about me. I am not a push over anymore. I am not gullible to their foolishness thanks to Reese. He thinks that a few texts during the past couple weeks is enough to keep me hanging on, well I have news for him. It's only because I desperately want to attend this concert which is the only reason why I'm actually still entertaining this brother or else that number would have been deleted from my phone ages ago, I just haven't got the time anymore!

Chapter 25.

Janet

I had a smile on my face and I was entertained. Things were going good with Michael but I still felt like there was something missing. My heart wasn't in it as much as his was. He was too nice and attentive to my needs. He always wanted to be with me evenings and weekends, it was becoming a bit overbearing. I needed my space. I needed time to breathe. Everyday I had to try and find some excuse not to meet up with him, or for him not to come to my house, it was actually becoming tiring. There was this feeling within me that something was missing, it would eat away at me every time I was near Michael and I knew exactly what it was!

When I was with Michael he catered to my every need. I didn't have to do anything, he was always there to do it for me. He made me feel like a queen but I also felt like I had lost my freedom, I was no longer the single independent woman. A fortnight ago we spent a nice weekend together, rolling between the sheets. It was the perfect way for me to release some built up sexual frustration which I didn't realise I had until Marcus came back into town! Seeing his physical person, wishing that I was the one laying next to him every night and feeling his warmth against mine was driving my imagination crazy! While Marcus had been absent from my life for so many years, I had managed to contain my true feelings for him. I was able to repress my sexual needs, push them to the side, but the sight of him had woken all the womanly feelings from within and it had hit me full force. I felt like a vixen again!

"Hiya babes. Look you've been working too hard gorgeous you need to relax"

"I cant Michael, I've got deadlines to meet and very little time" I closed the lid to my laptop and relaxed on the bed... this was going to be a long one!

"What's going on with you? I mean I haven't seen you in ages, we have hardly spent any time together"

"I've told you hun..." My voice was low and unconvincing, I knew Michael could tell that I was making excuses after excuses but he was just not giving up. He was determined to force his presence upon me tonight. "I just need some space at the moment... you know to..."

The stunned voice reacted... "What?... Are you serious? What do you mean?"

I could hear it in his voice. I knew Michael felt like he had just been shot with a bullet to the heart but I needed to get it out. I could not continue lying and stringing him along any longer, it was unnecessary and a bit cruel.

"This is all moving too fast. I just need some time to be grounded for a bit"

"What do you mean? Do you feel that I'm suffocating you?"

Truth was I did feel suffocated. I couldn't breath. He was everywhere I turned, emails, texts and phone calls. He was too overbearing, I wanted the attention but I needed it from someone else right now and it was not Michael!

"Look Michael, it's just that I have so much work to do and I just need a little space"

"I can give you some space. Sorry if I have been bugging you too much. Please don't shut me out"

"I'm not shutting you out. I'm just not ready for all of this"

"Ready for all what? Janet, I am here for you"

"I know you are and that's just a little overbearing at the moment. We haven't been seeing each other for no longer than a few months and I kind of feel like it's moving too fast. I mean, don't get me wrong I enjoy your company but I just need you to take things a little slower"

Unknown to Michael this was a frequent habit of mine. Some say it was my detriment but I just could not help it. It was innate to me now. Anytime a man got to close to me or tried to move the relationship further I got cold feet and pushed them away. Michael is a good man and I really do enjoy his company. He is what I need, someone who is level headed, focused, attentive and loyal. But I am just not ready for all this at this moment in my life. My head is too confused to attempt to be serious with someone at this stage. The man who I love was engaged to someone else and expecting a baby. I can't just pretend that I don't love him anymore, because I do and it pains me to think about them together, let alone him telling her that he loved her. But the reality was that their grass isn't too green!

"Janet, I just don't understand what I've done wrong. But I understand that you need your space for a bit, so I will do just that. I will leave you to let you clear your head and get whatever it is out of your system. I just want to make you happy"

He was so sweet, here I was telling him that I needed some space and he was being so understanding and supportive. He was not even challenging my decision. This made me feel a small fraction of guilt about ignoring his advances, his heart was in the right place but I just could not accept it at the moment.

"Look, I will call you Michael" Before he could respond I put down the phone and he was gone. Was I supposed to feel guilty? The feeling that was rushing through my head was a sigh of relief. I was just not ready for commitment at the moment. He was handy for elevation from my problems, but recently these problems had been more prevalent and I had ultimately lost the battle.

I had spoken to Leyah earlier in the evening and she had given me the full story on Reese's new fascination on being a full-time father. She speculated that his fiancée was pregnant and he wanted to get in more

211

training. Of course I told her that that was ludicrous until she told me her second suspicion, which made the first one look like a piece of candy. She had come to the conclusion that he was trying to gain full custody of Asia. Now I was not one to make assumptions, so I had to tell her my full analysis on this. Although I detested Reese due to what he put Leyah through: getting her pregnant and lying to her about his woman, I did not think that he was capable of plotting something so sinister. Yes he was the number one bastard, but he wouldn't take Asia away from her mother and from what Leyah has told me, I don't think his fiancée would stand for that. But I must admit that all the sudden attention was suspicious. Reese had to be planning something, that's for sure. I poured out the last drops of Hennessey and allowed my mind t o drift away from Leyah and Reese, managing to settle into thoughts of Marcus once again. Why do I want this man so much? Not having him in my life felt like I was incomplete. I did not feel whole with out him near. The touch of his hands was so relieving, the smell of his cologne was heavenly and the sound of his voice was breathtaking. It always sent sweet sensations through my body every time! This is what love does to you, it has you all twisted into submission. It takes over your thoughts and any principles which you once had, leaving you fully at its mercy. I need to release this pressure and there is only one way to do it.

I sat on my bed with my legs crossed and listened as the phone rang, holding my breath as I waited for the phone to be answered...

"Hello babes. I was just thinking about you"

A big grin formed on my face as my heart slowly regressed from the knots it had formed.

"Really? Great minds think alike then"

"Yes, definitely. How are you Jay?"

"I'm good. Better still. How are you doing? Did you sort out the thing with Jasmine?"

"Oh yeah. Yeah everything is good now. She was planning a surprise for me. She gave me a pair of diamond encrusted cufflinks saying 'Dad'. They must have cost a fortune."

I listened with speculative ears. That sounded like some far fetched cover up to me, but hey Marcus must know her better than me. He should be able to sense if she is lying, he is a barrister after all!

"Oh, well that was nice of her" I replied with sarcasm.

"Maybe I've just got her all wrong Jay. You know, maybe I'm just looking for faults in her for some obscured reason"

Wow, that woman must have some magic cuchie for real, because Marcus was gullible to fall for that one. She sure knows what she is doing. How could he believe such a stunt! Come on now she was on her phone, giggling and the way he explained it I would have never guessed it would have benefited him. I sat up to digest this, vex that my alcoholic comfort was empty.

"Oh okay. So everything is good now?"

"So, so. I've still got my eyes open babes. I'm not deluded with the fact that she has issues with my brother and she has way too many male friends. But I'm just trying to do the right thing"

I hated that line 'I'm trying to do the right thing' what exactly did that mean? You don't mind fucking up your own life because you made a mistake? You don't mind compromising your own happiness for the sake of another's selfish needs! I just couldn't understand why Marcus would do this to himself. I had always thought him as this strong smart man but this woman had changed him. He was obligated to compromise himself for his child. Really I should respect and commemorate this, but in this case I just could not.

"Where is she now?"

"Out as usual. Said she was going to some friend's house. I'm just really busy at the moment. I have to defend this client next week who is up on some serious murder charges. I've got masses of preparation to do."

"Oh sorry babes, am I disturbing you?"

"No, not at all. I needed a break to be honest. I've been at this all day. So babes, how is this 'guy' of yours then?"

"Oh yeah, he is okay. We are just taking it slow at the moment..."

Why did he have to ask me that? I was not about to sit and tell him that I have kind of kicked him to the curb, because I was not ready for a relationship due to the fact that I am in love with someone else, that person being *HIM*! "You know how it is at the beginning!" I lied.

"Yes, I sure do. Don't I wish for those days again! Trust me when I say that I would do things so much different!"

"Yeah, you and me both"

We both laughed. Speaking to Marcus was always refreshing, without even trying he would make me smile. He would make me forget all of my problems and the secret which I held from him, making me fall deeper in love with him all the little bit more each time. He made me realise why I love him so much and why I needed him to be a part of my life.

"Look, I'm going to warn you from now, Jasmine is planning a baby shower thing and she asked me for your number the other day. I reckon she is going to invite you to come and sit with all her shallow friends and talk about babies and men!"

"What? You know I'm not going to attend right? No offence!"

"None taken. Look, you have to come and represent my side. She has invited Trina too, she is definitely coming"

That put a different outlook on my attendance. Trina was Marcus'
cousin. I had met her a few times at his birthday celebrations and
holiday events but I hadn't seen her in about two years. She was
wonderful, full of spark. At the tender age of twenty seven she was
already divorced after getting married at nineteen to this Jamaican guy
who was just looking for an easy ride. They were married for no more
than two years before she was faced with his infidelity. Unfortunate for
her she had caught him in bed with his brother's wife and I mean they
were literally in her bed, between the sheets that she had paid for! That
was the last day he had seen her. She packed his stuff and threw him out,
but she didn't let it hold her back. She picked herself up and continued.
Continued with their three children and never looked back. She was one
strong woman. From the first time we met we got on like a house on fire.
We even went out raving together a few times. What I loved about her
was that she was on my level, she was a go getter and it helped that she
was able to pick up my subtle body language and gestures on off-key
individuals when we went out. You know those people you see where
you have to look twice and think *why would you even step out the house
looking like that'* or *'how long has she had that weave in her head'*!'
And I know our extra terrestrial sense will be in full force if I attended
the baby shower.

"Oh great. How is she?"

"She's cool. You know she hasn't even met Jasmine yet. She has only
spoken to her over the phone. I'm kind of worried about them meeting
up to be honest, because I'm not sure what mum may have told the
family after that dinner fiasco!"

"You're worrying for nothing. You're so funny. Don't worry I will keep
Trina in line."

Yes this was going to be an event not to miss. Trina could not stand fake
bitches and Jasmine fitted that description to a T! I could just see her
face now, with her fake smile. How could Marcus even think about
marrying this girl! Jasmine is so lucky that she is carrying his baby,
because she would not even have come remotely close to be a Walters
otherwise. Our conversation continued for another twenty minutes until
Jasmine walked back into the house. As soon as she heard that it was me

on the phone she insisted that she spoke to me. I took a deep breath as Marcus hesitantly handed her the phone.

"Oh hi Janet, how are you girl?" She said with her fake conceited voice like she actually gave a damn!

"Yeah I'm good. How are you and the baby doing?"

"Oh darling, this baby is taking over my body! I've put on so much weight. As soon as I give birth to this I'm hitting the gym. There is no way I'm going to lose my figure. If Victoria Beckham can do it, I definitely can! I've already found a personal trainer. Anyways enough about me, have you got anyone new in your life at the moment?"

I rolled my eyes. What was she on? Talking to me like we were old friends! The sound of her voice repulsed me, she was fake beyond reason. Look at her trying to pry into my life, hoping that I was still a sad single out here while she was engaged to be married. Huh, didn't I have news for her.

"Yeah, I have actually"

"Oh baby, you didn't tell me that Janet has finally met someone" She said with sarcasm as she shouted out to Marcus in the background.

"That's wonderful Janet. You have to bring him to the wedding!"

Yeah, yeah just rub it in my face. I could tell that she was loving this! Damn, yes I know you are engaged to be married to Marcus. I just hope that he see's sense before then or better still leaves her at the alter! Now that would be funny, she would have to eat humble pie for the rest of her life. Her publicist friends would love that!

"Yeah sure, anyway tell Marcus I will speak to him soon" I was trying to escape this conversation immediately but Jasmine was trying to make it as hard as possible for me. I rolled my eyes again as I sat listening to her constant interjections.

"Oh hold on before you go. I'm planning a baby shower and you just have to come. It is going to be so divine. I'm having smoked salmon, prawns, specially imported cheese from France and luxurious specially made continental cakes. I wouldn't normally eat such fatty foods, but the baby is my excuse. I've even got a party planner to come in and make it spectacular. I'm telling you darling, it is going to be an event you don't want to miss!"

My gosh, this woman was serious! Anyone would think that she was planning a huge televised social event! What does she need a party planner for? It's only a baby shower for crying out loud. I shook my head in sympathy. I sure feel sorry for Marcus, this woman is going to burn a hole straight through his wallet before the baby is even born.

"Yeah, sure I will be there" I said un- enthusiastically as I rolled my eyes in disbelief.

"Good, well I will post you out the gift list and invite hun. Take care of yourself. Smooches"

This woman was definitely unbelievable. I hung up the phone as I was still in a state of shock. This was the first time Jasmine and I had ever exchanged more than two words to each other and I could hear it in her smug voice that she was thinking in the back of her head that she had won. That she had succeeded in locking Marcus down. I just hope she doesn't think that she will be getting an easy ride. I paced up and down my front room as her voice had me all irritated and annoyed. Why did Marcus have to get trapped by her! She was a Black Barbie and a 'wanna be' celebrity. She was such a pretentious woman, Marcus deserved better even if it wasn't me!

Chapter 26.

Keshia

Two weeks had passed since I had spent the night in Kamarni's arms and we were spending even more precious time together. Making memories together. But we were careful, we were both trying not to be in a secluded intimate place with each other for fear that the sexual beast within us would be unleashed. We were lucky the first time, because I had the strength to say no. My conscience would not willingly let me put someone through the hurt and pain which Bobby had subjected me to in the past. I knew what it felt like all to well. On the other hand I guess every woman knows what it feels like at some stage in their life. If your heart hasn't been torn apart by a man at one period or another then you have not lived or experienced love at all. Kamarni was perfect for me, I just could not believe how well we gelled. We were like two fish dancing in the sea, the stars shining up high, dazzling in the sky. This is where we were meant to be, he was a fairy tale come true.

The bright afternoon had given us the yearning to be with each other, so we had decided to take a trip to the gym for a quick work out together, which had slowly moulded into a regular routine for us. It was a way for us to spend time together without having to sneak around and steal a moment. This was our haven, our place where we could be. Afterwards we would stroll down to Shakes R Us and have a Strawberry, Kiwi, Pomegranate and Cinnamon smoothie. It was a nice feeling to do something together. This is what all relationships should be like. I hadn't done anything like this with Bobby for years. It was foreign to him now. He was established in his relationship, which meant to him that all previous efforts were no longer needed. He didn't have to do the lovey-dovey stuff anymore. We didn't have to act like a new love smitten couple! Boy was he wrong. This was the stuff which kept a relationship together. Doing things together is what holds it together. My mother always said to me *'A family that prays together, stays together'* and I always tried to live to that proverb. Kamarni and I bonded together like we were the perfect couple, it felt so right. I missed him so bad when he wasn't around. He had worn on me hard! We spent so much time together that when he wasn't here I became increasingly envious of his woman, wishing that I was the one that he was with all the time, breathing in his air. Why couldn't it be me?

During one of our late night conversations while his woman was at work the problems with his relationship slipped into the conversation. I felt uncomfortable hearing this at first, but it gave me an advantage. It gave me insight and it filled in the missing gaps! It turned out that his fiancée was more interested in her own career than she was with his. She seemed to give him constant headache, moaning at him to find a *real'* job and to stop with this *'music thing'*. The emotion in his tone as he spoke told me how much it pained him to realise that she was no longer supportive of his dream, crushing it at every opportunity. I can't believe she told him that he was too old to be playing music in bars. I'm telling you she had to be tone deaf or something, because Kamarni's talent was not one to be ignored and pushed under the carpet. I sympathised with him, realising that it must be hard without the support of your partner. It is expected when you put your all into something you love that they be behind you one hundred percent, it is not something to be compromised or abandoned, it is a necessity! Through this revelation I understood the lyrics in his songs deeper, I felt it. It caressed my soul and made me understand that they were composed from passion, from the hurting within. It was personal for him. But like a typical man I don't think he was able to speak to anyone close to him as the fear of showing weakness held him prisoner. His music was a way for him to release and express his pain without being judged. I scrutinised my thoughts, baffled but intrigued at how they had been together for so long and not started a family. Allowing my curiosity to have the better of me I asked, but the answer I received almost made me regret that I was being so nosey. Kamarni paused before answering me, searching within for the least painful way to explain. Eventually he composed his words and disclosed the pain that his partner had been pregnant a few times but always miscarried. Now they had given up on trying, fed up of the pain that followed, retreating to the belief that if God wanted them to be parents then they would one day when the time was right. As selfish as it was, that was just fine with me. I just hope they wasn't due to receive that blessing anytime soon! I knew every aspect of Kamarni's life and I loved the fact that he was so free to share the information with me, yet I had failed to tell him the details of my background. He knew what he needed to know, just not the extended version. I was not ready and he didn't need to know really did he?

It was mid afternoon and the sky was clear and blue. Kamarni and I had strolled to the park to enjoy the rest of the day outside of the gym. We sat on the bench by the pond with our sunglasses on and watched the housewives play with their children and the squirrels who searched for nuts. He squeezed my hand a little tighter. I smiled into his eyes receiving his little gesture and acknowledging the presence it made in my heart.

"Keshia, this is scary because it feels so right"

"Babes I know"

"No you don't, you don't understand the predicament that I'm in. My feelings are deep. I can't stop thinking about you and every time I think about you this warm feeling rushes over my body" His words were rushed like he could no longer contain himself.

"Believe me when I say that I feel exactly the same. I don't know what we are going to do. But we are managing as friends babes. We've done it for months now"

"I know, but its killing me. I don't even want to think about you with another man all hugged up together"

"Well, just think about how I feel. I'm not hugged up with anyone at the moment, you are"

He hung his head in annoyance, his actions speaking a thousand words. As he rose his head up slowly a few of his locks swung before his eyes shadowing the dark lust which filled them. He moved towards me and engaged his lips with mine kissing them with an obsession, pleasure racing through the both of us like an electric current. His hands drifted across my face, holding it in place. My gosh we were in public, in broad daylight, has he lost his mind! Once again I wanted to break from the kiss but I was trapped, I was locked with his full lips holding me captive to the sweet feeling. The sensations swept through our bodies calmly for all to see.

"Lets go"

I obediently responded and rose up as we leisurely walked hand in hand towards the exit following the path towards complete desire. Before I realised we were back at his mothers house. We kissed each other passionately, allowing our hands to drift all over each others flesh. Paths of wet kisses raced around my neck before I felt the cloth of my vest disappear, which was quickly replaced with the warm sensation of a wet tongue tracing where the garment once was. The straps of my bra was next, carefully it was thrown to the floor. I moaned. The feeling that swept my body was too intensifying; a flood of emotions came rushing full force from my head to my toes. Now it was my turn. I quickly slid my hands up his strong back and helped him out of his green polo shirt, we fumbled up the stairs remaining in locked lips trying not to break the seal. He pushed the door open and without opening his eyes guided me to the bed. We dropped down in harmony on the soft mattress with his body all over my frame, giving him more access to do what he wanted. I relaxed and made it easy for him. He licked his way down the path of my neck to my stomach and back up around my erect nipples. My body rose to his touch, pleasing him silently. He took his hands and rubbed my aroused rose bush between my legs, feeling the reaction which he had caused he struggled out of his jeans and boxers. I felt his hard penis against my legs, making me want this man even more. He continued to caress my body, touching it like a prized Jewel. Taking his time to examine every inch with his hands and then his lips. His kiss was a bolt of lightning to my body. I could not do this anymore...

"Baby I want you. I want you now"

His breath was short as he replied "Okay"

He slowly inserted himself into me, gently, softly. I was filled with a rush of immense pleasure. All my sense was out the window. I felt his warm breath on my earlobes as he whispered.

"I don't want to lose you".

My body melted as he rocked his body slowly then sped up the pace focusing on the pleasure my body was receiving. The feeling was like no other and all efforts to hold on were flawed, my body let out the biggest explosion it had ever witnessed. He held on while I caught my breath back before rolling over onto his back guiding me on top of him. I rode his manhood perfectly, we were the perfect fit. He steered my hips towards his, pulling me closer, harder, faster. I leaned in and kissed his chest then slowly licked his nipples giving them a slight bite before retreating back to the action. He rose his body and lightly bit my neck, feasting on the love within. We were both groaning with pleasure, naked, joined together, until he shuddered from the rise of the eruption coming…

"Get up, get up!"

As soon as I rose, he exploded all over his body and my thighs. I flopped back onto the bed exhausted, feeling guilty for our submission. Kamarni ran his fingers up my back and towards my mouth. I gently kissed the tip of his fingers, peace overcoming the passion we had just shared. How had we allowed ourselves to surrender to the hunger for one another? We had given ourselves to each other in the comforts of his mother's house. Shit! What were we thinking, we didn't even use protection! How could I be so stupid? Worst thing I need right now is to become pregnant! How would I really explain that one? Well one consolation is that he didn't release his seed inside of me. What difference does that really make!

"Kesh, what are you thinking about?"

I sighed before answering. Trying not to look into his eyes I spoke with worry in my tone "Babe, we didn't use any protection"

"Its okay, I didn't cum inside of you"

222

"Yeah but that's not the only thing I'm worried about and have you heard of pre-cum?"

"Look, I'm good. I don't sleep around babes and if you're worried we can always go and get the morning after pill"

I shouldn't really trust his words. I had been caught out once before with the brutal truth of Bobby's infidelity in the past with a trip to the GUM clinic. But this was Kamarni and we trusted each other. We had made a silent agreement to monogamy within our little *'understanding'*. Plus his time was pre-occupied with me. He didn't have any time to add a third person into the mix.

"Yeah you're right. Sorry"

"Don't be. I shouldn't have been so stupid babes, but I couldn't help myself. Something just came over me and I had to have you. I couldn't fight it anymore"

I understood and squeezed him tighter as we relaxed and lay there in complete tranquillity, not making a sound. Holding each other close, reminiscing on the moment we just shared, in the bed where we first felt the closeness of each other a month ago. As I shut the door to my flat behind me I smiled to myself as the feelings came rushing back to me. The feeling of Kamarni and I conjoined in union.

Why did it have to be so complicated?

Why does life have to be so unfair?

•

Chapter 27.

Leyah

The D-day had come for Reese's mum's party. Why was I actually attending? I fully knew what I was potentially walking into. I looked in the mirror and put on my earrings as Asia fiddled to put on her white tights. Last week I had tried to call mummy Pearl and politely turn down her invitation, but as I knew she would she did not even let me get a word in during the whole call. That was her trick I knew it was a virtually impossible task but I had to try. Reese's mum always had a way about her where you just had to listen and obey when she spoke. She had been the authoritive figure for her two boys, not a girl child between the them, just boys so I understood why she was so firm. She was the full illustration of a strong black woman. I promised myself that I would only spend an hour at the party, drop Asia off and disappear. Yes I have to show my respects, his mother has been so supportive towards me while the rest of his family had judged and slandered my name. They saw me as the *'home-wrecker'*, like it was me who was pursuing him! I shouldn't let it bother me really, but I know that I am not yet in the right mental state to deal with the bitchy stares and gossiping behind my back.

I picked up my purse from the bed. Please God don't let any drama kick off tonight. I stepped into the night air from my car wearing an electric blue dress and matching heels with my black purse to tone it down. I thought that the colour would be a bit much and bring too much attention to myself but after consulting Keshia, she believed it was a good choice. I had to look stunning tonight, especially if Shantel was going to be here or even Reese's cousin Rachelle, who was close with Shantel and hated me like I was her worst enemy. It was just after eight thirty and the party had started an hour ago. I held Asia's hand as we walked towards the venue, hearing the sounds of Gregory Isaacs blasting out through the night air. She looked so cute wearing her little red and white checked Elle dress and matching red shoes, her gleaming jet black hair in three bunches. As we neared the entrance Asia was greeted by a middle aged lady who she recognised, she politely smiled at the couple and they looked at me and gave a friendly greeting. I knew that they must have been thinking in their heads *'Oh, so that must be her mother!'* They must have constantly pondered on what I looked like because I never socialised with Reese's family, the only time I got to see a few was at Asia's baby dedication ceremony and that was the close family members only. Tonight looked as though this was a family re-union. I smiled at the various people as we walked through the noisy lobby with Asia guiding me this time. Mummy Pearl had hired the banquet hall at her local community centre, which was just about adequate for the amount of people she had up in here. The hall was decorated with various orange and silver balloons, streamers and banners. The dance floor and the food area were separate, which was good. I hated having to juggle eating while I was being bumped into by someone's arse dancing. I looked up from spying someone's tempting plate of fish and heard the familiar voice come from behind us.

"Princess…"

Asia released my hand without hesitation and turned to give her dad a tight hug. As he lifted her up, he gave me a devious smile which lit up his eyes and said *'You look stunning'*.

"Thank you for coming Leyah. You look lovely." I smiled. "Let me introduce you to a few people"

"What? Why?" I said confused and worried.

"Everyone wants to meet you. I've told them so many nice things about you and they all love Asia. All I had to say was that she gets all her beauty from her mother… well most of it" He grinned, highlighting his model features.

Reese was so slick right now. I must admit he was looking really good tonight modelling a light grey fitted Italian cut suit, which magnified and praised his features. He knew he was gorgeous and he was working it well. I ignored his request and tried to divert his focus.

"Look, where's your mum I need to give her this gift"

I raised my hand bearing the huge silver gift bag which disguised a beauty gift package and voucher to attend one of the top spa's in London. Mummy Pearl loved to relax and pamper herself. She always had immaculate hair and nails. Asia and I felt that this was the perfect gift for her as she had more time to concentrate on herself now and she was more than deserving.

"Oh, okay. Sure! Come, let's go find her"

Reese led the way through the crowd, making numerous stops, peering through people and inquiring if anyone had seen his mother to which people pointed us in various directions. My eyes darted across the room anxiously, wanting to find her as soon as possible. I just hoped that I didn't walk into any uncomfortable situations... Shantel for one! He stopped again by someone who was sitting on the chair talking to an elderly gentleman. The persons face looked familiar, but I could not place where I knew him from. He was wearing a dark grey suit and lime green shirt with the top button undone fully displaying signs of a thick hairy chest.

"Hey bro this is Leyah. Leyah this is my brother Anton"

I stretched out my manicured hand to greet him, as I did he looked at me like I had just offered him my hand in marriage! He disregarded my welcoming gesture and rose up. He had to be at least 6'6 I thought. He stretched both his arms and brought me close to give me a hug, like we had met before. Anton was Reese's older brother. Unfortunate to the single ladies, he was married with two children and living in Los Angeles having moved over there ten years ago to play Pro ball. Regrettably following an injury in his third season he was forced into early retirement, but he was prudent and used it to his advantage by using what he had learnt by starting up his own Sports Agents Company and now two years later he is one of the top leading sports agents in LA.

"So you're the lucky lady who captured my little brothers heart?" He grinned, exposing his perfectly lined white teeth.

What!! I was stunned with his statement and a little embarrassed. I didn't know what to say in response.

"Sorry?... No I'm Asia's mother"

"Yeah I know…"

I looked at Reese sceptically, wondering what exactly he had told his brother. This was uncomfortable. I still didn't even know if Shantel was here or not.

"His words could have never described the magnitude of your beauty. It just wouldn't do you justice."

I blushed. Charm most defiantly ran in the Daniels family. Reese stopped a waiter passing by with glasses of wine and handed me a glass. I reluctantly accepted aware of the intentional considerate gesture.

"Thank you. So you're here for a few weeks?" I asked, focusing back onto Anton.

"Yes I am. I could not miss my mothers sixtieth! But unfortunately I had to leave my wife back out in the States, she couldn't get the time off work. You two would have got on great. I'm here with my twins Trey and Sondrey. They're somewhere around"

What did he mean by that statement? I didn't need to get on with anyone in Reese's family and why would he really encourage that?

"Oh, it's a shame she couldn't make it. Reese never told me that you have twins, that's lovely. I bet they must take after their father"

I analysed his features as he looked so much like Reese, except he was a shade darker and had a bigger frame. They had the same facial features and glowing eyes. I was astonished that considering the length of time Anton had been residing in the States he had not lost his English accent.

227

Only a few of his words evidenced his Yankee background and I must admit the sound was receptive.

"What is going on ere?"

I turned around to meet Mummy Pearl's huge grin, she extended her arms and hugged me. Both boys had definitely inherited their good looks from their mother. They were such a beautiful, loving family.

"Hey mum, have you seen Asia?" Reese asked.

"Yes, she is running around wid she likkle cousin dem. Leyah, you look lovely darling. You always do. Me so glad that you mek it."

"I told Reese mum. I don't know how he let her slip out of his fingers!" Anton grinned.

Before I could answer Reese jumped in…

"Well it wasn't me. She was too stubborn!"

I gave him a sharp cutting of my eyes. "Well… some of us were more deceiving than others" I added.

"Look here, you two make amends. Reese don't upset Leyah in here today"

Yes Mummy Pearl to the rescue, although Reese was her baby she made it perfectly clear that she did not agree with his behaviour. Her son's weakness was women and I had been one of the many unlucky victims.

"You' all come and get some food"

"Mum, Asia bought you a little gift" I handed her the package, as she accepted the gift with a thankful smile she gave me a kiss on the cheek, telling me that I shouldn't have. Of course that really meant; I'm glad that you did. I knew that she would love it. Moments later she was whisked off by some of her old friends to go and dance to the sounds of the great Bob Marley. I must admit, Mummy Pearl looked really good for her age and she was well trained on the dance floor. I doubt if I could even keep up with her. Anton became engrossed in conversation with a middle aged woman wearing a frilly red dress with black sheer tights and white heels. I discreetly laughed sighting her curly wig trying to help her stay young. I began to walk away when Reese turned and whispered into my ear above the loud music

"So what do you think of my brother?"

I laughed. "I noticed the similarities. You both are definitely charmers"

"Well, you know!" He winked.

"So do I have to be watching my back tonight? Where is your fiancée?"

"Huh? Oh yeah, no she isn't here. She couldn't make it"

"Oh yeah!" I looked Reese up and down sceptically. To be honest I was just glad that she wasn't here. Not that I will be staying long, but I just didn't want it to spoil my vibe tonight. The music was nice. I loved listening to revival music because it made me think of my own parents and the monthly parties my uncle formerly held at his house. That was when you witnessed 'dancing'. Yes our parents knew how to dance. They were the original wallpaper strippers! You would witness them dancing to the tunes, but the movement was almost invisible. The wining that took place was a shocking experience, but it explained why so many parents back then had so many children! We walked to get some food. Reese insisting that I had something to eat, not that he was the reason that I was getting food anyway. I had seen numerous plates passing my visual proximity and they all looked very tempting indeed. After I had devoured a large serving of the tasty Caribbean dish, I retreated to dance to the music. Finding a little corner in the back of the hall which was not too crowded, I pitched my plot. I watched people conversing and laughing and it made me feel a little uncomfortable standing on my own, as Asia was running up and down playing with her cousins. Eventually I had the occasional conversation with an older gentleman who was standing beside me, constantly asking me for a dance. It later transpired that he was Reese's grand-uncle. He was a funny old man, you know one of those elderly men that used to be a *'sweet boy'* back in his days and still felt that he had the touch to *'mack'* young ladies. I had to laugh, but I was grateful for his company, he made me feel at ease forgetting the uncomfortable situation which I was in. As I swayed to the sounds of Marcia Griffiths I felt a pair of hands capture my waist from behind. I turned around, angrily moving from the grasp upon seeing who was the figure testing his luck.

"Look, don't play with me in here. I don't appreciate it"

"Leah, sorry I just wanted to have one dance with you"

"Well, we don't dance. We don't do anything together accept care for Asia" I tried not to attract any attention to us. Fortunately the room was dimly lit and there were too many people to notice us. Problem for me was that I did not know who was family and who was not. I was not about to give people anymore reason to hate me. Reese was really testing his luck in here today. He must have too much alcohol in his system to even think that he is able to touch me like that. We haven't been that close to each other since before I found out about Shantel and I am glad. How dare he think that he still has rights to me like that, where he can just touch me and I will be okay with it.

"Sorry. Forgive me but you look really gorgeous tonight. Everyone has been complimenting you"

I was flattered, happy to hear that I had been noticed, but I could not let Reese know that I was pleased. "Excuse you! What have you been telling people?"

"Well wouldn't you like to know" He sniggered as his face was partially disguised by the shadows of the strobe lights. "Well I've been showing you off. Everyone has been asking who the sexy woman was in the blue dress. So I saw it fair to confirm that you were Asia's mother. Is that a problem?"

"Look I don't need people judging me in here tonight. This is exactly why I didn't want to come"

I was angry. I didn't want to be acting like a happy family. This was all a lie. Being here made it look like we were together, like I was his fiancée. When the truth is that I was the other woman that bore his child. Now I'm here parading like it is something to be proud of while his fiancée was away. Picturing what other people may have been thinking made me uncomfortable again.

"Look I'm going now"

"Why are you being so dramatic?" Before he could continue I was already saying my goodbye to Uncle Louie. As I finished I hastily walked towards the exit looking for Asia and Mummy Pearl as I did so.

"Leah, wait up. Slow down. You don't have to go"

"Look I only intended to stay for an hour anyway. Find Asia let me say goodbye" I turned to search the room when an elderly woman approached us with a huge grin on her face with her walking stick in her hand. Reese noticed her approaching and went over to her to help her steady herself towards us. He was so thoughtful. His mother had definitely raised him right. All her hard work was certainly not wasted, well not all of it. Heaven knows where he learnt how to mistreat women.

"Auntie Vi, this is Asia's mother Leyah"

Why is he doing this to me? My blood was boiling, I did not want introductions but Reese had once again put me on the spot and it would be rude of me not to respond. He was such a selfish bastard, always thinking about himself. I plastered a smile on my reluctant face and shook the frail woman's hand as she spoke.

"My goodness isn't she a pretty lady. I can see where Asia gets her beauty from and the two of you make such a lovely couple"

"Oh no, we are no longer together" I stated making it clear to both parties present.

"Yes, it is a shame. You young people always play around with your relationships. Once you have a child together you will never be able to part. It is Gods will and you mustn't disobey him any further"

"Auntie Vi, we don't see eye to eye" I added.

"Look here! I don't want to hear any of that nonsense. If you can lay down together, you must be able to commit to each other"

I respected the morals of elders. They were right, it should be like that and back in their day it was like that. Now society was too free and promiscuous. Commitment was no longer a necessity; it was an inconvenience to most. Reese retreated, wanting to look like the innocent obedient one, clearly not wanting to own up to his part in this. That he was the reason behind all this drama. Why was everyone trying to put us together, like they were unaware that he was engaged to someone else?

"Sometimes it just doesn't work out Auntie Vi"

"Yes but you two must work it out. You look lovely together, you do and all children need a stable home. I gwan pray for unnu"

She was right, we did look stunning together tonight. I glimpsed the reflection of the two of us standing side by side silently complimenting one another. But little did Auntie Vi know, Reese was the prototype of a playa. All that glitters undeniably isn't gold. After eventually finding Mummy Pearl and my daughter I was able to leave. I hurried out the exit trying not to bump into any more relatives, passing Anton smoking outside with a few other guests. His face lit up as he saw me and then suddenly dropped as he saw the expression on Reese's face who was close on my heels behind me. Trying to avoid anymore conflict I quickly wished Anton farewell. He held onto my arm, not very pleased that I was leaving already but he could tell from the look on my face that I was not in the mood to stay any longer. In an attempt to ease the tension and the assumption that I looked like a 'babymother' that was hard work, I promised that I would see him before he goes. He was adamant that we should all take the kids out for dinner before they fly back to the U.S. and to no surprise Reese was happy at the prospect, loving the way that

232

the children were a good excuse. I don't know what had come over me, but the words of Reese's Auntie Vi had annoyed me in some sort of way, I just needed to leave quickly. Of course Reese tried to put on the façade of a gentleman by offering to walk me to my car, despite me telling him that I would be okay. Anton stubbed out his cigarette and forced me to accept Reese's good gesture. I reluctantly agreed as I didn't want to give off a bad impression, not that I cared what Reese's family thought of me but I did not want Anton to have more weight for the fire. I waved goodbye and noticed the brothers give each other a wink, like Anton was wishing Reese good luck for something. Luckily for me, my car was not parked too far down the street. I did not like the idea of being in the company of Reese on a one to one basis and I could feel that he felt he had earned some sort of victory for this gesture. What really was his game tonight?

As I neared the car I searched for my keys in my bag and unlocked the doors.

"Leyah, I need to speak to you for a second"

Before I could answer he had opened the passenger side and let himself in.

"Reese, look I just want to go home. Can you please get out of my car?"

"Look I know that I have been stupid in the past and I have caused a lot of hurt and pain for you. But as you can see everyone see's something which we don't..."

"Oh yeah, and what is that then?... Is it that they think you're the perfect idealistic, ambitious black gentleman that's rare like gold dust? Is it that they cannot see the real inconsiderate, lying cheating bastard for which you are?"

Reese sighed. "Look how long are we going to bicker at each other like this?"

"Have you got amnesia or selective memory? You are the one who has done all this. You are the one who has been the cause of the

233

dysfunctions in our communication. So don't be acting like it is something trivial to get over quickly, because it is not! And don't you ever touch me again!"

I could feel my anger rising, this man was so arrogant! How dare he tell me to stop being angry at him! Am I just supposed to forget that he broke my heart into a thousand and one pieces! It may be easy for him to just close his eyes and forget it happened, but it's not so easy for me!

"Leyah. You don't have to be so angry all the time. I've apologised and apologised and I am truly sorry. I wish I could turn back the hands of time, but I can't. So all I can try to do is make it better."

"Huh! Don't worry about me. Just worry about Asia and Shantel! And what is the deal with all that? Why is your family acting like she does not exist?"

"No they are not. It's just Anton. He doesn't really feel her, he thinks I can do a lot better. And Auntie Vi, she's old, she doesn't know what she is talking about"

I rolled my eyes at the flaky answer I received. I knew that Reese wasn't telling me everything. His eyes were wondering about in its sockets rapidly. There was more to this story, but right now I wasn't really interested, I just wanted him out of my car. My hands were becoming sweaty. His head was rested on the headrest, his lips moist. Looking at him in that position reminded me of our first date, when we sat in his car for hours outside my house engrossed in conversation. Remembering that moment unconsciously made me subdue my anger towards him. It was a horrible feeling because I wanted to hate him, I wanted him to feel the pain which I was feeling, but it was all melting away. I have to try and maintain my feelings towards him. I have to fight!

"Leyah. You look really exquisite tonight. I love that dress you are wearing. It looks good"

"Reese, do you have anything constructive to say because I want to go now?" I said with a harsh tone, clearly irritated.

"Yeah… urm. What time do you want me to bring Asia home tomorrow?"

"Well I'm going out about six, so can you keep her until Monday and take her to nursery?" It had totally slipped my mind that I was due to attend the date with Lucas tomorrow for the concert.

"Why? Where you going tomorrow night that you won't be home for eight?"

"Excuse you. I do not have to answer that, as it is none of your business!"

"Yeah… well. I'm just wondering because I thought that Asia came first"

"And what is that supposed to mean? How often do I go out? I take care of my daughter full time. Yes it is time you looked after her more! I thought that's what you wanted?"

"Look I'm not judging you. Yes you do take good care of our daughter. I'm sorry; it's just that I'm looking out for you!"

"Well don't!"

"Okay. Don't worry I will take her to nursery Monday…and Leah, thanks for coming. We appreciate it. I know this must have been hard for you. But you still came. You're a tough cookie Leyah and I love that about you. I always have"

"Please don't love anything about me. Channel your energy else where!"

"Look I'm telling you what I feel"

"Why? It is not going to change anything. I would like you to just keep things simple"

"Okay Leah. You sure you don't want to stay for a bit longer. I saw the way which you was stepping to Sizzla"

I tried to hold back my amusement "No thank you. I've got to go"

Reese turned and looked me dead in the eye. His eyes were lethargic. I could tell he had drunk a fair amount and it was only ten o'clock. I did not intend to stay out this long. His lashes fluttered as he blinked, I always adored the long length with made his eyes look so sensual. I can't get lost in this…

"Goodbye Reese"

"Okay, I'm going. You sure you don't want to come and embarrass me on the dance floor. Remember when we went to that dance in Barbados and we won that competition?"

I laughed recollecting that night. That was one of the good times we had shared. We had decided to attend the seventies night that the hotel had put on and we had fully dressed up for the occasion. Reese wore a pair of lime green bell bottoms with a purple butterfly collar shirt and red platforms. I on the other hand was dressed in a red and yellow flowery thigh dress, with electric blue platform boots and a huge black afro wig. That night was amusing. We were both stone drunk and pulled out all the old dance moves which we remembered for the dance competition, winning first place.

"Why would you bring that up? Even if I went back on the dance floor, you wouldn't be able to keep up with me"

"Yes I would. I learnt a lot from you that evening"

We both sat in hysterics thinking back to the moment, the tension disappearing between us.

"Look. Let me go"

"Okay, but I have never had so much fun with anyone else as I have with you"

I ignored him and watched as he opened the door and got out. Before he shut the door he peered back through and said goodbye in a voice which sent tingles down my spine. Damn, I must be so sexually deprived that Reese has the ability to make me feel like this. He shut the door, knowing what effect his words had just had. I hate him so much. It was a skill of his, which was his expertise. I drove off watching Reese walk back to the hall in my rear view mirror, gosh he was one sexy specimen.

The next day I woke, I reminisced on the nice dream which had excited me last night. The regular occurring dream of me and Boris Kojoe walking down the aisle. How I wish it were a reality or even close in the fact that I had a man at least. Well on a positive note at least I had a date tonight. I had the prospects of obtaining a long deserved social life. Late last night I had received a text message from Lucas stating that he couldn't wait to see me today and confirming the time we had to meet. It felt strange that I was actually anticipating this date tonight. I knew that I had issues in regards to men and I had very little faith. But although Lucas had shown some familiar signs, I was able to take note from Keshia's advice and live for the moment. I wouldn't hold Reese's behaviour against Lucas. I would go out and enjoy our date. Lucas was his own person and I should treat him as such. Damn, I hated listening to others advice. It made me feel like I was too trivial, like I was always over-reacting. I had every right to, didn't I?

As I began getting ready, nervousness rose in my stomach. I was excited about going to see Musiq Soulchild. This was the concert of all concerts to be this year. Lucas had said that he had managed to get hold of good seats, I don't know exactly how he happened to pull that off but he ensured me that he had. I was hoping that I wouldn't have to keep looking over the masses of heads to see. I decided to dress in some light denim skinny jeans and a backless silver top. My hair was up in a quiff with the back out, with flawless make- up. Luckily I had recently gone out shopping with Janet and she had forced me to purchase some new items. Dating was foreign to me. I hadn't done it in ages so there was a lot which I had to learn. I paced up and down the room as I noticed the time, it was now quarter to seven. The concert started at seven! Lucas had said that he would pick me up at six, where the heck was he! It was not an easy journey, we had to travel all the way to Hammersmith. I hated being late, we would miss half the opening acts. I picked up my mobile and called his number, waiting for him to answer…

"Yeah, babes I'm on my way. Give me fifteen"

"Okay. But can you hurry up please we're going to miss half the show?"

"Yeah, sure. I'm on my way"

He clicked off the phone. Now I was becoming infuriated. I was sitting waiting for this man and he was almost an hour late. I was a sitting duck right now. A further twenty minutes passed and still no Lucas. I tried his mobile again and this time it rang out. I stood mad, my skin boiling with rage. There is no way we are going to get there anytime soon. What was he playing at? Again I tried his phone and it rang out. Ten minutes later and there was a knock at the door. Finally he had arrived I thought. Although I was angry at him for making us late, I checked my attitude and thought that there must be some logical explanation. I grabbed my bag, re-applied my perfume and checked my hair in the mirror before opening.

"Hey, how comes you're still at home?"

I looked on in disgust. Embarrassed and upset at the unexpected visitor. "What are you doing here?"

"Well. Mum told me to bring over some food left from yesterday for you, but I didn't think that I would catch you still here, but mum insisted"

"Don't bullshit me Reese. You have come over here to be nosey! Why can't you just stay out of my life!"

I started shouting, I was annoyed and irritated. Lucas had stood me up and now Reese was here to witness it. Can my life get any worst! He stood at the door, not knowing what to say next. He could tell I was pissed off and I was definitely taking it out on him.

"Look, sorry but I just brought you food"

"Yeah thanks. What else Reese? You gonna stand there and bloody laugh"

"What are you on about?"

Before I could reply my mobile started ringing in the front room and I dashed to answer it. Lucas name was flashing on the screen…

"Hello who's this?" Came the unfamiliar hostile female voice.

"Excuse you?"

"Who is this? Lucas is my man and I want to know who is phoning his phone!"

"Look, there must be some misunderstanding…"

"Yeah, there must be. Let me tell you something you dirty bitch. Don't be calling back this phone again yeah!"

"Listen. You do not know who I am and I suggest you talk to your man about this! And don't be cussing on my phone because you are making yourself look like such a fool right now."

"Well, fuck you. All I am saying is don't phone back this phone"

"Gladly!" I hung up.

Blood pressure was definitely raised now. How dare she call my phone and cuss at me like I knew he had a woman. How typical. Why does this always happen to me. As I turned around I forgot that Reese was present. He had come into the house having heard me raise my voice and now he was standing in the doorway looking at me with speculative eyes.

"Piss off Reese. Don't even bother say a word. Just bloody get out my house. I'm fucking fed up of this shit!"

He stood leaned on the doorframe not saying a word.

"Did you hear me?" I bellowed.

"Leah, stop swearing, its not you" He walked towards me. I was trying desperately to fight the tears that were trying to defeat my pride. As he moved closer, he attempted to hold me in an embrace. I tried to push him away but the tears began to fall and all inhibitions were lost. I held onto him and cried my eyes out.

"Its okay" He said as he rubbed my hair and allowed me to let out all the frustration.

He stood there patiently, the more I cried, the more embarrassed I became because this was happening before Reese. He was witnessing me at my lowest. I was weak and vulnerable right now and Reese had seen this before, he was previously the cause of it. Now someone else had caused me to breakdown. Strong Leyah had lost.

I began to calm down and my heart rate regulated. Reese pulled me away from his grasp and looked me in my face which was smudged with black mascara.

"Leyah, its okay. Don't worry about this man. You're beautiful and it is his loss. Just as it was mine. You don't need anymore of this bull!"

"It's your entire fault. Don't touch me" I stressed tussling to get out of his grip, but he was stronger and maintained me there in his strong manly grasp.

"Listen…listen to me…"

I struggled to get out of this uncompromising situation, but I failed. I could feel the passion erupting from within. The reactions of Reese being considerate and caring was a thorn in my side. He looked down into my eyes and pressed his lips against mine. I wanted to fight him off but I couldn't, all I could do was react. My body needed this, the touch of a man. He kissed me passionately, deeply, with sincerity. My body relaxed and went with the flow, it felt too good. His tongue tasted like sweet succulent peaches. My feet began to buckle underneath me, but Reese was aware. He was ready to hold me up, to be my rock. He relaxed his frame and leaned against the wall holding me close, continuing to suckle at my partly glossed lips. His arms holding me in a tight embrace. He got caught up in the moment and squeezed a little tighter… the foggy cloud that had made my judgement hazy disappeared and I was able to think straight again…

"Stop! Get off"

"Sorry" He let go of my body and rubbed his closely shaved beard, savouring the moisture on his lips. He looked as confused as I felt.

"Get out. Please. Just go home"

"Leyah I'm sorry"

"Don't! Just go"

His eyes fell to the floor, then he reluctantly walked out the lounge and out the front door.

What was I thinking? How could I be here kissing this bastard! How could I let him in like that? This is what Shantel was worried about. Shit, this is what I was worried about. Yes I was still attracted to him but I didn't want us to be here like this. I hate him, he is the epitome of a playa and here I am giving him leverage. Shit, we kissed!

Have I lost my mind?

Chapter 28.

Janet

I strutted up the expensive path which I could tell was recently completed. It glistened in the sweltering sun and not a scratch tarnished the surface. I opened the patio door holding the yellow gift bag in my hand as my finger rested on the bell, waiting for someone to answer. Through the thick walls I could hear the soft sounds of some soul playing from inside the house, then the familiar frame opened the door.

"Hi. Janet. I'm so glad that you could make it. Ohh and who is this?"

I kissed Jasmine on both her cheeks before answering. "Jasmine this is Michael, Michael this is Marcus's fiancée Jasmine"

Michael held out his hand for Jasmine to shake, but instead she moved forward and recited the same greeting we had just shared.

"Nice to meet you Michael. I've heard so much about you"

She eagerly took the gift out of my grasp, which I had made Leyah shop for on my behalf. I was not strong enough to shop for a gift for Marcus's unborn child which should have been mine. It was just too hard for me to deal with. I still didn't even know what I was actually doing here!

We followed behind Jasmine as she escorted us into the stunning garden, it was amazing. They had so much space and just as expected Jasmine had gone all out for this baby shower. They had white canopies throughout the garden, stone statues of babies and water fountains adoring the surroundings. There were even fully clothed waiters walking around with drinks and hors d'oeuvres, this definitely must have cost a bomb!

Although we were still on my assigned break, I had decided to bring Michael along with me today because I didn't want to be here looking like a sad single, watching Jasmine parade about with my Marcus! Being vindictive she hinted that I should bring my partner along because all her friends were attending with their other halves. I wanted to look happy as well. Even though it was all pretence, I was trying. Michael was happy to receive my call after his numerous attempts to contact me which I purposely ignored. Some how it felt like he didn't even mind that I was using him for my convenience, I mean he must have figured it out by now. I suppose he was just happy that I had finally introduced him into my personal life. He hadn't met any of my close friends apart from Keshia and Leyah and that was because they were both there when I met him, or else he would have been a myth for at least three months, if he had lasted that long! Michael grabbed two glasses of wine from the passing waitress and stood adoring the scenery. I admired the way he dressed, he looked the part. We both looked the part coincidentally co-ordinating with each other in lilac and blue.

"Wow, so your boy is loaded?" Micheal asked.

"Not really, he just works hard for what he likes and his woman likes to spend it as fast as he makes it"

He sipped on his wine, watching the other guests. "Well his house is lovely. His woman isn't too bad either. You make her out to be some sort of witch!"

Yes I had given Michael the low down on my bitchy turbulent relationship with Jasmine. He had to be prepared for all the sly remarks we would be making towards each other, having slight little condescending digs from time to time.

"Look, don't let the pretty face fool you" As I finished my sentence, Marcus came walking towards us from inside the house. A smile lit up from my face as I witnessed his grace. He was casually dressed, wearing

243

a pair of white linen trousers and an egg yolk yellow crew neck cashmere jumper. He looked amazing.

"Hey Janet, you made it"

We greeted each other as we usually did, with a hug and kiss of the cheeks, but this time not lingering like we would typically do when we hugged, aware of all the eyes that would be on us if we did. No one seemed to understand our friendship, let alone appreciate it. Although I held strong romantic feelings for Marcus it was not publicised. It was not like we were having an affair!

"Marcus, this is Michael"

They shook hands cautiously. Like they were both protecting their territory, sizing one another up. This was the long awaited day for each of them as they had both heard so much about each other, but had never been able to put the face to the name. Michael wore a plastic smile on his face. I knew this expression as it was what he used when I first told him about Marcus and every time I mentioned his name.

"So you're the famous guy, that's taken my friend away from me"

Marcus said, trying to make light of the situation. "She hardly has anytime for her old mate anymore"

"Well… what can I say. Janet is a very special lady" He grabbed my waist, trying to prove something to Marcus. I just stood smiling uncomfortably, trying to keep up this façade while welcoming his kind words.

"Yeah she is"

Marcus gave me a smile, which sent warmth through my body and made me blush.

"Well I'm glad that you both made it" He said casually.

"Thanks for the invite. I've never actually been to a baby shower anything like this!"

"Yeah I'm sure you haven't Jay, Jasmine has gone all out for this. Any excuse for a party and she will do it. I said to her, aren't baby showers supposed to be a room full of women talking about babies, pushchairs, labour and breastfeeding?"... Michael nodded in agreement... "And she looked at me like I was an alien. She had the cheek to tell me to get with the times. This was what a baby shower in 2008 entails!"

"Well she sure is ahead of the celebrity D-List game!"

"That's right, I can't' even keep up! Well have you guys had anything to eat? There's a buffet table over there"

Marcus pointed towards the side of the house where there was a pink canopy and streamers.

"Oh, yeah we'll grab something in a bit. Love the house by the way"

"Thanks Jay. I'm just trying to get it all in order before the baby comes. To be honest I'm not fully prepared as yet"

"Well you better hurry up, you have like what?..."

"Yeah, just over a month" Marcus said.

"Wow, your woman looks good for eight months pregnant" Added Michael, feeling left out of the conversation.

"Yeah, she is carrying well"

"My daughter's mother put on so much weight when she was pregnant".

I looked at Michael as he made that comment, not appreciating the fact that he was being inconsiderate to the poor woman who had to go through nine months of body invasion. I had seen pictures of his nine year old daughter Sparkle, she looked just like him. Michael was very forthcoming from the beginning that he had a daughter. She was the apple of his eye. He would do anything for her, although from what he had told me and what I had seen, her mother was a total bitch! What you would call a 'babymother' from hell! She was crazy! He had told me that a year ago she had tried to get him stabbed just because he wouldn't give into her demands when she wanted. Hearing that and other stuff she had done made me think twice about even dating him. I was way past getting phone calls from 'babymothers' and dealing with the continuous drama. I did not need it in my life at my age, but luckily she hasn't been a problem... Yet! We stood looking awkward, trying to get over the tension between the two male dominants, then Jasmine called over to Marcus from the other end of the garden. Okay I admit it, yes she did look radiant wearing a nice flowered white maxi dress hugging her bump. It made her look like a pregnant runway model. Everything about her was precise, even her hair was done with precision. I could understand why Marcus was captured by this serpent. I even caught Michael admiring her on more than one occasion, but she wasn't a threat to me, she had nothing on me! I looked around trying to act like I wanted to mingle, but the event was filled with Jasmine's colleagues and friends from her social circle. All the women where over-done with maximum make-up, looking like they had studied the latest fashion from Vogue magazine. The men who accompanied them also looked like male models, sporting perfectly lined eyebrows and recently manicured hands. Only the odd few were looking like 'normal' men, not worrying about their personal appearance, drinking beers and talking about football... what a night this is going to be!

"My gosh Janet!" Came a loud voice from behind me.

I spun around stunned. To my surprise there stood the familiar 5'2, dark chocolate woman with her black and red curly weave.

"Wow, Trina. You look well. How are you?"

Greeting each other with a hug, we admired how well we both looked after so long. I was finally relieved to have someone else to talk to. Someone who would be a positive critique like myself. Michael was no good, he was praising Jasmine for all her hard work and effort, not seeing her for who she actually is and it was beginning to irritate me.

"Damn, I feel like I have stepped into Barbie world! What's with all the plastic?" Trina looked around with disgust on her face, amazed at what she was seeing. "So where is this Jasmine that has my cousin all smitten and turn fool?"

Michael and I both laughed. I scanned the garden and searched for Jasmine, locating her with Marcus talking to a couple wearing matching Kente cloth outfits at the rear of the garden.

"There she is at the back with Marcus"

"Huh! Wow. I never knew my cousin liked such fake, prep up women! She looks like she had that make-up painted on! Well, I better go over and say hi. Back in a few"

Trina walked towards the hosts, swinging her little hips as she went. I laughed recollecting her witty and comical personality. She was definitely fun to be around and you were guaranteed to have laughs.

A few hours passed and Jasmine continued to strut around the party like she was Victoria Beckham, collecting the gifts and placing them on the fully decorated gift table. I yawned as I was becoming bored. Michael had left me to attend the boys room and he was taking so long that I knew he must be idolising the house and using the opportunity to network. I stood tapping my feet on the patio watching Trina in deep conversation with one of her relatives. As I turned to scan my surroundings in the hope that something would relieve me from my boredom, Marcus came walking towards me with a cheesy grin on his face.

"So Jay, that's your new guy huh?"

"Yes. That's him"

"Well. To be honest I wouldn't have pictured him like that. Didn't really think he would be your type!"

"And what do you mean by that? How do you know what my type is?"

247

I looked at him, trying to read his thoughts.

Marcus laughed "Well… he just doesn't suit you"

I was offended, not for me but for Michael. How could he say that?

"Marcus, he is a nice guy. Why are you always so protective over me? Can't you just be happy for me for once? I always supported you in your relationships. Even now, you know that I am not too fond of Jasmine, but I came. I come here and smile up with her, just for you. Because you are my friend and I care for you!"

"I know Jay. Sorry. It's just…"

He looked into my eyes lovingly, making me hold my breath, wishing that the three words that I have always dreamt about him saying escaped his lips. But I knew it wouldn't, it's not like this was the most appropriate place for him to make such a confession.

"Its just I feel the need to protect you. I don't want to see you with any and anybody. I want the best for you"

"Marcus, I'm a big girl now. I can look after myself"

"I know you can babes, but that doesn't stop me from wanting to be there for you, like you have been for me in the past"

"Thanks" I was weak. "Anyway can we change the subject?"

He smirked. "Yeah…sure"

"So how much did this extravagance cost then? I see she is still rinsing your pocket!"

"My gosh Jay. This woman sure knows how to spend other people's money! I mean, was there really any need for all this? This is all a show for her friends"

I shook my head in disbelief. "Well you must know what your doing! Or maybe you're Mr Boops!"

We both laughed as we had discussed this topic numerous times recently. I always teased him about him being her sugar daddy. Jasmine treated him like a credit card and because she was pregnant Marcus had to oblige. Trina returned and joined the two of us, interrupting our private joke.

"So cuz, you really went top scale with this so called baby shower! This isn't no baby shower. This is a rave!"

"I've told him already!"

"Look both of you shush! Jasmine likes to go all out and have the best!"

"Yeah we have noticed! I would do the same if I had a sucker like you!" Trina joked.

"Listen I am not no sucker! We both agreed on the particulars of the baby shower"

Me and Trina laughed as Marcus tried to defend his loss of control. We all knew that he had no power over any of it.

"Yeah right! Marcus please! I know you and this pretty face has you sprung! Remember that little coolie girl next door to Nan's when we was young that used to always rinse you for your strawberry bonbons?"

Marcus smiled remembering the girl. "Listen, that was different. She had the prettiest smile"

"Yeah! You have always been a sucker for the pretty ones!"

He pushed her playfully, embarrassed at the recollection. I had a feeling that he knew he was in too deep and had no control over what was happening to him right now. He was no longer in forefront of his life. Jasmine had assigned that role eight months ago and virtually had him by the balls for the next eighteen years!

I slipped out of my court shoes, relieved to finally be back in my house with normal surroundings. I relaxed back onto the sofa, listening to Michael rabbit on about how he had made a few new contacts with some of the guests. He was good at networking, seeing the importance of getting to know people as he assured me that you don't know when they will come in handy.

"Jasmine's, really nice babe. She speaks so highly of you"

I rolled my eyes, as I was fully aware of Jasmine's techniques. "Really?"

"Yeah, she said that you are like a best friend to her because you and Marcus are so close. She adores the friendship which you two have"

Now I knew this was a load of bull. Jasmine has constantly expressed her disagreement of our friendship and I have been on the receiving end of her verbal abuse on numerous occasions. I knew what she was trying to do! She was trying to become friends with Michael, so that I could look like the paranoid one. '*Yeah, everybody feel sorry for poor innocent pregnant Jasmine!*' The scheming bitch!

I answered Michael sarcastically "Does she really? Maybe the pregnancy is making her lose her memory!"

"Well I like her"

"Good for you!"

"Well, baby. I'm so glad that you brought me along. Marcus seems like a cool dude, except when he pulled me to the side to have a few words"
I jumped up stunned. "What! When?"

"You must have been somewhere with Trina. He was like sort of threatening me. Telling me that I better treat you right and not hurt you, that sort of stuff"

I silently smiled, thinking that was just like Marcus. He had always approached the guys at college that liked me and put the frighteners on them. At least I know he still cares.

"So what did you say?" I questioned.

"Well I told him that I am going to hold you like this and maintain a smile on your face for the rest of my days" He demonstrated his words by slowly caressing my face whilst holding me close.

I examined my thoughts. He is trying, Marcus is taken now and I suppose if I can't be with the one I love, then I should love the one I'm with.

Well at least try!

Chapter 29.

Keshia

Bobby was due back any moment now. I stood impatiently in the crowded arrival lounge waiting for him to descend from the gates. My time with Kamarni had ceased. It was now time to return back to my old life and pretend that I was not struck by the love bug. The time apart from Bobby had given me a chance to think about where I wanted to be, who I wanted to be with. I loved Bobby but I realised that I was no longer in love with him. He did not make me feel the way Kamarni did. I know it's not guaranteed that Kamarni and I would be together, but I feel that I owe it to myself to be happy.

"Baby, I missed you so much" I was greeted by a big tight embrace and kisses which swept me off my feet as he grabbed me and spun me around.

He put me down looking intensely at my body in my tight skinny jeans and tight white vest, licking his lips. I could tell exactly what he was thinking! He smiled at me seductively and I unleashed the words that welcomed a lie as I told him that I had missed him as well. I just couldn't tell the truth, I felt compelled to respond. Truth was that I had hardly missed him at all and that I had shared my body with another. Lying was the right thing to do right now. This wasn't the right time and he seemed so happy to see me.

I looked on as Bobby said goodbye to some of his friends from the cast and we departed to walk to the car. Holding my hand and pulling his large LV case in the other, Bobby gave me the run down on the men who he just said goodbye to and what the set was like. We neared the car park entrance almost bumping into a blonde Australian Tourist, pushing an overloaded trolley. A pretty light skinned woman wearing a pair of extra tight jeans and an extremely small orange top which strangled her breast called over to Bobby with excitement. Bobby jumped nervously at the sight of seeing her.

"Oh, Melissa. Hi"

"I was trying to catch you at the baggage lounge. We definitely have to meet up now that we are back" She said with lust in her tone.

Bobby turned and looked at me with unease on his face, plastering a smile in an attempt to convince me not to worry... that the interaction was innocent. But it did not settle my unease and Bobby was shifting uncomfortably.

"Melissa, this is my '*girlfriend*' Keshia"

Melissa looked me up and down with her false eyelashes before opening her overly glossed mouth.

"Oh hi. I've heard so much about you. Bobby is such a great actor, he is just the best and thing is he doesn't actually know it. We had so much fun out in Ireland."

I don't know if it was me being paranoid, but it was like she was indirectly trying to hint something to me. Whatever it was she was suggesting, I didn't like it.

"And who might you be?" I said trying to remain calm and conceal my annoyance.

"Oh, I am only one of the make-up artists, not an actress yet. But working with Bobby has been an honour" She said with her cheap coloured lip gloss forming a suggestive pout.

Bobby sharply interrupted, feeling the heat rise between the two of us. "Well, Melissa take care. We gotta run"

"Oh yeah sure. Well we must all go out for a drink. You have my number. Ciao"

Melissa walked off in the opposite direction strutting her six inch heels, enticing the men that passed. I watched her, annoyed. I did not like the look of her, she reminded me of one of those women that would sleep with anyone in order to get to where she wanted to be in the business hierarchy. Bobby began walking at pace, quickly trying to avoid any questioning, but it was burning in my soul and I had to confront him about our little encounter…

"So, why was she so happy to see you?"

"Huh?"

"Don't act dumb. Why have you got her number anyway?"

He quickly rubbed his low cut hair, giving him time to think of something soothing to say. "Look, don't take this out of context! She was the make-up artist on the set. We all associated in the evenings and went out for drinks, that's the only reason why I have it"

"Oh yeah? Well the way she was looking at you told me different!" I snapped taking my hands out of his grasp.

"Didn't you hear her say that she has heard a lot about you? Babes I couldn't stop talking about you. I missed you so much!" He turned and nibbled at my neck.

"Stop! Look I'm serious!"

"Yes baby!"

I cut my eye at him knowing that this discussion was pointless. I was not going to get any answers now. We continued our path towards the car to commence the long awkward journey back to our humble abode. I was irritated after meeting that woman. I knew that there was something that Bobby failed to tell me, thing is I don't know why it bothered me so much. I had spent the past couple of weeks with my dream man, the perfect man to my existence and here I was being a big hypocrite. But really, I was the innocent party in all of this wasn't I?

Chapter 30.

Leyah

My head had been hurting me since that dreadful night last week after Lucas woman had dropped the unexpected on me. I hadn't spoken to the lying, cheating, bastard since that day. He had left countless messages on my phone but I had decided to spare him the verbal execution, it was a waste of energy. I didn't need to answer his calls and hear all the rubbish which he was guaranteed to divulge- *'Oh she is not my woman', 'Its not like that', 'She just still wants me'*. I knew it would be a bunch of nonsense escaping his dark deceiving lips. I don't need this kind of drama in my life. I have had a life times share! Now look what old drama had reopened its wounds because of that! Mistakenly I had leaned on Reese's hard manly shoulders in my moment of despair which led to gravitational force pulling us together for a passionate kiss. I still can't believe that I stooped that low. I kissed Reese! I was still angry with myself for allowing it to happen. I should have broken the kiss, stepped away, but I couldn't. I just couldn't dress back!

It was Sunday night and Reese was due any moment as usual to drop Asia off. I was pacing in the front room anticipating his arrival, trying to avoid any regurgitated conversations about the event! I had been peering out of the curtains for the past fifteen minutes when I noticed the familiar four by four driving down my road. Now it was crunch time, the way which I handled this situation would determine all future liaisons with him. I had to put the message across that it was never to happen again! It was a huge mistake to participate in that kiss!

I opened the door before he could knock and greeted the two familiar faces. I was trying not to anticipate a reaction, but the situation became more awkward than I predicted. I didn't know where to look, my eyes darted round like a football trying not to focus on one position too long.

I was so ashamed with myself and I felt terrible. Reese picked up on my apprehension and understood the awkwardness of the situation. Retreating, he gave Asia a quick kiss goodbye letting her run inside. He didn't even attempt to say anything about the kiss or do his normal routine of trying to wind me up! He just uttered a quick good bye and walked back to his car. I hastily closed the door, knowing that one glimpse could potentially ignite the feeling which he left me with after he departed yesterday night. Knowing Reese this was all a big game to him. He must be loving the fact that I still love him, that I responded to his kiss! Hold on a minute! What am I actually saying? I don't love Reese anymore, I can't. I'm just vulnerable because another man had let me down; another man had proven my theory right! All men are the same! I just can't believe that Lucas had a woman, he seemed so sincere. The way he was hounding me at the beginning made me want to trust him, believe in him. I knew I shouldn't have listened to Keshia and Janet, I knew I should have just stuck to my own philosophy. The only way a man can hurt you, is if you let them. My past avoidance technique had worked, now I know I must definitely revert back to it and be the ice queen which I once was! I just can't believe myself, my one weakness Reese, had caused me to lose my senses for that brief moment! We had shared a passionate kiss behind Shantel's back.

I took another sip of my glass of red wine which I had been consuming for the past hour trying to deliberate on my thoughts. Asia was fast asleep, which meant another boring night in for me. I was slightly envious of my friends who had company, they had someone to keep them occupied. Even if it was someone who they didn't want to be with long term, they still had someone to talk to, someone to share the evening with. I had no one, not even a back up! My daily evening ritual had become depressing. I would come home sort out the dinner, spend some time with Asia, put her to bath and bed, wash the dishes and then come and relax in front of the TV, play some music and read another pathetic romance novel! It was depressing thinking about how my life was. It was nothing like how I had pictured it would be at this age in my life. I had no excitement. The most excitement I experienced was hearing about all the drama in Keshia's life, now even Janet had more to tell then me!

I rested back in the armchair, dazing at the TV until I heard a faint knock at the door. I rose up suspiciously and cautiously walked towards the door. I looked through the spy hole... the image I saw instantly put me in a confused state. My body froze and my heart began to beat wildly as I turned the lock to expose the unexpected guest...

"Sorry I just needed to see you quickly. I need to get this off my chest"

"Why didn't you just call?"

"I couldn't. I needed to see you face to face"

My heart continued to pound in my chest as I let him enter past the threshold. His large frame walked into the lounge at ease, rubbing his beard.

"What is it now?"

"Leah, our kiss last night made me realise how much I have missed you, how much I yearn for you. I know that you hate me and you think that I'm just doing this to play games with you, but you need to understand how much I need you right now"

I took a deep breath, analysing his face as he spoke. Worry clearly written over his face. His stress lines in his forehead were dominant. His eyes deep with anticipation to the reaction I was about to present.

"I'm sorry you feel that way!"

"What! You're sorry?"

"Yes I am, because I can't help you. I can't say the same Reese"

"You're talking rubbish. I know you felt that kiss, I know you did. You responded to me. You..."

"No I did not. I didn't want you to kiss me. I don't want you near me! Go home to your fiancée Reese! Just go!" I shouted raising my voice then retracting as I remembered Asia upstairs asleep.

"I am not going anywhere! Leah Leah, I love you and I always have. I don't know what I was doing with Shantel. All I know is that I'm not doing this anymore. I'm not pretending!"

"What? Go, before you say something you regret. It is not fair for you to play with peoples hearts Reese. I'm not going to allow you to play with mine anymore!"

As much as I hated him, I still loved him deep down inside but I could not let myself be vulnerable to his sweet talk again.

"I told you I'm not playing!" His voice was authoritive and his eyes stood firm in contact with mine as goose pimples shot across my bare arms.

"Yes you are, you done this before remember?"

"I'm leaving Shantel!" He spurted out.

"What?" I said shocked.

"I don't want to be with her anymore"

"Look just get out. I don't need to hear this"

He touched my hand in an attempt to soothe my anger that was rising from within. My head was beginning to spin, the wine was taking hold at the wrong time.

"Leyah, look I mean what I am saying!"

I took hold of his arm and pulled him out of the room and towards the front door not wanting to hear another word. I wanted to believe him, I wanted to take hold of him and let him take control of my body with his, but I knew it wasn't right. I thought I had let go of the past a long time ago and set myself free from my emotional connection with Reese. I had to fight the feeling, but what if he was telling the truth about leaving? Where would that leave me? Nah! I don't need to be picking up a man like him, he did it to her so he would only come and do it to me! I must keep it in perspective; he is the scum of the earth!

"Leyah, I'm pouring out my heart to you right now!"

"Bye Reese because I'm not listening to this bullshit anymore"

I opened the door with my free hand and pushed him out. He didn't put up much of a fight after landing on my doorstep. As the door closed a sense of regret overpowered my heart. I leaned against the back of the frame and exhaled. I knew that I still loved this man but I had been deeply hurt by his lies. I felt for him so much. I thought that he was the one I would marry, but obviously he had another agenda. What he had said tonight could not surely be true, I was confused. I didn't want to ever be one of those women who ran back to the father of their children on a casual basis. I refuse! But Reese had me weak right now and it wasn't helping that I had not engaged in any form of intimate sexual attention in approximately eleven months, and yes I was tired of using the rabbit! My thoughts drifted and I was plagued with the image of Reese's naked body across my own, with beads of sweat dripping off our bodies merging together. My body melted as I visualised his masculine body. Thinking whether his biceps still bulged like they used to or if his body still shuddered when he released his load. Stop! What am I doing? I turned to walk into the kitchen when there came that faint knock again…

As soon as I opened the door he grabbed me by the waist and drew me close, placing his sweet moist lips upon mine, sucking every last bit of life out of my breath. I put up no resistance as I fumbled with the back of his shirt reaching my hands alongside his muscular back as he gently pushed me against the wall. He started to fumble with my skirt but then decided against it, opting to slowly caress his hands up my thighs, squeezing them delicately as he moved up towards the centre. The intoxicating heat from his body felt so good, I needed to feel him close right now. He drew back and looked me dead in the eyes like a lost puppy who just found his way home. I stood mesmerized as he took his left thumb and ran it along my bottom lip, at that moment I knew I had lost all will to fight and could feel my body responding to the heat which was developing between our bodies. I had to draw him closer… I bit his

259

finger softly and invitingly. He smiled seductively and continued his way up my thighs until he reached my red panties. He took his hand and continued to caress my pelvis underneath the soft lace until finally deciding to draw my red barrier down. By this time my love was so wet and inviting. My panties slowly dropped to the floor while I used the moment to grab him closer. He felt how much I was yearning for him and continued to kiss me… forcefully but passionate.

"Ohhh baby I want to feel you" He groaned as he fumbled with his trousers.

I took my hands from his back and attempted to undo his trousers eagerly on his behalf. Once I managed to get the restricting fabric down he placed his hands onto mine and placed them inside his boxers… damn he was so hard, all I could think was enter me now. He moaned as I rubbed my hand across the head of his magic stick.

"Awww, let me take you, let me take you now"

He proceeded to lift up my skirt and raise me to level his pelvis as he slowly entered inside of me. My feet were barely touching the floor. Right then the moment felt so good and I could feel my juices flowing with every stride and every motion he made. We were pressed against the wall making our bodies limited in the movements we could make so I had to trust him to balance my weight and let him take over my body, total control of my body! It was such an intoxicating feeling, I felt powerless and it felt good. This fine sexy milk chocolate man was having his way and doing what he pleased with my body. He was pumping in and out of me and my body was weakening at the knees. His mouth lowered to my right breast and he slowly licked his tongue around my nipple whilst still inside of me as solid as ever. The feeling was so intense I could not take it anymore and I reached my climax as he made a deep thrust inside of me. Groaning I smiled. He brought his head up and looked at me with his seductive dark brown eyes, while he licked his lips biting the bottom one as he drew his mouth once again towards me. He broke away and pulled his firm hard manhood out of me and lifted me up to the bedroom. My head was spinning as he laid me onto the bed and removed his shirt, taking his hands and parting my legs, slowly running them up my calves and thighs. He then took his fine lips and tongue and followed that path, stopping at the outside of my most intimate place he entered making sure that he pleased me more than himself. My legs began to weaken again as my body shuddered. Once he was satisfied that I was enjoying the feeling he began to speed up the pace. I could feel every motion and damn it felt so good. He swore he would never do this.

"Reese, stop I'm about to cum again. I can't hold out…"

"Babe cum, I wanna taste you"

"Baby I'm cumin…I'm cumin"

I had released the built up sexual frustration once again. Reese came up and looked at me licking his lips, he flipped me onto my stomach and again he took his hard manhood and thrusted deep inside my swollen rose bush. Deep, deep inside, we both began moaning in complete ecstasy. He felt so good. It felt like our bodies were two entwined locks of hair, twisting and turning with every blow of the wind. He held me so close like a china doll not wanting this moment to end. Sweat was dripping from both of us and he was holding on to the last stroke like his life depended on it. With every thrust he moaned and groaned. It felt so good to have this power over a man. I sunk my nails into his back while he grabbed my hair passionately with one hand while rubbing my sensitive spot simultaneously with the shaft of his penis. His strides became faster and deeper, I could feel his heart beating faster and faster as though it was racing with his body inside of mine.

"Baby I'm cuming, I'm cuming!" He moaned before exploding with an enormous climax. My body reacted in a way as if to never let him go as I felt every muscle in my intimate place clench.

"Damn baby, you feel so good. I missed you so much. I missed the way you feel. I missed the way we feel together"

He kissed my forehead.

We lay still. I looked up at the ceiling and allowed the calming of the atmosphere to bring me back to reality.

"I can't believe we just did that. I can't believe that we are here again!" I uttered, trying to regain my breath.

"Its okay, it's going to be different this time. I love you and I am willing to admit that now!"

"What do you mean you love me! How can you love me? You're with someone else for crying out loud!" I sat up suddenly becoming conscious of the mess I had just woven myself into for the sake of my own selfish needs.

"I'm surprised Asia hasn't mentioned it to you"

Looking at him all puzzled I answered. "What?"

"Shantel moved out last weekend. That's the real reason why she didn't come to mums party"

"What? How come?"

"She kept pressuring me and I couldn't lie anymore. I told her that I didn't love her. I don't want to marry her and I definitely did not want any children with her! Things haven't been good with her for a while. Well to be honest it's since the day I met you. I just knew she wasn't for me!"

I looked at him gobsmacked, raising my hands to my mouth. I didn't want any part in breaking up his relationship with Shantel.

"Don't worry its not you. She wasn't right for me full stop. I don't know why I stayed. I realised that it was doing more hurt than good to be honest, and she became increasingly negative towards Asia, and then she kept talking about having a baby. I just couldn't do it and from then I knew I was in the wrong place." His eyes became small and sympathetic.

"Reese, don't think that I am going to welcome you with open arms because you have had this sudden realisation! You put me through so much shit! You hurt me so deep!" He leaned in towards me and kissed my head again. I moved in disgust.

"I know I did Leah and that was purely selfish of me. Back then I was young and I didn't know what I wanted. Like I told you before I fell in love with you and things got deep between us. I know I should have told you from the beginning about Shantel and I apologise for that. It's just that I didn't want to lose you"

"Oh, well you executed that with precision now didn't you! How did you really think you would have gotten away with it?"

"I didn't think babe. I just looked at things with tunnel vision. Nothing else mattered"

"Yeah, you did that alright!" I sighed pulling the covers closer to cover my shame.

"So where do we go from here?"

I ignored the question put to me and let the words repeat in my head. Reese knew not to ask me again, so he resorted to making the best of the moment at hand because he understood that this will not come to pass again!

We lay back in the bed holding each other and I made it clear to him that he had to leave before Asia woke, there was no way I wanted her to see the two of us together or him in our house so early. No way! I know that I should really make him leave tonight but for now I just wanted to succumb to having a man in my bed again, laying with the male species! Although he was still a lying, cheating bastard, it felt good to be held again. I buried my dizzy head in his short woven chest hair and drifted to sleep.

Chapter 31.

Janet

It had been a month since the superstar baby shower and I had once again distanced myself from Michael. It had now become an automatic reaction. I had begun to use him at my disposal, at my request. Thing was he was only too happy to oblige! Any contact was good enough for him at this stage and he did not want me to cut him off completely. I didn't want to get attached to him, no way. I couldn't, my heart wouldn't let me. It belonged to another. Using him to cancel out any feelings which I still held for Marcus was not working. I was feeling increasingly stressed recently, which I attributed to the fact that Jasmine was soon due to give birth to Marcus's baby. I was constantly anxious and breaking out in little panic attacks daily. I was not the one to be around at the moment. I hated the fact that I still had not been able to control my feelings for Marcus. I mean he was out there coping, getting on with his life, preparing to be a father and here I was making myself sick with worry about him progressing. Him being trapped by that bitch! Why can't I get over this? I need to let go and stop letting this eat away at me. But it tore away at me constantly, I was consumed with envy. Why did I let my stupidity take control of my feelings? Why don't I just open up to love and welcome it when it presents its face? Now love was loving someone else. Love was making a life with another. Love was bringing a part of that love into the world!

I was so glad that he had managed to postpone the wedding until after the birth of the baby. It was all too soon for him to get married and have a baby in such a short space of time. It was a war zone for Marcus trying to convince Jasmine to put the wedding on hold, but the facts were in front of his face and he recognised the problems which it could potentially bring. Everyone told him he was rushing into this all too soon and that's what he had told her, with the use of various ammunition which he built up over the past couple of months. She had no other option, so she eventually agreed. They were already having problems living together, why would you then go and put yourself in such a situation where you will be trapped, stuck and tied into the commitment legally? Yeah he was having a baby with her and that was basically the same thing. But at least if anything goes wrong he will only have to look after his child and not feel obligated to look after her and her lavish lifestyle. Not that I am an advocate of men leaving women to be single mothers, but the women have to take some responsibility. I am not going to let an innocent man throw away all the chances he has of real happiness for the sake of this money hungry pretentious bitch! My father had once told me that only once in your life time you will meet your true love and if you lose that love there will never ever be anyone that comes close. I truly believe in my heart that my true love is Marcus. Now all I needed to do was work on my coping strategy to deal with it. I had lost him and I was to blame.

No one but myself.

I buried my head into the pillow, tossing and turning from the disturbance of my nightmare. The sheets were tangled in my body as I tossed my legs about. I looked at my glass bedside table thankful to be awakened by the sounds of my mobile phone ringing. I always left this on in case of an emergency and right now I began to realise that this was a call which I would have thankfully missed!

"Jay, Jay"

"What's wrong?" I replied in a sleepy but anxious voice. My body was conscious that it was the early unsociable hours of the morning.

"I'm a father!"

My heart sank to the pits of my stomach as those three words echoed throughout my ears, giving rise to a nauseous feeling erupting from the pits of my stomach. It was a horrible feeling which I was not expecting right now. I lay motionless and speechless in my bed listening to the excitement in his voice. Why was I feeling like this? Like Marcus becoming a father was a surprise for me! I had known this day was

265

coming but today it had become a reality. September 30th would be a day which I would never be able to forget!

The forced words escaped from my mouth as I finally trembled a response. "Congratulations... I'm happy for you babe"

"It was amazing Jay. I watched him being born, it was beautiful. You should see his full head of hair, his tiny little toes. He looks just like his daddy"

A tear rolled down my eyes as the realisation and resentment took full hold. My world had officially collapsed.

Chapter 32.

Keshia

I slammed the fridge door. Why was it that everything Bobby did was annoying me recently? I was noticing every bad irritating habit. My blood began to boil by the slightest little things he did. He would leave a tiny drop of juice in the fridge, leave the toilet seat up, leave his dirty boxers on the damp bathroom floor and forget to clean the sink after shaving. Ooh that got on my last nerve! I poured the milk into my tea trying to calm myself down. Since Bobby had returned from Ireland, I noticed that he was overcompensating for something which I just couldn't put my hands on. He was acting like we were this loved up couple again. All this had thrown my plan out of the window, I couldn't find the right moment to discuss where the relationship was going. I know any woman would think that I was mad right now, but I knew Bobby and for Bobby this was unusual behaviour, especially as we've spent the past three and a half months apart! Yeah fair enough absence makes the heart grow fonder, but there was something unusual. Something was definitely not right. I tried not to let it bother me too much as I concentrated my thoughts day and night with Kamarni. Thoughts of him would tip toe into my mind and consume anything which I was thinking about at the moment. I would regularly reminisce on the night we shared together, which would make my body tingle as the sensations rushed through my body again. It was virtually impossible trying to spend quality time with Kamarni now that Bobby was back. My whole routine had to be re-designed again. There were no more late night conversations and we were no longer able to meet up freely and enjoy the passing day together. I missed it. Don't get me wrong I still spoke to him, but it wasn't the same. To defuse Bobby's suspicions I had told him that he was a colleague from work who I was working with on this new project. Well it wasn't totally a lie, he was working with me as one of the mentors for the youths on my mentoring project. So I wasn't totally guilty of that lie. But I knew that I couldn't leave my phone around for his pondering eyes to see, because curiosity would surely kill the cat!

We sat on two different ends of the sofa in knife cutting silence, watching a repeat episode of Dr Who. Tension was gripping the air until we were finally interrupted by the sound of the buzzer. I jumped up grateful. Yes, this would be Kyle. My baby brother had called earlier to tell me that he would pass by later in the evening. I was a bit sceptical at first because this was unusual for Kyle and I knew that this was an indication that there was trouble laying ahead somewhere. It was nice having my brother around and I was thankful that he finally got on with Bobby, especially after Kyle found out about his frequent infidelity acts! Kyle really wanted to physically hurt Bobby after hearing the full story. It wasn't that Kyle wasn't the same type of man, but he was angered at the fact that someone had the audacity to do it to his sister. Although he is younger than me he felt the need to protect me, when really he should be protecting himself. A few months ago I had to rush to Kings College hospital after receiving a phone call from Darren who was one of Kyle's friends, he almost scared me half to death! Apparently they had been involved in some sort of altercation with another guy at a club and Kyle ended up being stabbed. Instantly I thought the worst and fear consumed my body, I was cold with terror. Luckily it wasn't fatal. He took one in the arm and the other in his back. I couldn't cope with losing my brother, especially by the hands of another. But I knew the lifestyle that he was living meant that his life expectancy was no more than twenty five! Death and injury was a frequent visitor to me due to the area which I grew up in and the field that I chose to work in. Many of the young boys that I worked with across the years were either in a gang or knew gang members. Even if they didn't want to get involved in gang culture they were connected in some sort of way. Many got caught up in the fast life; they had no value for life anymore. No belief in themselves and what they can achieve. The reality was it was a scary life out here and there were many more victims to come.

Kyle walked in and greeted us both, placing his three phones and car keys down on the glass coffee table.

"Yo sis, what's going on?" He turned and greeted Bobby "You cool bro?"

"Nothing much. How are you?" I responded, giving him a hug.

"I'm good, I'm good. You know Kerry's seeing some yardie man?"

"What! You're joking, what did Kirk say?"

"Well, you know he's mad! Said that he is not doing anything for her again! Bwoy I had to go there and hot up the brudda!"

"Why are you getting involved for? Just keep out of it!"

"Nah, the brudda is some punk! He is all knocking her about in front of Raynelle"

"What!"

Raynelle was Kirks four year old daughter. Unfortunate for her, her mother was a well known hoe! She was loose in the community! God knows why Kirk slept with that in the first place! Kerry was a frequent coke head. I had tried to get Raynelle out of that environment when ever possible, but since Kirk got locked up the battle became infertile. Kerry used Kirks incarceration as an excuse for Raynelle to stay with her. We all knew that she was just worried about losing her benefit money, she had no motivation to work or do anything positive with her life and unfortunately she was only twenty two and already had three kids. Don't get me wrong she is a pretty girl or I should say 'used' to be, but now she had deteriorated. Her looks were beginning to fade and her drug use was becoming hard to disguise.

"Look I'm gonna have to call her again, because I'm not running the risk of my niece witnessing that shit or even becoming a target!"

"Sis, don't worry I've got it. The dude is some wanna be dealer. I've got my soldiers on him!" His face was serious, he had a look which I knew too well. He always had this look before he went to go and beat up boys on the block.

269

"Kyle don't make this a messy situation!" I knew how hot headed my brother was and that he would do anything for a bit of conflict, but this was not one of those situations which needed such intervention. Bobby intervened in the conversation and tried to reason with Kyle, but as per usual it was just going in one ear and out the next. Kyle was ignorant to the laws of the social norm, he was more swayed by the ways of the street and nothing would stop him thinking like that. The fast life was his choice no matter how hard people tried to show him different, it was more glamorous.

The next hour led to a game of dominos and of course Kyle won two out of three games. Bobby was a sore loser, blaming it on being a dumb West Indian game and his brain was too advanced for such simple games. Kyle and I both looked at each other and laughed, knowing that he was pissed for not winning. Then right on cue one of Kyle's phones began to ring. Once one started the rest would follow suit. The life of a hustler. To my disapproval, I could hear Kyle making various drug deals on the phone and instructing his 'workers' to move certain amounts of supplies to a range of places and meet up with prospective clients. I really hated what my brothers did, but unfortunately they were products of their environment and they did what they thought was best to survive. I knew Kyle was much smarter than this and I often tried to convince him to leave the streets and gain real employment. But the glitz and glamour the 'streets' provided was too much for him to exchange. In his head he believed that he had too much to lose. A nine to five could never support the lifestyle and respect which he believed he had gained over the years. Soon he would be in a cell next to Kirk. I shook my head thinking mum would roll over in her grave. I munched on my apple as Kyle expressed good bye with a nod of the head towards Bobby. He walked towards the front door with his Armani jeans half way down his backside, exposing his black designer boxers for all to see with his trade mark tight white t-shirt clinging to his muscles which he maintained by attending the gym five times per week. Then there were his over colourful Nike Trainers which all the youths of today seemed to wear. People often said that he looked like a bigger version of T.I. but to me he was just my little brother! I followed him to the door trying to convince him to let things slide with Kerry.

"Kyle, please try to keep yourself out of trouble and leave that Kerry alone to do what she is doing. I will sort out Raynelle"

"Sis, it's gone too far for that!"

When he said those words I knew that something terrible had already happened and Kyle was now in too deep to turn around. All I could do was pray that no one would get hurt. We exchanged an embrace as I silently expressed my love for my younger brother. He was all I had left. After Kyle left the night seemed to drag. I felt so empty not hearing Kamarni's voice as often as I was used to. It was pure torture for me. The more I tried not to think about him the more thoughts of him entered my mind. Wondering what he was doing, thinking if he was holding his fiancée right now, hoping that he didn't kiss her in the same way which he kissed me, hoping that he didn't make love to her the way we did. Part of me was ashamed of my thoughts of Kamarni, because it was disrespectful towards his woman, she had every right to capture his every attention. This was a breach of trust of my relationship, although in contrast my relationship was not a bed of roses right now. I was still suspicious as to what had really happened between Bobby and that 'make-up' girl, but I didn't really have any hard evidence which I could use as an excuse to exit this inert commitment. Since his return the 'make-up' girl had been consistently calling his phone and sending text messages. But what made it worst was not only was Bobby trying to hide it, he was doing very badly at it. He was straight up slipping. Yes, curiosity got the better of me at times and I had to read one of the texts. But it did not cure the suspicion, she was good. Her text lead on to nothing. She was not direct and blatant; she was playing the game too.

I suppose there is only one way to catch a rat!

Chapter 33.

Leyah

The next morning I awoke to find Reese gone, leaving his scent drifting behind. I looked over at the clock which displayed ten past six. The memories of the sin committed a few hours ago were still fragrant within my white bedroom, but somehow I didn't feel any regret. It was what I needed. No I shouldn't have done it with him but who else would I have released with? Reese had to have known that this was a one off. I quickly shook my hair out convincing myself that nothing more would come of it. Ever! I was definitely sure of that!

Asia was still blissfully asleep in her bed. I was thankful that she hadn't woken in the night and seen her parents hugged up together like two loving parents should instead of the frosty reception which we normally embraced each others presence with. I carefully shut her bedroom door trying not to disturb her so early, allowing myself to have a few more hours to myself. The more I analysed the situation that I had gotten myself involved with and what Reese had said about Shantel, I felt guilty. I felt sorry for her. She obviously loved Reese, she proved that by standing by him like he was the last man on earth. The break up would have surely been hard for her and hearing that she had moved out, wow! I know if that was me Reese would have to be the one moving out. There would be no way I would leave my home that I had lived in for the past couple of years. No way! There must be more to this story than what he is saying.

I walked around the scene which witnessed the passionate session a few hours before, retrieving the evidence and stripping the bed down. There was no way I could sleep on those sheets tonight, the smell of Reese was everywhere. I smiled thinking about the sensations he gave me last night. Why did he have to be the one, my perfect fit! He knew everything about my body and how to please it. That was his advantage. I was not going to let him fool me again. I have to be careful with this situation. There was no way this could become anything more than what it was last night. A few hours later and Asia was awake, her peaceful face resembled her father so much. I bent down to give her a kiss as she looked up at me reminding me of the love which conceived her. The love which I had revisited a few hours ago. I hastily prepared her breakfast, putting the washing machine on in the process just as my phone began to ring.

"Hello"

"Morning beautiful"

I closed my eyes as a hot sensation went trough my body. I didn't want to have this involuntary reaction, this was not good! I walked out of the kitchen, not wanting Asia to overhear the conversation as kids have a habit of repeating things they were not meant to hear.

"Morning, what do you want?"

"Wow, did you wake up on the wrong side of the bed? Look I just wanted to see if you was alright. I didn't want to wake you when I left because you looked so sexy sleeping"

I smiled, knowing that he always had a way with his words that would make me blush. Come on Leyah keep focused!

"I didn't want you to think that what I was saying was bull! I'm serious"

"Okay, just stop there. What happened last night was a one off and it is not going to happen again. You fulfilled your purpose and lets just leave it at that! It was a favour which I needed and you obliged. Thank you. Now let's just move on and go back to how we were before"

"I beg your pardon! Are you trying to tell me you used me? Leyah I don't believe that for a moment!" He said with sarcasm.

"Listen to what I'm saying. It is not going to happen again. So leave it. Don't mention it again!"

"Fine! But you know I love you. I always have"

I tried not to let his words weaken my heart. Reese was still Reese and I had to remember where we had come from and how we had ended up like this. Everything he tried to say in his defence I cut him down, nothing was going to penetrate me anymore. Maybe Reese was sincere in what he said last night, but I was not ready for this. He was not ready for this and there is no way I am going to let him hurt me again. One time was enough for me. I've had enough of men now for a lifetime. They were only good for one thing and I received that thing last night.

Chapter 34.

Reese

Yes the wall had finally come crumbling down. I knew it was only a matter of time. All I had to do was wait for the right moment and the time was last night! As much as she tried to deny it I knew she still wanted me. She can never resist me, no matter how hard she tries to move on, she can't. I'm the best man she has ever had and will ever have! Yeah back in the day I enjoyed being a playa. I wanted the best of all worlds. When one woman pissed me off I would just go to the next. I wanted a comfortable life. But then I met Leyah and she changed it all. I had to deal with all these 'emotions'. They were foreign to me and when she got pregnant I felt something which I had never experienced before… a sense to protect her and my child, but that didn't work out how I planned! Shantel made sure of that!

I know I often don't make the right decisions, but I had to do what was best for me back then or else I wouldn't be as successful as I am now. But now, last night made me realise that I almost lost a great thing. Those strange intensifying emotions are back and I think that I love her and there is no way that I am going to lose her again. I have to make this work, but I have no idea how to. Leyah has made it clear that it is not going to go further than last night, but I know her weakness is me and what I laid down on her last night, she will be yearning me for weeks. She will soon pick up her phone asking for more. If not I will just have to use dirty tactics!

Shantel leaving was pure drama, she mashed up most of the house in an angered rage. Calling me a bastard, a liar, telling me how much she hated me. Yeah she was right, I had been all those things to her I admit that. But sometimes to be successful in life you have to hurt people along the way. She was not for me. Living with her became utter torture.

I got fed up with her pestering me for sex, trying to impregnate herself. Accusing me of shit! I had been trapped with her for long enough. Finally my business is doing well. I had built up my clients and I didn't need her extra stress. I mean yeah I know being with Leyah might be worse, I did her wrong in the past and I will have to live with that for the rest of my life, but I am truly sorry for that and I want to prove it to her. I'm getting older now and I know where I want to be. I hate not being with my baby girl everyday. She deserves two parents constantly.

This is the right thing to do. I will prove it to her…

Chapter 35.

Janet

I looked on as Marcus took his son carefully out of the car seat. I wanted to fade away and disappear, this was the first time I was seeing his little baby. I don't know if I can handle this just yet. What if the baby was a spitting image of him? What if he had the same smile?

My Marcus is a father!

Marcus looked on with pride admiring his little creation. I could tell that he was ecstatic. He was definitely a proud father, gleaming with joy.

"Jay, look at him. Look at my little boy. I can't believe I'm a dad"

"Neither can I" I struggled, faced with the reality of my mistake, my ultimate sacrifice. He raised the baby out of his coat and handed him towards me.

"Oh no, I can't. I don't like holding babies"

"Jay, shut up. Hold him while I sort this out"

I stretched out my hands and carefully took hold of four week old baby Joshua Cruz Walters. Jasmine had wanted to name him after a celebrity baby but Marcus was dead against it, there was no way he would have his son looking like a 'wanna be' celebrity with some ridiculous name. So Cruz ended up as his middle name, much to her disapproval. Joshua blinked out of his sleep and looked up at me with his bright grey eyes which startled me.

"Wow, where did he get these bright grey eyes from?"

"I have no idea. I suppose Jasmine has white in her family. When we noticed them she gathered it must have been a throw back from somewhere"

I remained impartial, analyzing baby Josh noticing that his skin was also much fairer than that of his parents and despite what Marcus said he had not one feature of his. Why was I looking into this so deep? This jealousy thing is really getting out of hand now. I'm being too critical.

"He is cute Marcus"

"Yeah he is. Just like his dad. I thought I better bring him out to come and see his Auntie Janet, seeing as she hasn't made the effort as yet. Plus Jasmine needed some rest. He wakes up exactly every three hours! Without fail screaming for food"

"That's why I'm not ready for this whole baby malarkey anytime soon!"

We both laughed.

"Jay, you better hurry up, you know the old biological clock is ticking"

"Shut up you! So how is everything going apart from little man keeping you up at night?"

"You know, it is actually quite good. I love being a father Jay. I mean Joshua just keeps me going. I look at him and feel so proud. That's my son. That's a piece of me! I'm up making bottles, changing his nappy, bathing him and it feels great. I never actually thought that it would be with someone like Jasmine though. I always thought that maybe…"

His eyes began to wander around the room clearly showing a sense of reluctance which he tried to disguise by quickly stopping in mid sentence and changing the subject. "…But anyway, how's things with you?"

"Marcus continue with what you were saying"

"Nah it's cool. It's cool. Jasmine just keeps doing really strange things. She didn't even want me to bring him over. Asking me a number of questions like where you going? Why you taking him out? What time you going to be back? I mean he is my son too. I felt like I was in the dock! It's like she doesn't want me to take him to see my people she just wants to show him off to her people! I'm not accepting it Jay!"

"Don't worry, she is just being an over protective mother"

I tried to be the good friend and ease his mind but it was suspicious behaviour. Something wasn't right. Marcus sat and talked for a further few hours before Leyah and Keshia came round wanting to have a look at the new addition. Coming to gloat in my face about what I had lost and what could have been mine. When they arrived they both began fussing over the baby wanting to hold him. It was nice when they were this young. I just wished that they stayed like this forever. I loved the smell of babies, they had this nice natural baby smell which gave me a feeling of security and protection. I t always made me want to squeeze them closer. Baby Josh seemed like a natural ladies man, just like his dad. He was happy being treated like a prized possession as he was passed around making not one disapproving sound. We sat in my conservatory drinking cocktails as the rays from the sun warmed up the room. The conversation was all about fatherhood as we bombarded Marcus with questions. Keshia being extra nosey and inconsiderate to my feelings opened her big mouth and asked if he was getting any sex yet since Jasmine gave birth!

"What, don't all look at me like that! I'm just curious! How long do you have to wait?"

Trust Keshia!

"Nope I'm not, well not just yet. She had a C-section. I was disappointed with that but she was adamant that she didn't want to go through the tribulations of a natural child birth. Said some foolishness about she wanted to look as good as Victoria Beckham after she gave birth!"

We all burst out laughing almost spitting out our drinks in the process.

"Where did you find her from again! You sure do pick em!"

"Tell me about it!"

I looked on adoring Marcus as he fed the baby his bottle. He was so natural at it, who would have thought it! My heart bled as I watched on wishing that it was our baby that our friends had come to adore because we were the proud married parents to this little gem. But it was not, I was no where near being a mother, let alone being with a partner. We all sat talking and having a laugh, talking about the good old days and the days which were ahead. It was not a future that I was looking forward to. I had always hoped that one day I would be sharing it as Mrs Walters. That dream was now far beyond my reach because of my own personal fears of rejection and loss. I had lost the best thing in my life to a self absorbed, money grabbing chicken head. It was the hardest thing I have ever had to accept. It wasn't only that I couldn't have him, but I knew he could do a lot better. I returned back to the conversation with a fake smile on my face pretending that I was okay, trying to hide the thoughts that burdened my head. Keshia looked at me then at the baby she was holding in her arms. I knew that look and that look was thinking the same thing as I was earlier. His baby was beautiful but why was he so pale with grey eyes and light brown hair. Neither of us said a word as Marcus looked elated and we were all happy for him. He was happy. We just shared discrete glances not wanting to spoil his joy and enjoyed the rest of the evening.

Chapter 36.

Marcus

I drove into the driveway noticing an unfamiliar silver BMW M6 Convertible parked in my spot. Curiosity engulfed my mind as I parked up next to it, giving me a feeling of unease. I looked at Joshua who was sleeping comfortably in his seat, innocence beaming from his little face. Reality adorned on me every time I looked at my son. I was responsible for this little life and ensuring that I protect him with everything that I have. He was now the most important thing to me, nothing else seemed to matter. Everything that happened in my life previously seemed so insignificant now. This is what life is about. Being happy!

I unlocked the door, stepping into the house hearing the sounds of an unfamiliar male voice talking with Jasmine. I walked along the wooden floorboards, quietly creeping into the lounge holding Josh in his car seat. As soon as the door moved Jasmine spotted me and jumped, clearly startled at my entrance. The owner of the unfamiliar voice turned around immediately to see what had interrupted their discussion. Looking at me standing in the doorway he sized me up with his eyes.

"Oh, baby your back already" I could hear the trembles in her voice which indicated that I had stepped into something which she didn't want me to uncover.

"Yes! Is that a surprise for you?"

"No... it's just that urmm... I didn't expect you. I mean I didn't hear you come in"

I looked towards her suspiciously, then towards the stranger in my house sitting on my sofa with a glass of Brandy in his hand. I looked back at Jasmine my eyes demanding an explanation.

"Oh... baby urmm... this is Ty. He is a friend of mine from Youdas"

"Where?"

"Oh you know, that little public relations firm I worked for a while back before you and I"

As I racked my head, the unexpected guest reached for a hand shake. His face looked awfully familiar. I set the car seat down carefully before raising my hand out of respect to comply with the gesture.

"Oh, well Ty just stopped round quickly as he was in the area. Actually he was just about to leave" She looked at him with a look which begged him to go along with it. "Wasn't you Ty?"

He quickly caught on to the unsubtle hint. "Oh...yeah!"

I looked at his glass still half full. He quickly downed the rest of the brown liquid before raising himself out of his more than comfortable position. "Urmm, nice meeting you. Jasmine, we must catch up again soon"

My blood began to boil as realisation struck me in the stomach. As Ty stood up fully he looked me in the eye with an expression which made my body turn cold before looking down at Joshua briefly, then heading towards the front door. Jasmine quickly got up and followed him. I stood frozen with anger, my fists clenched, unable to move. What the hell was this man doing in my house and why was Jasmine acting so guilty! A thousand answers went around in my head, trying not to let two plus two equal four! Jasmine reluctantly entered back into the room trying to hide the situation which was just before my eyes, focusing on Joshua like it didn't happen.

"Oh my pumpkin. Look at him sleeping, I better go and lay him down in his crib"

"I don't think so Jasmine. We need to talk!"

"Baby talk about what? Has he been good?" Her voice trembled once again.

"Like who the fuck was that man in my house?" I said trying to be calm and not let the arising anger take over.

She laughed uncomfortably. "Why are you swearing babe. Don't be silly, he is just an old friend!"

Anger enraged within me, irritated at the fact that she was playing games and treating me like an absent minded fool!

"Don't fucking piss me off! Why the raass does my child resemble this man Jasmine?"

"What are you talking about babe?"

"Stop bloody playing games. I come into my house to see some red skin man sitting on my chair comfortably with light brown hair and grey fucking eyes. What do you mean you don't know what I'm talking about?"

"Look Marcus, it's not what you think" She pleaded.

"Oh yes it is!"

"Baby, he just came round and I just... I just!" She started crying and becoming hysterical, but I was determined to get an answer.

"Don't do the bawling Jasmine it's not going to work this time. Why the fuck does my son look like this man?"

She fell to the floor unable to compose herself. "I'm so sorry, I'm so sorry!... I didn't know"

"Don't fucking play me like that. You knew alright! You fucking knew and you brought that man into my house! Into my fucking house! Are you out of your mind? Well you must be, you must!"

"Please Marcus, listen to me… I didn't mean to…I didn't know. I just thought that maybe…maybe, he would have been yours"

"You thought! You fucking thought! Don't make me laugh! How could you not have known? How long were you going to lie to me? You evil bitch!"

"Please Marcus don't. I made a mistake!"

"A mistake! That's an understatement. I am the one who made the mistake. Thank God I didn't marry you. I just knew something wasn't right. Everyone knew it"

"I love you. I love you Marcus. Please don't punish me for this!"

"Punish you? I don't give a damn about you! You didn't think about me. Why should I give a damn about you!"

"Let me explain please"

"There is nothing to explain. Pack your shit and leave!"

"What? Leave? I have no where to go. You can't kick us out. What about our baby?"

"Our baby is not *OUR* baby. It's *YOUR* baby, *YOUR's* and that fucking Ty you had sitting in my house drinking my fucking Brandy! You better go and call his arse! Why would you do this?"

I looked down at Joshua stirring in his sleep. My son who I had loved for the past month was not my son. I had been deceived in the worst way. I wanted to crumble up and cry. I loved this little boy. Jasmine had kicked me right in my gut! I knew Josh didn't look anything like me but I didn't want to accept the truth. I had hoped that it was a throw back gene like she had said. It was possible after all. But now everything was so much clearer. I had been played!

What am I supposed to do now?

Chapter 37.

Keshia

I was pacing around the flat waiting for Bobby to come back home, thinking of how to approach this situation. The twit had accidentally picked up the wrong mobile this morning! I told him it would cause problems in the future having the same phone but that was me being paranoid of my own wrong coming to light. Luckily for me I had erased all evidence out of my electronic time bomb. But Bobby, Bobby wasn't as smart. If you're going to do wrong make sure you cover your tracks!

My blood was boiling and my heart rate was racing. I was fuming! Initially I didn't realise that he had taken my phone this morning until I heard it ringing. That was not my ringtone! This bastard was really taking the piss, he was really taking me for a fool! I thought we had overcome all the past fuckries which he used to carry on with but obviously not! I just knew it, I knew it! I knew my instincts were right, but I never thought the pain would ripple through my body like it did. I was handicapped by what I had seen. How was I going to approach this now! Fuck this shit there was no way I was going to take anymore of this again!

I stormed into the bedroom and reached up for the suitcase Bobby had just returned with. Rage driving my actions I opened all of his drawers and furiously threw all his belongings into the case. Recklessly some of his clothes lay scattered everywhere. I just wanted his stuff gone. As I grabbed his trousers and blazers out of the wardrobe something dropped out of one of the pockets landing on the floor. I stopped dead in my tracks and looked carefully… there was no way that I was seeing what I was actually seeing!... It was true, fucking bastard! Tears ferociously escaped down my eyes making my mascara bleed and run down my cheeks. I was here once again!

How could he do this to me again! Doesn't he learn? Well I definitely do!

I continued determined, grabbing as many things of his as I could, filling up a couple black bags in the process! I was so angry shifting through his shit. I managed to throw his toothbrush and shaving stuff in one of the bags before stopping in my tracks as I heard the door opening…

"What are you doing?" Came the shocked voice.

"Take your fucking shit and fuck off out of my life!"

"Kesh, what's going on?"

"Don't play dumb with me don't take me for no fool Bobby. Is this what you came back for?" I threw his phone at him viciously, hoping it would hit him in his head leaving him unconscious, but I missed!

"Look talk to me"

"Oh, now you want to talk you nasty dirty fucking tramp! I should have never listened to your lies! Take me for a raass fool yeah! Look at this" I threw the object which had dropped out of his pocket. "Yeah explain this now!"

Bobby looked on in shock, speechless not knowing where to start or how to even start!

"Look, it's not what you…"

"Save it! I'm not stupid, for once in your life be a fucking man and own up to it! Tell the bloody truth Bobby! You can't even do that can you! You don't even have any respect for me, don't you think you owe me that much!" I walked up to his face shouting in anger, wanting to hit him but not letting him get the better of me. He stood silently with the sonogram photo in his hand. Watching on as I threw his belongings at him.

"I'm sorry. Kesh I love you and I'm sorry"

287

"Sorry doesn't cut it anymore. You mean to tell me all this time you been running around with that make-up bitch until you get her fucking pregnant! When were you going to tell me Bobby? Huh?"

"Look I'm not even sure if it is mine. She slept with a few of us up there!"

"Oh, and that makes it okay! You bloody slept with this bitch with NO protection and you come back here and stick your dick in me! Urgh. You know what fuck you Bobby!"

"Babe it's not like that! I used a condom but it broke… and she just kept bothering me. I don't want her"

"Well you better change your mind, coz I don't want you! She can bloody have you! And to think you had her flaunting up in my face knowing that you had slept with her! Oh my gosh, it all makes perfect sense now! That's why you were so jumpy at the airport!"

"No, no it wasn't that!"

"Save it. Come out of my face" I pushed past him and went to open the front door.

"Kesh, please don't do this. Let me explain! Babes I love you. Please. Please"

"Get out!" I screamed.

"Kesh!"

"I don't want to ever see you again! Let someone else put up with this shit! I'm not doing it!"

He looked on remorseful, remorseful to the fact that he had been caught. He saw in my eyes that I was not playing and it was not the time to try and make amends. He stopped and picked up his suitcase trying to close it shut. I eagerly looked on with pain tearing through my soul that I had to go through this again! He took each bag out to his car until the final bag was left. He turned round and apologised once again, which was met by frosty silence as I stood in the corridor. His plea was not going to work this time. He walked out the door with his keyboard in his hand placing the key to the flat on the table, knowing that there were not any reprisals he could make for his big fuck up this time. He turned and walked out of my life once again with his head hung low! This time I knew it would be for good. As the sound of the door shut behind him I broke down crying. Not knowing if it was out of happiness that I had finally been able to let go or if it was that I was going to miss him. All I knew was that this was the start to a new beginning.

Chapter 38.

Marcus

After strong deliberations with myself I knew it wasn't right to kick Jasmine and the baby out. I mean he was practically my son, I love him. I had raised him thinking he was my own. Now that the truth was out it didn't excuse my behaviour to act irrational. I'm not that cold hearted to do a wicked thing like that. I know what I have to do for Joshua's sake, it wasn't his fault that his mother is a lying cheating tramp! Hate over shadowed any bit of feelings or thoughts what I had for Jasmine, she was the cause of this unbearable pain ripping through my heart right now, because of her promiscuous ways my house was no longer a home.

I gathered my suitcase with my most needed items and carried my holdall with a few suits. I was not going to come back here until she was gone. I exited the master bedroom and walked straight in the direction of Joshua's room where she was sitting crying. I felt nothing. I felt no pity, no sorry for her, just nothing. She brought this on herself. Entering the room with my luggage in tow, she noticed me and looked up with her swollen makeup smudged eyes, trying to beg for sympathy but it was met with my cold blank stare that said nothing.

"Look, I'm not doing this for you. But I'll leave. You just make sure you're out of here within the next week and don't take anything apart from what you brought in here!"

"But Marcus you don't have to do this" She blurted out, pleading with the unreasonable. "We can make this work"

"Don't say a word. It's just poor Josh I feel sorry for. If you are not out within a week I will have you legally removed. Don't play with me"

She started her bawling again with her hands in her face. It hurt me to leave my son, my boy. I loved him so much but I cannot do this. She had lied to me for over a year and the truth was he wasn't mine. His real father was in my house today and no matter how hard I tried to forget that image, everything of Josh was him. I walked up to his Moses basket and looked on him, silently sleeping without a care in the world. His little chest rising as he breathed his small hands curled in a fist. My first born. I gently bent down and gave him a kiss as a lone tear rolled out of my eye. I gave him one last look before turning and walking down the stairs, ignoring the desperate pleas from Jasmine.

The front door shut behind me and I felt like my world was over!

I had no direction anymore.

I was lost.

I pressed the remote key and unlocked the car. Throwing my suitcase in the boot I jumped in the driver's seat not knowing where I was going to go. There was no way I could go to mum's I couldn't deal with her mouth right now. I sat in silence with my eyes filling with water, not knowing what to do next. I better just book into a hotel for the night and figure something out. I've given her a week and if she knows what is good for her she better be out way before then.

Shit! How did I let this woman pull the wool over my eyes! How did I let her fool me like this? That bitch! I slammed my fists onto the steering wheel enraged. My fatherhood had been stolen from me. A piece of me had been ripped out. I was no longer complete.

Chapter 39.

Janet

I jumped up out of my sleep hearing the desperate sounds of the door bell ringing. It was twelve thirty in the morning, who would be crazy enough to be banging my door down at this time? I threw on my dressing gown and rushed to the door where I was greeted by the shadow which I knew all to well. As I opened the door the heartbroken, confused face pushed past me in desperation for solace.

"Marcus, what's wrong?"

He looked up at me with tears in his eyes then he broke down on his knees. I didn't know what to do. I had never seen him like this before. Never! What on earth could have happened to make him react this way? I knew it only had to be something serious. Very serious! I stood there and cradled his head while he held on to my legs, releasing what he needed to let out.

"Marcus, hun talk to me"

It was difficult at first to understand what he was trying to say but through his despair and visible pain I deciphered that Jasmine was the cause. What has that woman done now to have broken him down like this? After twenty minutes I had managed to calm him down. Helping him off his knees I ushered him into the front room to take a seat. He sat for a while shaking his head in disbelief, but I was still unaware to what had disturbed him like this and altered his composition. His reaction was now beginning to scare me. Finally he began to talk…

"Janet, you were right. Everyone was right. I tried to do the right thing, I did and look werc it got me!"

"Babes, what are you talking about?"

He took a deep breath before continuing "My son, Jay! My son! That bitch lied to me. He isn't mine!"

My breath stopped in my throat not wanting to understand the words that had just escaped his mouth, but before I could respond he continued clearly shocked.

"I went home and this man was sitting all up in my house Jay. Jasmine started acting strange and then I looked on this man and he looks just like Josh! She lied to me Jay. The bitch made me think that he was my son, fully knowing that he wasn't. I almost married her Jay!... Josh isn't mine!" He buried his hands in his head grieved.

Oh my gosh! I didn't know what to say, what does he mean Joshua wasn't his? How could she do this?

"Babes, don't worry, don't worry" Was all I could say. I hated seeing him in so much pain. Marcus loved this little boy and then to find out that the baby you knew as your own was not yours! Damn, what could I possibly say to make him feel better! I couldn't turn back the hands of time. All I could do was comfort him in his time of need and let him release.

"How could she do this? I knew she was no good. I knew it. But I had to be there for her and the baby! She knew that he wasn't mine, she must have known from the beginning! She wasn't even going to tell me Jay... imagine if I hadn't come home and seen this dude in my house she would have led me on for how many more years!"

"Marcus, you didn't do anything stupid did you?" The thought triggered in my head, like a light bulb had just switched on. I knew Marcus had a temper on him at times and a situation like this could easily make the calmest person react irrationally. The adrenaline rush would just take over! Just imagine seeing a next man up in your house, looking like *your* baby! Damn!

"I didn't do anything. He got up and left. I was so mad, I just told her to pack her shit and leave but then I couldn't put her out on the streets with Josh. It wasn't right. I told her to be out within the week. I'm going to book into a hotel."

"Don't be silly, you can stay here. I'm not going to let you stay in a hotel!"

Marcus tried to decline my offer but there was no way I was going to let him stay in some hotel when I had more than enough space. I couldn't believe what that bitch had done. I tried to warn him, something just wasn't right with that woman! I just knew he was too good for her. But I would have never thought that she would do something as calculated as this! I sat and listened as Marcus told me the whole situation and what he intended to do about it. I could see the pain he was feeling right now and I wished I could just reach in and take it all out for him, but I couldn't. From the moment he arrived at my house his phone was constantly vibrating. He slowly reached over to his jacket and threw the phone on the floor. As it impacted with my wooden floor it shattered into pieces. It was clear that Jasmine was trying to call him, wanting to beg for forgiveness. Now was definitely not the right time for her lies. What could she possibly say to make him forgive her? This is something which is unforgivable! This was like a talk show! This never really happens in real life does it? Yes it did, because it was right here on my best friend's door step making him look all vulnerable and lost. What was he going to tell people? How would he ever overcome this?

Chapter 40.

Leyah

I walked up to unlock the front door trying to rush whilst trying to ignore Asia's whining and little tantrum. I fumbled for my key when I heard this male voice behind me. I turned around and was greeted by a young ginger haired spotty delivery guy holding a large bouquet of red and white roses. Obviously he must have the wrong address, there was no way these flowers were for me.

"Excuse me are you Leyah Rogers?" He continued.

"Yes I am"

"Then these are for you"

The young delivery boy handed me the bouquet of flowers. Asia looked on intrigued with her pushed up face. I was only glad that it had managed to calm her down. I signed and watched the delivery guy rush back into his van, speeding off to his next delivery. Anticipation came over me and I couldn't wait to get into the house and open the card. Who would send me such a lovely bouquet? I rushed Asia up to her room, unimpressed with her behaviour. Following the reprimand she stomped her little feet all the way up the stairs. Fortunate for her my mood had been calmed by this beautiful surprise. I laid the flowers down as I searched the back of the sink cupboard for my only vase which I hadn't used in a long time, in fact the last time it had any usage must have been after I gave birth to Asia. I carefully took off the card before unwrapping the subtle pale lilac outer packaging of the flowers and arranged them in the vase. The aroma which the they released was breath taking. I had forgotten how lovely fresh flowers smelt. Enchanted by the scent I picked up the card and slowly read the message…

"Because you're special. I Love you and miss you. R"

I inhaled. I should have guessed! Reese was trying his hardest to wear me down. Since my mistake which led to our night together over a week ago, he had been constantly trying to prove to me that he was trying to change. He consistently called telling me that he wanted to be with us, to be a family and how much he loves me. But I couldn't let all his talk distort my judgement and throw all my senses out of the window just because he thinks he has had this sudden epiphany. Reese will always be the epitome of a playa! And that was not what I needed in my life. Fair enough people can change but Reese can't change. Look at him. He got rid of one woman and now he wants to replace her as quick as he can. No way, it will not be me! I mean he hasn't even waited for her side of the bed to get cold! What kind of man does that! Only Reese! Yeah I thought about it, I thought about actually being a family unit for Asia's sake but there was too much to lose. There was no way I was going to lose my sanity again! He broke me down to a place I never want to visit again! If I let him back I would be condoning his behaviour. Disagreeing with myself. But what about Asia? She needs her father.

He can't change!

But what if he could?

Chapter 41.

Keshia

I sunk in the bed trying to drown out my sorrows with a bottle of Remy. I hadn't spoken to the girls in a few days because I was strategically missing their calls. I couldn't face it all right now. Bobby was gone and I had boxed up the rest of his belongings. It still hurt that he had done this to me again! The fact that he had got another girl pregnant was just all too much for me. There was more to think about than my wounded pride. He had put my life at risk again and I could never forgive him for that. Luckily for him my check up at the clinic came back all clear! Thank God for that! Some may say I got what I deserved, because I had cheated on him as well. But his actions were worse; he had gone that step further and got another girl pregnant. There was no need for him to cheat on me this time, I had trusted him and before he left for filming he had promised to make it work. More fool me for listening to that. Yeah my mind was on Kamarni at the time, but that was different. I hadn't been physical with him by then. As much as I may have lusted and adored him, I had been faithful, so to speak. Bobby's unfaithfulness had been calculated! The bitch had smiled in my face with her fake self, telling me how great he was! I just knew she was talking about more than just his acting!

My life was a rollercoaster at the moment and I didn't know when it was going to end. Nothing seemed to be going right. Kyle had been low key after his 'madness' with Kerry's baby father. Unfortunately after he had received a few broken bones and bruised ribs he decided not to hold his beating like a man, he reported it to the police, giving them my brother's name as one of his attackers. Then Kamarni had been a bit distant lately because his woman had been off work for a few weeks. That meant that I was all by myself and I was sure feeling it! Jealousy overpowered my senses. Kamarni had the best of both worlds while I was now left out in the cold. I was not his main priority. I was not anyone's main priority anymore. It was lonely. I had no one to talk to! No one to put a smile on my face, no one to hold me close in their arms while we giggled together, nothing! I had wallowed in my misery for too long, allowing it to take over. I didn't want to do anything. What did I do wrong?

A few hours passed as I sat in my house clothes tucked up in my bed for another day, sporting un kempt hair, listening to some reggae music, trying not to hear any soppy tunes. I took a large gulp of the Remy, succumbing to the feeling before I was disturbed by a phone call. It sat vibrating on the floor as I contemplated whether to answer it but my inner self gave in as I realised people must be worried about me by now. I looked at the flashing screen and saw that it was Kamarni calling. Finally he was returning my call after I had rung him last night in my moment of weakness, but I hung up disappointed after receiving the greeting of his answer phone. I was in two minds whether to accept the call recognising that I sounded like crap. I watched the phone as it continued to vibrate. I knew it would be wrong for me not to answer, it wasn't his fault for all this and I needed a bit of cheering up.

"Hi"

"Keshia, are you okay? You sounded a bit upset in your message last night?"

The sound of his caring voice made a lump form in my throat, forcing back the tears I replied.

"Yeah, I'm fine" I lied, but it didn't last for long. The lie itself made me realise the truth and I broke down and started crying, telling him everything, from how Bobby had introduced me to this woman who I now found out may be carrying his child, to kicking him out of my flat. Kamarni was speechless. He didn't know what to say, but he tried his best to give me some words of comfort so that I wouldn't do anything irrational. I don't know whether he was thinking about me or the implications this would have on himself, but I could hear the fear in his voice.

298

"Do you want me to meet you later?"

I paused and thought about this carefully. Kamarni was my breath of fresh air and it may do me some good to see him considering I hadn't seen him in the past two weeks. I needed to feel wanted right now. For someone to hold me close and tell me that it would be alright. But my mind was racing a hundred thoughts. I needed to make Kamarni mine now, there was nothing stopping me. Nothing at all in my way. It was just for him to realise that here is where he needed to be. Bobby wasn't good for me and I knew this, but having Kamarni in my life was where it felt right. Yeah he has a woman but that's not my problem. I'm going to get mine.

"Yeah that would be good" I replied, smiling with my thoughts.

Chapter 42.

Janet

He looked so hopeless laying on the bed lost in his thoughts. I stood and watched him, waiting for him to reply with a lack of urgency.

"Jay, what did I do wrong? I was good to her. I didn't cheat on her after we became 'official'. Why?"

This was not the answer to if he wanted a cup of coffee. I slowly entered the room thinking about what I could say to make him feel better, to help put that beautiful smile back on his face, but nothing came to mind. The situation was so deep that nothing could make it go away. I sat on the edge of the bed reaching out to touch the long back which I often had indecent thoughts about.

"Babes, you did nothing wrong. She is just a self absorbed inconsiderate woman who only thought about herself. Some people just don't think about how the impact will effect others. Don't let her defeat you"

Marcus turned around and looked up at me with a determined look in his brown eyes. There was no spark but a glimmer of hope.

"Your right. I've got to get on with it. She is the one who lost out, forget her. I think I will have that cup of coffee now babe" He smiled.

I was happy that he was finally making some progress. He had been at my house for three days now, avoiding the world. He hadn't even gone to work because he didn't know how to answer peoples meddling questions about how he was coping with fatherhood. Even his mum had called wanting to know what was going on because she had been calling his house looking for him. To her surprise and contribution to a false heart attack, Jasmine had scornfully told her that he had left. Although Marcus was close with his mum, he just didn't want to explain it to her at the moment and pleaded with me to fill her in. I obliged doing the best I could with the understanding that I had gained over the past few days. As soon as I told his mum the story I could hear the anger down the phone but I knew by the tone in her voice that she was thinking '*good riddance to bad rubbish*'. She had never really liked Jasmine. In fact no one did, they just tolerated her for the sake of Marcus and the baby. But now that the baby was not his, there was no need to hold back.

I walked back up the stairs with Marcus coffee in my hand. Reaching the top we unexpectedly bumped into each other as he exited the bathroom, with nothing hiding his modesty but a black towel clinging to his waist. Steam escaped from the bathroom, tantalising my senses and making the moment seem more romantic than it was.

"Oh sorry" I uttered as his wetness touched my arm. A sensual look passed his eyes in response.

"It's me that should be saying sorry. I thought I'd better get up and get ready for work"

I looked on in total awe. I had forgotten how sexy he was but now his nakedness stared at me, enticing involuntary reactions within. I watched on a little too intensely as water dripped off his chest. Oh how I wanted to lick those beads off with my tongue. Marcus moved to the side, interrupting my indecent thoughts and making my heart rate slow down.

"Is that my coffee? Thanks"

I handed him the mug, forgetting that I had been holding it all this time. Closing my mouth I watched his firm buttocks walk off into the guest room. He was surely one fine specimen, how on earth did I ever let him get away! Why on earth would Jasmine need to cheat on him and produce a child, silly woman! Well at least I can appreciate why she would have tried to hold on to him and lie. Not that I condone her behaviour, but I can see that she knew he was the bomb and no woman should ever willingly give 'that' up! I recovered from the unexpected interaction, turning to retreat into my bedroom to finish getting ready for work, but I was all dishevelled. I couldn't think straight. Marcus had me all hot and bothered for intimacy. I put on my clothes wondering what it felt like to be all up and personal with him again. How his skin would feel next to mine, reunited. I stood with my eyes closed reminiscing on the night we shared. Reliving the moment and wishing the moment was right here again. I would enter his room and whip off that towel, while he devoured my body with kisses. Passion racing, our bodies interlocking and heart beats thumping. Knock, knock… I jumped out of my thoughts, grabbing for my blouse as I instructed him to enter.

"Jay, look thanks for letting me stay here. I just wondered if you had anything planned for Sunday evening because I want to cook you dinner, just to say thanks. You're a good friend and I appreciate you so much. You've put up with a lot from me"

"Don't be silly babes, that's what friends are for"

"I know, but you would do anything for me and I love you for that"

My heart melted as he spoke, sincerity escaping his tone. I looked down blushing.

"It's nothing, believe me. You're my friend for ever. I will always be here for you. Sunday's good, I have nothing planned"

I just uttered the last word when he came towards me raising his hands towards my neck. My heart stopped, silently hoping that he would reach across and hold me in a tight embrace, placing his lips on mine while I tasted his smooth lips, but to my disappointment he took his strong hands and un-tucked my collar. I let out an uncomfortable laugh, not wanting him to notice that I was secretly wishing for something else.

"See and you can't do without me. You can't even get dressed without my assistance! So Sunday is booked then"

I looked at him disgruntled but amused at his commentary. I love this man so much.

Chapter 43.

Keshia

My heart was racing in my chest anticipating his arrival. I had given Kamarni my full address this time. I wasn't in the mood to go any where and there was no point hiding my location anymore, I had nothing to worry about. Bobby was definitely not coming back into my life and Kamarni didn't fit the profile of a potential stalker. My only worry was making sure that I was looking my best, I needed some tonight. My body yearned to be touched by Kamarni. I hadn't seen him for a while and I wanted him to know exactly what he had been missing. I admired myself in the mirror looking at my strategic outfit. I stood wearing my red seductive Ann summers lingerie set, which I knew would get Kamarni's desire racing with one look. Pleased with what I saw I covered my nakedness with my red and white silk flowered dress, which gave that sensual seductive feel and made my silhouette look like a model. Everything was perfect. The strawberry scented candles were burning and my classic slow jam CD was playing. I was ready for seduction.

He walked through into the strange surroundings looking amazed at what he saw before him. He stopped and smiled, clearly taken a back by the backless dress and the sweet scent which paraded throughout the flat. Not wanting to let the mood digress I quickly embraced him in a tight hug. Holding him so close that he could feel my heart beating through the thin fabric, squeezing him as tight as my arms would allow, breathing in his scent, missing that manly smell. He mirrored my gesture for the first few minutes, then becoming tired of the restricted movements he let go. I released him, locking my lips with his passionately, trying to show to him how much I had missed him. As our lips engaged it somehow didn't feel the same, something was missing. I removed my lips feeling uneasy, retreating from the feeling of being desperate. Kamarni didn't say anything. He just had this blank smirk on his face and tried to put me at ease by caressing my arms. I tried to let the sensation filter through my body as I ushered him into the front room in an awkward silence. He submissively followed my shadow carrying a bottle of red wine in his free hand. I could tell that he felt uncomfortable being here. His body language spoke a thousand words. I saw the nervousness in his eyes, but he was trying to play it off cool trying not to show any apprehension. He grabbed my arm and turned me towards him, making my whole body twist with obedience.

"You look amazing by the way" He spoke breaking the brewing awkward silence with desire in his tone.

"Thanks" I beamed. At least all my effort wasn't wasted after all. He looked around cautiously before relaxing down on the edge of the sofa with his legs open. I looked on intrigued. All I wanted to do was hold him tight in my arms all night. I need to hold him close, smell his heat, feel his warm hands across my body, feel him inside of me. I handed him the bottle opener and he proceeded to open the bottle he brought with him, pouring us a glass each. Yes this was going to get the mood going, hopefully it would help him relax a bit. We sipped on the cheap wine which made him loosen up, allowing me to take advantage. We sat on the sofa and hugged up as he told me about his week. I listened attentively as he told me about the drama with his school friend, which made me roll in laughter. It was good to actually laugh about something after all the sadness I had experienced these past few weeks. This is what I loved about him. He could always put a smile on my face, soon making me forget my problems. I rested my head on his chest and gazed up into his eyes, I was lost. His locks hypnotised me as he moved. Noticing the lust in my eyes he grabbed the back of my head and kissed me with all the built up frustration he had inside him. I reacted, happy that he was giving me what I needed. Quickly I removed his shirt, kissing his firm chest and examining his strong torso. I wanted to show him everything tonight! I had to give it all I had. I stood up and gave him a full view of my dress before slowly and seductively raising it up above my hips and taking it off… stripping before his eyes… enticing him with every move I made. He abruptly stood up, unable to take the teasing anymore, grabbing me by the waist he pulled me onto his lap.

"You look so beautiful. I missed you so much" He whispered through his heavy breathing.

I fiddled with his trousers trying desperately to undo them while trying not to come across as eager. It finally gave in and he quickly removed the garment allowing me full access. I moved in and pleased him, watching him squirm with pleasure, guiding me with every stroke. He reached for the latex sheath out of his pocket, making sure that we were protected this time. As soon as it was on I jumped on him like a wild beast, desperately wanting to release my own sexual frustration ahead of his, wanting to get at least three orgasms before the moment ended. True to my expectation he obliged my need and on the third stroke we came together, harmonising our perfect symphony, right there on my sofa. The sofa where I once laid with the man I thought I loved, but being with Kamarni showed me that it was nothing but lust. Pretence. My need to hold on to something which was obviously no longer there!

We lay there holding onto each other, using each other as an escapism. Escaping from the realities of our lives, the real happenings of time. I knew that this was going to be difficult, but I just needed to have him in my life, for the rest of my life. He was perfect. We were perfect. His woman was a distant reflection in the horizon. She meant nothing to me. As long as I didn't think about her I would be able to get through this. I mean he is here for the taking and if he willingly lets me take him, that's not my fault. It's hers!

I positioned my head across his chest looking up at the ceiling. Kamarni was fast asleep in-between my sheets. I dared not move for fear of him waking up because I wanted him here, I wanted him to stay here until the sun woke him up. I slightly looked up at his peaceful face, feeling a little guilty that I was lying with someone else's man. I knew he wasn't really able to stay out all night because his missus would surely be expecting him to return home, but who am I to wake him up? Surely he should know that he is supposed to stay aware of the situation and not fall asleep. It's not my problem. I stopped thinking and let the sleep take control and guide my guilt to a land far away where my dreams were in control of my future and I sure hoped that it was a promising future that involved this fine man beside me.

305

Chapter 44.

Leyah

Reese had been coming round daily, dropping things off for Asia. I knew his little game he was trying to play. He was trying to win me over by submission. By getting Asia to get used to her fathers daily presence and then resenting me for not letting him be here. Ohh I hate him so much. Why couldn't he just leave the situation alone!

I sat down on the breakfast stool and rested my elbows on the table. The more I told him not to come, to stop doing what he was doing the more he tried harder. I was frustrated, I didn't know what to do. Mummy Pearl must be in on it too because she had been calling trying to get me to come round for Sunday dinner for the past two weeks. I loved his mum but I just didn't need to be at her dinner table with Reese, acting like nothing had ever happened. Why should I yield just because he has become this 'conscious being' now that he has broken another woman's heart and tossed her to the curb! I have to stick my ground... but the pressure is getting to me. Reese was one attractive man and he knew how to work is sex appeal! The night we shared rocked my world. It was what I needed and what I had forgotten. I felt like a woman again, but that was not what I needed! I need more than just sex! I need stability, love, commitment and definitely faithfulness. I can never trust Reese. Never! Seeing him was becoming uncomfortable because I knew he would be dropping his regular comments in regards to me giving him another chance. A chance to make it work. I took a deep breath realising that he would be coming to collect Asia in a few hours. I rubbed my face knowing that I had to mentally prepare myself for this encounter. The ice box stance was needed.

He stood confidently in the front room, watching me tidy away Asia's toys.

"Hey look, don't take this the wrong way. I'm not doing it for any praises but Asia mentioned that you've been a bit stressed lately. Well that's s not exactly how she put it but I took it that way. So while you got some free time on your hands while she is with me, I thought you should relax"

I turned and looked at him offended! "Excuse you?"

"I know, she's going through the late terrible two's at the moment. So I took the liberty and booked a spa day for you and two friends. Here"

He handed me a small gold envelope while I looked on bewildered! Damn he was good. These are the things that made me fall in love with him in the first place, the nice spontaneous romantic gestures! He knew I was a sucker for these things. The ice wall slowly melted...

"Look, I'm not accepting this. I don't need you to do anything for me!"

"Stop being so stubborn! Go and relax yourself, you deserve it! I don't expect anything. I'm just showing my appreciation"

"Appreciation for what?"

"For being such a great mother. You do a great job"

I just looked at him blankly and kissed my teeth before calling for Asia to hurry up. Yes I would take the gift because he was right I did need it and who am I to turn down such a great gesture.

I waved them goodbye as they got into his car and drove off. I slowly walked back into the living room to search where I had thrown the envelope down in an attempt to act like I wasn't bothered in front of Reese. Finding it on the mantle place I opened it and looked at the details instantly noticing that the booking was at one of London's top spa's. Yes the girls would love this, this was going to be us tomorrow. He knew what his unscrupulous behaviour was planning. He wanted to try and get Janet and Keshia on his side as well. Two extra tickets huh! Who else would I take with me but them! Well we will sure take advantage of this situation. I picked up my mobile and dialled their numbers to tell them the exciting unexpected plans for tomorrow. We sat in the expensive luxurious spa excited, holding a glass of champagne, laying on our backs waiting for our massage therapists to arrive to give us the hot stone treatment. This was the life, Reese had done well. I needed to take advantage of this and I'm glad that I had.

"Wow, Reese sure pulled out all the stocks for this. You really need to reconsider getting back together" Keshia said impressed as she sat up to sip on the pricey champagne.

"Are you out of your mind? Have you forgotten the hell which he put me through?"

"Exactly Keshia, come on. Just because he bought her a few gifts, flowers and treated us all to this nice expensive spa trip it doesn't mean that she needs to instantly forgive him and jump into his arms. She at least needs to milk it for a bit longer!" Janet said sniggering.

"Well, I'm just saying! It's better the devil you know! And he looks like he has changed"

"Yeah, you should know that shouldn't you! I mean the amount of times you let Bobby get away with some shit you've become an automatic doormat!" I bitched.

"What! I have you know I am no longer with him actually!"

Janet and I both looked at each other shocked, rising up from our positions. When did that happen? How come she never told us?

"Keshia, what do you mean you are no longer together?" Janet asked concerned.

"Well, it's all long really. He slept with some woman when he was away. She is saying she's pregnant so I kicked him out. Not going to listen to his lies anymore, there has been one too many! I tried but he's not willing to change. That's what I mean when I say that you should give Reese a try. He is making a lot more effort!"

"How did you find out? Why are you so cool about it?" I asked ignoring her last comment.

"Look I'm past caring now. I needed a couple days to digest it all and get on with it. So I have done that now. I didn't tell you guys because I didn't need you all feeling sorry for me. I just had to deal with it on my own!"

"But we would have been there for you" Janet confessed, hurt that she didn't come to us.

"I know that's exactly what I didn't want! I needed to be there for myself "

We understood where she was coming from, but we were still upset that she felt like she couldn't confide in us. We always told each other everything especially something as major as this!

"Anyway, let's get off my drama. I'm happy now that he is gone. What's new with you Janet, coz we know what's up with Leyah" She queried with a devious tone!

"Well, Marcus is staying with me for a few days"

"What? How comes? Where's Jasmine?" I said shocked! Wow we all had confessions today! There was so much we didn't know about what's happened this past week!

"Well, you all are going to find out soon. But Joshua isn't Marcus's baby. Jasmine lied and he caught her with the real father all up in his house…"

I gasped, shocked with the story. How could a woman do that? Marcus is such a lovely guy. A very rare breed and she took full advantage of him. We all knew that the baby didn't look like him, but who would have thought it! Janet continued to explain the story in detail as the Italian masseuse started our treatments. Keshia tried to convince her that this was her chance to make her move while he was weak and vulnerable, but Janet was not hearing that. She was not about to take advantage of her friend in this fragile situation. It was weird listening to all the things going on which neither one of us had a clue about. Some would say that destiny was speaking, our times where now here.

A time for change.

Chapter 45.

Janet

I glided back into the house feeling like a new woman. I shut the door behind me and the delicious aroma hit me full force.

"Jay, your back already. How was it?"

I stood surprised as Marcus walked towards me with his sleeves rolled up and his top button undone on his striped Polo shirt. Looks like his hard work at the stove had made him hot. He leaned in and helped me take off my jacket while I told him all about the Spa trip. Even he was impressed with Reese, but he had to admit that it was a low blow but a good desperate attempt. As I watched him work his way around the kitchen, my body was filled with unusual warm sensations that raced through me. I knew exactly what the cause was. It was the realisation of someone cooking me dinner as I came home. I actually had someone asking me how my day was. I was coming home to someone already here. I took a deep breath, exhale. I sat excited at the table as Marcus brought out the main starters of melon and prawns. I looked on suspicious with the chosen unusual combination. He picked up on my hesitant approach as I picked up my fork.

"Just try it Jay, trust me you will love it!" He said with a comical tone. I smiled. "Your not trying to poison me are you? I mean the last meal you cooked me was when I came to visit you down at uni and you made me pot noodles!"

We both broke out into laughter, remembering the original meal of Spaghetti Bolognese which Marcus prepared had burnt, leaving him with no other option but noodles.

"Look I've come a long way since then babe. Trust me"

I took my first mouthful and savoured the sensations. To my surprise it was delicious. I licked my lips in enjoyment as he proceeded to serve the main course of honey glazed salmon, barbecue chicken wings and rice with Greek salad with a special secret twist which he didn't want to share with me despite my constant pleas. I tucked in amazed at how delicious the meal was, I couldn't have asked for more. I looked on in total amazement; I really never knew he had it in him. I picked up my glass of wine as Marcus refilled it once again. Making another toast, we toasted to *'friends, change and happiness'*. Gosh I wish this man was mine forever.

He was everything I wanted.

Everything I've ever wanted.

We finished up and I helped him clear the table while he prepared the dessert. My imagination took hold of me again allowing me to wish it was him with whipped cream and strawberries laced all over him, but instead I had to settle with rum cake and custard which was delicious. I took my last spoonful enjoying the intoxicating sensations as he laughed at me confessing that he had cheated by asking his mum to bake it. I just knew it was too good to be true for him to have made. I smiled gratefully that he had actually gone out of his way. He had really showed me his appreciation this evening.

"I'm glad you enjoyed the meal Jay"

I looked at him in admiration, wondering why any woman ever let him get away. Why did I let him get away?

"It was so nice. I might have to lock you away and keep you here as my slave to cook my meals"

We both laughed as we relaxed in the lounge watching a DVD, talking about the future and more positive things as I tried to keep his mind off Jasmine and Joshua. I knew he had been missing Josh immensely, who wouldn't.

312

"You remember how we use to do this all the time back in the day Jay. You wrapped up in my arms on mum's sofa as we watched The Real McCoy?"

I laughed remembering the moments. "Yeah, those were the good old days!"

He grabbed me pulling me closer re-enacting those moments. My head rested on his chest as he comforted my loneliness, bringing me to tranquillity. He smelt so good.

"Jay, where did it go wrong?"

"Huh?"

"You know… we were so good together. You were my best friend. My everything. I trusted you like no other. You went through everything with me. I… I love you Jay"

My heart stopped. Did I just imagine those words? The sincerity in his tone? The confession of 'real' love? I blinked ferociously making sure that I wasn't in a dream. No it wasn't a dream. I need to respond but I couldn't respond my mouth had frozen in the shock!

"Did you hear me Jay? I Love you. I always have. I was afraid to tell you because after that night in Manchester you just shut me out. I've had no control over my life recently and now I feel like this is a blessing in disguise. I'm not afraid to tell you anymore Jay. You don't have to tell me the same but I need to let you know how I feel"

I shifted from my position looking him in the eyes, searching for any doubt. Was this the wine talking? Or was he serious?

I took a deep breath. "Marcus I love you too, I wanted to tell you for the longest but I was afraid as well… and then when you told me that you were engaged and expecting a baby I felt like my whole world had crumbled"

He gazed down at me with love in his eyes, happy with my response but with regret that the confession didn't come sooner. I stared back at him noticing that the glimmer was back in his eyes. The passion that I had once known was back. He leaned forward and kissed me, passionately, seductively. My whole body melted like it was a block of warmed up ice. The taste of his tongue was better than I had remembered. I was lost in the experience, the experience of Marcus all over again. Forgetting all my worries and anxieties about the realisation of my feelings, I just wanted him to know how much love I had stored inside of me for him. We tongue wrestled on the sofa for the next half an hour enjoying the feeling, the renewed sensations. Our hands caressed each others skin, delicately yet eager whilst the ripples shot through our bodies.

"Baby, let's go upstairs"

"Are you sure?"

I looked him dead in his eyes and whispered. "Yes. I'm not afraid anymore"

He held onto my waist as I ushered him to my Boudoir. As soon as we reached the threshold he raised me off my feet, carrying me over to the red cotton sheets in his strong arms. Exhale. He looked at me with his eyes still embodied with love. Just then I knew for certain that his feelings were true, they were deep like mine. He kissed me gently, taking his time to make my inner body scream with desire. As much as I couldn't control myself I tried to match his pace, holding on to the eruption that wanted to explode. I fiddled through his tenderness trying desperately to take my dress off so that I could feel his skin against mine, but he gently grabbed my hand wanting to do it for himself, whispering in my ear as I surrendered to his request. My body tingled as his hands glided over my ebony skin, raising the material over my head exposing my matching black lace knickers set. He looked on admiring what he saw, taking in every inch of my body.

"You're as beautiful as I remember"

I looked away bashful as his hands glided around my pelvis. Now it was his turn to remove some garments. He slowly unbuttoned his striped shirt exposing his strong defined torso, accompanied by a few chest hairs. I reached forward and kissed his chest then slowly glided my tongue over his nipples. He moaned in agreement. I could feel his manhood pressed against me desperately in need of release from the restriction of his trousers. I kindly obliged, releasing the caged animal. Marcus was grateful and lent in kissing my breasts in return, pleasing each one simultaneously. I have never wanted someone so bad like I want him right now. But I was savouring the moment. I didn't want it to end. I didn't want it to feel like it had in Manchester after I had kicked him out. He finished teasing my upper body, stopping for a moment to catch his breath. Smiling at me, pleased at my aroused state he whispered into my ear that he would be back, demanding me not to move. I lay there exposed as he exited the bedroom and went downstairs. I hope he wasn't paying me back for what I did to him. A few minutes passed and I became suspicious, as I was about to call out to him he returned. He looked at me with a cheeky grin and moved closer whispering more sweet words into my ears as he nibbled on the left and then the right. My body shuddered making me lose all senses which I once had. He rolled me over onto my chest, moving my hair out the way, kissing a path of soft wet kisses down my spine. My body heated up once again while I dripped in other places, ready. Suddenly I felt something cold run along my back then I felt his warm lips following the same path. I whined in ecstasy, bewildered with the sensations that ran across my entire body.

"Do you like that?" He asked.

"Yes" I panted.

I always knew he must have been the master at love making and now once again I was experiencing it first hand. I had lost control.

"I love you" I confessed as I lost all inhibitions and succumbed to the feeling of total ecstasy.

He put on the barrier and entered home as it invited him in. Calling out his name, anticipating his arrival.

I was fulfilled.

I was no longer empty.

This is where I wanted to be for the rest of my life. In total bliss, perfect harmony. Our bodies intertwined as we rolled between the sheets, pleasing one another. Dancing to the rhythm that we made together. There was no moment in my life that was as perfect as this.

"I love you more" Marcus declared.

Chapter 46.

Keshia

Kamarni woke in a panic, tugging his arm up from underneath my head. He looked straight at the clock sitting on the shelf opposite, realising that he had fallen asleep for longer than he needed to again. I laid in the bed unmoved acting like I was unaware of his predicament, looking on as he jumped out of the bed with his bareness, desperately gathering his clothes. It was past nine o'clock. How would he explain this one this time? I shrugged my shoulders not really caring for his difficulty. It wasn't my problem! Shaking the loose strands of hair from my face I rose my hot body from underneath the sheets watching Kamarni's frantic behaviour with amusement.

"Shit. I need to go. Where's my socks?"

"Babes you're going already?"

"I got to go. My woman is going to kill me. Look at the time! How did you let me fall asleep?"

I looked at him disgruntled not bothering to even answer him. How dare he blame me, like I was supposed to be his keeper! Huh, he had another thing coming. I'm not the one in the relationship! Still rushing around like a Tasmanian devil he continued looking for his clothes, reaching under the bed he finally found his missing sock. Hurriedly he shoved his foot into it, quickly proceeding to put on his size nine timberlands. I was surprised that he actually took time out of his mania to kiss me on my lips whilst telling me that he would give me a call later. Before I could respond he was gone, out the door with the scent from the aftermaths of sex left behind. Once again I was left lying on my bed alone. Wallowing in the steamy aftermath of last nights love making, realising that I was

317

now the '*other*' woman. The one thing that I had hated, I had become. I sat up wrapping myself in the soft blanket. How did it ever get to this? I looked around the room engulfed in the sin. The lies, the deceit! I was sleeping with someone else's man and he was not making any effort to leave his woman! Not that I had asked him to, but we had become an item more or less. He was here servicing my needs and chilling with me at least four times a week. It was more than sex, we had a connection. A connection that was hijacked by his uncompromising selfish woman. He didn't need to be with her anymore, he had me and we were meant to be!

I sat flicking through the TV, listening to Janet's over excited and elevated mood on the other end of the phone. Something definitely had her acting like a kid in a candy store today. I grudgingly listened on thinking that this was how I should be feeling after I had spent the night with the man of my dreams, the man who I wanted to share my forever with. However, my forever did not look like it was going to be soon. Janet finally stopped nattering and ended the conversation after convincing me to meet up with her and Leyah later on this evening for some drinks. After our conversation I still wasn't sure what had tickled her fancy, but she was definitely elated over something. Maybe Michael had proposed to her...nah! She wasn't really feeling him. Forget worrying about her, I need to worry about my life right now! As soon as I placed my blackberry back down on the coffee table it rang again. There was the well known ringtone… Kamarni. My heart jumped.

"Hi babes" I heard a long release of breath come down the phone. "Kamarni?"

"Look… Ermm she knows…" He said in a whisper.

"Huh?"

"We can't do this any more, my woman knows about us. Someone saw us together. There's pictures!"

"What the fuck? What do you mean?"

"I love my woman, okay. And I can't mess with you anymore!"

318

My heart froze and sank into the pits of my stomach. "What do you mean?"

"…It's over!"

"But… but…" With that I heard an angry voice instructing him to hang up the phone and then he was gone. I sat in shock, my mouth open not fully understanding what I had just heard. Am I dreaming? Yes I must be. I just imagined that phone call. I blinked back into reality and looked on my caller list, gasping… It wasn't a dream. Kamarni had just broken up with me. I was not having that. I dialled his number back enraged at the lack of explanation and the cold bluntness of it all. The phone rang out as I paced up and down the room, so I rang it again. Four calls later and he finally answered.

"Look, please don't call me. My woman's going mad"

"Listen, you listen to me yeah. How dare you tell me that it is over like that after everything we have been through! You're not happy where you are. Leave her and come to me" I pleaded with desperation in my voice, bearing no shame towards the situation. "She can't love you like I can. I thought we had something here!"

"Well you thought wrong, I'm sorry!"

"Who's that? Is that her? Tell her to get off your phone! Tell that dirty bitch to get off your phone now! I can't believe you…" Came the voice ranting in the background with rage and pain. I gathered it must have been his woman. I could hear the distress in her voice but I still wanted to try and convince him to leave. I was who he needed to be with. I was the one who supported his dreams. I was the one who encouraged him to approach that record company. I was the one who loved him like no other could.

"Please Kamarni" He hung up the phone. In the shock I cried, not knowing what to do next. Although I had blatantly done wrong I didn't want to retreat. I didn't want to lose the one thing which I loved more than life itself. He was my soul mate.

I sat and cried on the linen, mascara staining my sheets as I shed all the pain that I was experiencing. We both knew this day would come. I thought it would work in my favour but it had not!

Chapter 47.

Leyah

Keshia and I sat waiting for Janet to enter the busy wine bar. We were sat at a round table with raised cushioned chairs at the back of the venue so that we had full view. This used to be our frequent spot back in the day when we were all single or in need for a quick local retreat from the endless relationship problems and lack of it. You were always guaranteed to hear some good music in soothing surroundings. We hadn't been here for a while, yet nothing had changed. There was still the sleazy door man with his tubby round belly and greasy jerry curled hair who always tried to check me. Like I would *ever* be that desperate! And the short middle aged man who was always in here alone, no matter what night he was here, wearing a black vest showing off his puny muscles. I laughed as I observed my surroundings realising that some people were really pathetic or maybe it was just plain desperate! I looked up over my glass of margarita and saw Janet floating through the entrance. Keshia sat there downing her third shot of tequila not caring about her environment.

"Hey girl" I rose and gave her a kiss. She looked stunning, her skin glowed with a strange auburn tone. She must be definitely getting the '*good stuff*' from somewhere!

She leaned towards Keshia and greeted her before taking a seat, starting a short conversation about why she was late, apologising for the rush hour problems on the Victoria line. I was so glad that I didn't need to take the tube for work that was one place I did not want to be during commuting hours.

"So? What is going on? Lets cut to the chase, you're the one that called this gathering Janet" Keshia slurred. "How comes you look all happy?"

"Well" She shifted getting herself comfortable, licking her glossed lips and leaning closer. "It's finally happened"

Keshia and I looked on baffled, what had finally happened? What was she on about?

"Me and Marcus! He told me that he loves me. I told him the truth, how I really feel about him and we've decided to give it a go!"

"What? When did all this happen?" I reacted, stunned putting my hands on the table.

"He just mash up with his fiancée the other day!" Keshia said, her eyes barely open.

"I know but that was destined to end. He was only with her because he thought that she was carrying his baby! He confessed to me that he had been in love with me all this time. All this time we had both been afraid to tell each other"

Janet went on to tell us all the details and the steamy bits as well, going through plenty cocktails as she did. I was really happy for her. Finally she had given into her inhibitions, her true love desires and let it be what it was meant to be. They were perfect for each other, always have been. But she pushed him away, kept him at arms length, damn she almost lost him for good but now it had all unfolded, it was like a love story. I just hope it works for her.

We continued talking about Janet's new encompassed love, giggling and smiling like I was the one who was head over heels. Keshia reluctantly shared the moment, downing one cocktail after the other. I watched her puzzled. I could tell that there was something troubling her. She was drinking way more than usual and this was a sign that she was blocking something out. She always did this when she wanted to forget about something to avoid thinking about the reality of what ever it was that was bothering her and I know something was definitely troubling her. As strong as she was or made out to be she was still a woman and her feelings could get hurt as well. Janet stopped rambling, also noticing

Keshia's distant mood. Giving me the silent nod to delve into the sensitive questioning. I approached with caution. As soon as I did Keshia quickly became defensive and then exhaled a tearful release.

"I've become the woman I hate. I've been fucking with Kamarni and now his woman found out and he's left me... he left me so cold! I can't believe he would do that. We were perfect. I thought he loved me. I love him. I can't live with out him. I need him!"

We both looked at each other in amazement. We knew they were a little too close to be just friends, but we thought that it was all innocent lust! Now the truth was out, she was fucking with someone's man knowing that he had a woman and now she was upset that he had chosen his woman over her! How could she have let herself fall in love with him? Why would she put herself in this vulnerable situation? Janet knew my view on the situation, although she didn't agree with it she understood more than what I could so I left her to continue the conversation and verbal comforts.

"Look don't even worry about it. He wasn't right for you. Come on now, he cheated on his woman, he would only go and do it to you. You're too good for him?"

"He would never do that to me. This wasn't supposed to happen!" She cried.

"I know but it did. Now you just got to be strong and move on. Move forward. New year, new start!"

I sat and took all her words in. Anyone who cheats can never really change can they? It's in their blood. They've tasted the sweet sin of promiscuity, having their cake and eating it too. Reese can never be faithful. He will never be that perfect man that I need.

"It's all good for you to say. You're all loved up with Marcus and you Leyah you got Reese running you down like you're the last woman on earth! All I've got is nothing! Everything that I can't have!"

"Now hold on a minute! No one told you to run after someone else's man! You made your bed now lie in it! You never appreciated your relationship anyway, you both were messing around" I didn't want to say it so bluntly but the harsh approach was always the best approach. Although Keshia was my girl, I didn't agree one bit with what she did. Fair enough I felt bad that she had gotten hurt, but it was her own stupidity that led her down the path of heartache. She only had herself to blame. Keshia looked at me with venom in her eyes. I stood my ground, sticking to what I had said. Janet tried to defuse the potential eruption that was about to explode by putting down her drink, looking us both in the eye and demanding us both to cool down.

"Look you can't help who you fall in love with. I didn't plan to do this it just happened. Look at you and Reese..."

"My situation with Reese is nothing like this!"

"Yeah it is! How long did it take you to fully let go after he confessed to having a fiancée? And I know there must have been times where you needed him to satisfy your itch!"

"Listen, you done wrong! Admit it! This isn't about me! You knew the situation and you let this man do you like that! Get you all weak and vulnerable! Look at you, this is not the Keshia I know!"

She put her head down in shame. "Yeah, your right. I knew it all along. It's just... it's just that it hurts so much. I didn't mean for it to go this far"

"You know it's not initially your fault, it takes two to tango"

"Yep, and tango we sure did"

Keshia began to perk up, wiping the tears from her eyes with the red tissues that were on the table. We ordered another round of drinks while we sat and discussed the men in our lives and the shit that we had to put up with! Was being in love this painful? Did it mean that we would have to sacrifice our integrity and beliefs in order to find true love? Would we have to put other things before our heart in order to avoid heartache?

324

The feeling that lets us know we love someone is something that words cannot encapsulate. We have all been slaves to the love drug!

After we had sorted out our differences over many rounds of cocktails and rums we ended the night and said our good byes exiting the venue in our merry state. The night was cold, I wrapped my scarf tightly around my neck blocking out the bitter weather. It felt good meeting up with my girls and discussing our problems, although sometimes we didn't hear what we wanted, it was nice to hear a second view. They were like sisters to me, yeah we argued but we were never able to stop talking to each other for longer than a few days. We had a special bond, one which I never had with my sister.

As I stepped onto my doorstep I thought about Reese and how things would be if I gave him another chance. He would be a half decent man if I trained him well and put shackles on his feet! He knew how to romance a woman, he was financially stable and he was devoted to his daughter. But was that enough? I would be constantly worrying about his possible acts of infidelity, whether he had another partner or family out there. What if the words coming out of his mouth were lies! Look at Kamarni, he was such a lovely man I mean he sure pulled the wool over my eyes. I would have never guessed that he had a woman by the way which he used to look at Keshia and huh he sure had charm just like Reese. Damn, there seemed to be an epidemic around! All the sexy fine men were lying cheating, scandalous dogs! Is there no normal men left out there? Is monogamy not a word which men can speak fluently anymore? I stepped through the hall throwing my bag down on the floor as I entered, kicking off my silver heels. I relaxed in the comforts of the silent house relieved that Asia was over at Reese's tonight. He had offered to watch her so that I could go out and have some time to myself. I was stunned by his suggestion and he was acting a little too happy to collect her from nursery which was a deviation from our normal Friday routine. I was still trying to get used to his odd behaviour and him actively being there at the drop of a hat, but for now I will just enjoy it! The light on my answer phone was blinking which could only either be my mother or Reese's. No one else really rang my house phone. I walked over to the phone not desperate to hear the message but irritated at the flashing light. As I went to press the button to play the message the phone started ringing. I held the receiver to my ear and as soon as it touched I could hear Reese's voice ranting...

"My gosh, where have you been? I've been trying to get hold of you for the past two hours! I've left numerous messages!"

"Why didn't you call my mobile? What's wrong?"

"Your mobile is going to voicemail. What if it was an emergency? I was worried about you?"

I kissed my teeth. "Don't worry about me, I can worry about myself. What's the matter? Is Asia okay?"

"Yes she is fine. What happened to your phone?"

"Reese please! My battery is dead! And it's none of you business anyway!"

"Look, something could have happened to you…"

I huffed. "What do you want Reese?" I was becoming irritated.

"Leah, I just… I wanted to hear your voice and make sure you got home safe. It's late!"

"I'm a big woman Reese! I'm not Asia, I don't need protecting out here. I've survived this long without you here! So don't think that you have some sort of role in my life all of a sudden!"

I heard the pause in his breath while he contemplated his next move. Reese was diabolical, I didn't even want to give him a reaction about him wanting to hear my voice, because I was afraid. I was afraid of how I felt. I wanted to hear his voice as well. I had just been thinking about him and he had called. He could be so sweet and caring at times, this is what I was afraid of! Afraid of letting him back in, letting him back into my heart. It had started again. I had noticed how his voice was making me weak again, the bass in his tone was similar to Barry White. It was erotic and sent warm shivers down my spine. My breathing began to get deeper, intense. I was feeling hot everywhere rising to the familiar bait. I needed to terminate this call quick!

326

"Well you know I'm okay Reese. I'm going now!"

"Leah, are you sure?"

Sure about what? Why was he trying to weaken my defences with his indirect approach of sincerity?

"I'm fine Reese, good-bye!"

I quickly hung up the phone letting out a sigh of relief. How was I going to get through this again? It took me ages to get to this point in the first place. Why couldn't he just leave it to be the way it was. Let me carry on hating him! Now I could feel that I was crumbling. No not for him, please God, not for him.

Chapter 48.

Janet

I stepped into the warm house with the sounds of Mary J. Bilge singing throughout the dining room. As I walked further into the light I could see the naked flames of candles along the walkway guiding my route. I was emotionally apprehended, unable to make sense of the sensations which I was feeling. Romance had hit me at full force. I couldn't control the smile which beamed from my face exposing the feeling within. Marcus stood there with a single rose in his mouth looking as sexy as ever. He walked up to me like Prince Charming in Cinderella and took my hand, causing my heart to melt again. This couldn't be really happening to me, all my dreams were coming true. This is exactly how I had expected it to be. How I had imagined it would be. He held me close, looking deep into my eyes proclaiming his love for me silently. The thought of being Mrs Walters entered my head once again as he searched my eyes for the love which was within.

"Baby, I missed you. I'm not going to ever let you get away again!"

This had undoubtedly been the best week of my life. I had been wined and dined by the man I had desired for a lifetime. We had proclaimed our love for one another during many passionate moments together. Nothing else mattered as we were together in perfect harmony. We were the perfect fit.

Tomorrow was Jasmines final day to have vacated his house and I was not anticipating the moment at all because it left me with uncertainty. I didn't know if Marcus would be moving back into his house or staying here. All I knew is that I had gotten used to his presence and I didn't want to have to be alone again. Having a man around was a new feeling to me, but it was comforting. This is what life was about having someone special to share it with. Someone who was my Adam and I his Eve. I was his rib.

I proceeded to put my towel around me watching Marcus wet body laying on the bed. His brown skin melting into the sheets, when the interruption of my phone ringing intruded the aftermaths of the love making session we just shared. I called over to Marcus to answer it as he was nearer than I was. I watched as he answered, his voice inviting the caller to respond. All of a sudden his eyebrows raised. I knew this look, something was not right!

"Look, I don't know what your problem is…You better ask Janet about that not me. I'm sorry if you couldn't live up to the expectations!"

My eyes darted in their sockets as I reached over and took the handset out of his hands hearing the raised voice of Michael on the other end. He hadn't called in a while, giving me my well deserved space. Although he had been begging for weeks to take me out for dinner I had frequently declined whilst strategically missing his calls. I thought he would have understood by now, obviously he was persistent.

"Hello. It's me"

"What the hell is he doing answering you phone? Furthermore what is he doing at your house this time of night sounding all chilled?"

"Michael why are you acting like this? You and I are not together. I've explained this to you"

"So you mean to tell me you just go and jump in bed with the Marcus. How long has this been going on? You were sleeping with him all along weren't you? I just knew something wasn't right between you two! Janet, how could you do this? I have feelings for you!"

"Listen, I knew my feelings for you were not true, we've discussed this. Marcus and I are together now. I'm sorry but I love him. I always have" I felt awful breaking it to him like this so cold and unemotional, but he was just not getting my subtle hints that I no longer wanted to see him. The straight blunt approach was always the best approach wasn't it? I could hear the emotion in his tone, the sound of tears welling up. Oh please don't let this man cry down the phone.

"Look Michael I'm sorry, I have to go. Take care of yourself"

Marcus held my waist, sympathising with my dilemma. He knew it was hard for me to let people down this way, but it had to be done. I had to clear out my closet, no holding on just in case. No back up plan. I had what I wanted right here finally. I rubbed his naked firm thigh as I rested my head on his chest. Hopefully this would be the last of the drama in our lives for a lifetime. But I knew that this would be wishful thinking.

Chapter 49.

Keshia

I lay stretched across my bed, staring up at the ceiling having deep thoughts with myself, analysing where my life was after twenty eight years on this earth. I was definitely not at a place where I wanted it to be, I was supposed to be happy, I didn't want to be like my mother. She went through a number of dysfunctional relationships, brief encounters and men getting her pregnant and then leaving her. I don't want that to be me. I don't want to mirror her experience. Pain tore through my heart and sent knots through my stomach as I reflected on my past relationships. Then it hit me, I was attracted to dysfunction. All my past relationships were messed up in some way, deep down I knew that they were all a waste of time, destined not to last but I held on to a false sense of security. Being with Bobby was all that I knew, it was what I was used to. I knew that we had a very slim chance of surviving *'till death do us part'* but we both held onto the dream. The dream that one day we would be perfect. But it was far from a reality. We both came into the relationship with 'issues'. When we got together I had just split up from my ex Jayde due to his infidelity. He had me over insecure, going through his phone, calling up girls and cussing them off. That was me back then, the stupid ignorant woman who was fooled by his charm! When all along it was him who was the instigator in all of it! My relationship past was abysmal. I always chose the wrong guys. Look at Francis, he was sweet and kind but too placid. He would do anything I asked, no questions equal to boring. Then there was Chase, good conversation but there was not an exciting bone in his body. I had to be the one who was always taking charge and thinking of things for us to do, again boring! Oh and not to forget Edward who chased me for years, trying everything to get me. He had a good job, his life was together but he just wasn't my type. He even asked me to marry him but I needed more. I don't know what it was that I was looking for but I just needed excitement something challenging not a relationship where I could guess what would happen day after day. Maybe I made the wrong choices in life. Maybe I was looking for something that just wasn't there. Indirectly looking for a reason to fail. To beat the inevitable.

Why did I always want something that I couldn't have?

Something that ultimately causes me pain and heartache!

Tears rolled ferociously down my face as I sat and thought about Kamarni. He was a good man, we would have been good together. I needed him. The magnitude to which I missed him was unexplainable. Why did I have to let myself get caught up? That was not like me, how could I let this man get me weak? I didn't know who I was anymore! What was I going to do now? Everything had failed! I wanted to pick up my phone and call Kamarni but I wrestled with myself not to, not wanting to cause him any more problems, not wanting to cause his woman anymore unsuspecting hurt and pain. Really she didn't deserve it. She was lucky she had caught herself a damn good man. Although he cheated on her, he loved her. He chose to stay with her. Saying those words made my heart pain even more. The thought of him loving her was not what I wanted him to do! However, I knew that it was what it was! But I didn't want it to be. I wish I could just turn back the hands of time...

I laid there with the pills spread out on the bed, quickly downing a glass of water. My worries started to fade away as my eyes became heavier. Blinking, I tried to defeat it but retreating as I realised that it would take me to a better place... A place where I would feel no more pain...

Chapter 50.

Marcus

There was no sign of the convertible as I approached, the blinds were drawn and the letters were hanging out the letterbox. I took a deep breath before pushing my key through the hole. As I stepped into the passage I released my breath, the house was cold and uninviting. It didn't feel the same. I cruised downstairs checking all the rooms before reluctantly walking up the stairs to do the same. They had gone! Janet wanted to come with me to give me some support just in case Jasmine was still here, knowing that it would be difficult for me, but I had to do this on my own. I needed closure. The place I had shared for the past five months was now empty. All that was left were the memories. I sat down in Joshua's room which I had decorated in blue and white with Winnie the Pooh wall mounts. His little pine crib lay empty. I walked over to the rocking chair and sat down picking up his little teddy bear which mum had given him at the hospital. It smelt just like him. I looked around the room as I held the bear close to my chest. There was nothing left, there was no life left. I quickly forced back the sensations which were trying to erupt within. I was a man, I didn't need to cry!

Walking through to the bedroom I could smell her scent. The scent of deceit and lies. Everything that was hers had gone. The wardrobe doors were open exposing the space which I had now reclaimed. It was a symbol that I now had my life back again. I was no longer trapped in a world which was not mine. I was free. I was free to love the person who I had always loved. The person who I had always wanted to give my everything to. I smiled as I viewed my reflection in the floor to ceiling mirror.

Yeah I'm back!

Chapter 51.

Leyah

I rushed to the door with my towel wrapped around me, water dripping on the stairs, leaving wet footprints in my trail. I opened the door knowing that it was Reese. I watched as he entered inside with Asia asleep in his arms.

"Is it alright if I take her upstairs?"

I gave him a cynical look. Obviously I was not about to stretch out my arms and take her from him, letting my towel drop to the floor!

"Of course" I answered with attitude as he stepped back and took a good look before climbing the stairs to put Asia into her bed.

Trust him to come at this time, just as I was relaxing in my nice bubble bath that I had decided to take with my latest romance novel in order to kill some time. I closed the front door, conscious that Reese was now in my house. How did it get to this so quick? One minute he was the epitome of all evil, unable to step foot in my abode. Now he was a frequent visitor, like we had some mutual agreement. Like the script had changed to include him after everything that he had done! Anger rose within me as all the pain resurfaced and began to dismantle the good mood which I was in. Quickly trying to escape from that place I wrapped the towel tighter around my naked body and went looking for my dressing gown. As I was about to step into the bathroom Reese came out of Asia's room bumping into me.

"Oh sorry" He licked his lips as his eyes caressed me with his look.

"Excuse you. Did you change her into her pyjama's?"

"Of course!"

I stood uncomfortable. Heat rising between us.

"So did you like the flowers I sent to you?"

"Look, stop trying to woo me. I'm not the stupid young girl which you met and was able to fool! Stop wasting your money and sending them because I'm going to start throwing them straight in the bin!"

"Look, all I want to do is let you know that I'm sorry. I made a mistake. Well a huge mistake and I just want to make things right between us"

I watched his eyes as they trailed over my exposed flesh, desire burning through what he saw.

"Reese, yeah, yeah you've told me this a number of times. Look excuse me, let me go and put on some clothes! You can see yourself out"

As I brushed past him I noticed that he had made no attempt to leave. He stood firm in his lilac jumper, black jeans and Prada hat, his tall toned body hugging his clothes as he posed. Exhale.

"Look, I want to talk to you" He slurred with a slow seductive tone.

"Well do what we normally do and call me!"

"What's the point, I'm here? Finish your bath I'll wait!"

"You wish. Just say what you got to say" I stood with my hands folded across my chest.

"Well firstly I need to tell you how beautiful you look…"

I huffed, retreating to my original destination and grabbing my dressing gown off the back of the door, urgently putting it on over my towel in frustration. My body was beginning to give involuntary reactions again! I walked out with my face showing that I was becoming impatient, directing him downstairs.

335

He smiled raising his brows "Nice"

I sat down on the sofa instructing him to talk. I knew he had nothing really constructive to say but I still allowed him to occupy my time, interrupting my evening, not that I had anything better to do!

"Leah Leah. I'm sorry if you hate me..."

I instantly sucked my teeth, offended once again with his choice of words. Like I didn't have a right to hate him!

"...Wait hear me out... I know I wasn't the best man back then. I done wrong. I know this but what I said to you the other night I meant it. I want us to be a real family. I want us to be together and grow together. I want us to grow old together. I know that you think I'm just chatting the same old bullshit, but I'm not. I'm pouring out my heart to you. This is where we are meant to be" He placed his hands on mine. "I love you. You need to know how much I love you"

He leaned forward and I allowed him to place his moist lips on my lips. I closed my eyes and pretended that it was all okay, that everything was going to be okay. His lips moved to my sensitive place as I gave him access tilting my head to the side. My breath sped up, my chest rising to the pleasure my body was receiving. I had lost. I had lost the battle...

We woke with our bodies still joined together, our hands interlocked with one another. I looked in his eyes searching for the truth, looking for sincerity. I found it, it was there. He looked straight back at me with his long lashes and promised.

"I'm going to make you happy for ever"

Those words sent a calm across my body. A sense of peace. The battle was over. I no longer had to fight with myself, with my feelings. I had surrendered to the love which consistently bellowed from within.

"Mummy, Daddy!" We both looked up and smiled at Asia's beaming face. This is where he was meant to be.

Chapter 52.

Janet

We lifted up the last cardboard box and carried it together, into the house. Everything was perfect. It felt complete.

Two months had passed and everything had changed, changed for the better. Marcus rented out his house and was moving into mine. The decision for him to make the change was well needed. He needed a fresh start, a new beginning or in our case a continuation. We had finally become one.

My 10 carat platinum rock beamed on my finger as we placed the box down on the wooden floor. He glanced up into my vulnerable eyes and smiled, the smile which sent love tingles straight through my body. He took me by the hand and kissed me passionately.

"I'm never going to lose you again"

"And I'm never going to let you go again! I love you. Happy new year babes"

About the Author

Cassandra M Porter, born 27th July, grew up in the South of London as one of two children born to her West Indian parents. From a young age, she dreamt of writing and publishing her own novel and would write short stories in her spare time.

As a single mother to a nine year old, Cassandra has juggled parenthood with full time employment and her studies. She obtained a Bsc in Psychology followed by a Bsc in Criminal Justice and a Diploma in Probation Studies. She has been part of the Youth Offending Team Panel and currently works as a Probation Officer.

Through ***If Loving You Was Easy***, Cassandra has carefully captured the realities of the modern day relationship; a process which has taken three years to bring to fruition. She draws her inspiration from life experiences; both personal and professional. She strives to be a positive role model for her son and to encourage and empower others to realise their potential and aspirations.

Cassandra continues to feed her natural flare for creative writing and is currently working on the sequel to this inspiring novel.

Join her mailing list at: cassiemporter@signaturekisses.co.uk

Lightning Source UK Ltd.
Milton Keynes UK
11 September 2010

159722UK00002B/7/P